PUBLIC ORDER IN THE AGE OF
THE CHARTISTS

Frontispiece

MAJOR–GENERAL SIR CHARLES JAMES NAPIER

PUBLIC ORDER
IN THE AGE OF
THE CHARTISTS

by

F. C. MATHER

MANCHESTER UNIVERSITY PRESS

© 1959 F. C. MATHER

Published by the University of Manchester at
THE UNIVERSITY PRESS
316–324, Oxford Road, Manchester 13

First Published 1959
Reprinted with minor corrections 1966

To
MY MOTHER

Printed in Great Britain by Butler & Tanner Ltd., Frome and London

PREFACE

*Order is to be valued as the basis of freedom; only in a well ordered
society are the members of society really free.*
William Temple, *Christianity and Social Order*, p. 60

As Professor E. L. Woodward reminds us in his book, *The
Age of Reform, 1815–70*, one of the great distinguishing
developments of the nineteenth century in England was
"the organization of a civilized social life". The age was one in
which tremendous strides were taken in adding to human happi-
ness by improving the machinery of government. By the reform
of local administration insanitary towns were swept and drained,
slums were cleared and parks and libraries provided, whilst the
establishment of professional inspectorates, acting under the
control of the central government, brought about the effective
regulation of hours and conditions of labour in factories and the
exclusion of women and children from the mines. One aspect of
this general progress has been treated by the historian less systematically than it deserves—the conquest of mob disorder and the
creation of institutions able to maintain the public peace. The
reason for this neglect is not difficult to find. The historian,
especially the writer of general history, is a natural Whig. His
sympathies are with peoples against governments, with political
reformers against conservatives; and his attitude towards popular
disturbances has been not infrequently that expressed by John
Richard Green, commenting on the disorders of the Regency
period in his *Short History of the English People*, that "the real
danger to public order lay only in the blind opposition to all
political change which confused wise and moderate projects of
reform with projects of revolution".

This book, however, is written in the conviction that the
elimination of riot from English social life—surely one of the
outstanding achievements of the nineteenth century—cannot be
explained adequately without reference to the improvement of

the machinery for enforcing the law. Its purpose is to analyse, and describe the working of, that machinery in an age when new methods of maintaining public order were being tried out against a powerful current of unrest. The first chapter is devoted to a study of the problem of disorder. It is purposely brief and general, for it is intended merely as an introduction to the main theme, and my aim has been to avoid, as far as possible, retelling the story of Chartism and the Welsh Rebecca Riots, which can be studied in detail in works of great authority. The latter consideration has also induced me to deal in general terms, at the risk of over-simplification, with the theme of the concluding chapter, the study of the machinery of public order operating as a whole against disturbances. The writing of this chapter has been prompted by the need to counteract the defects of the analytical approach which is followed in the central portion of the book.

My thanks are due to Professor Arthur Redford of the University of Manchester, who guided me to this subject and introduced me to the discipline of historical research; to Dr. W. H. Chaloner and Dr. T. S. Willan, also of Manchester University, to Dr. G. S. R. Kitson Clark of Trinity College, Cambridge, and to my colleague, Dr. A. J. Hanna, who have read large portions of the typescript of this book and offered many valuable suggestions. Miss D. M. Marshallsay of the Parliamentary Papers Research Library, Southampton University, has advised me on the compilation of the index. For such imperfections as the work retains, I am myself wholly responsible.

I am also indebted to Professor G. M. Trevelyan, O.M., who lent to me his copy of Mandell Creighton's privately printed *Memoir of Sir George Grey, Bart., G.C.B.*; to the Commissioner of the Metropolitan Police, who granted me free access to the records of the Metropolitan Police Force, and to Mr. A. H. Hannay of New Scotland Yard, who guided me in the use of those records; to the Postmaster-General, who permitted me to consult the letter books preserved at the G.P.O., London, and to Mr. G. W. P. Devenport of the G.P.O. Record Room, who assisted me with his advice; to the Librarian, Windsor Castle, for permission to use the correspondence of Queen Victoria in the Royal

Archives; to Sir Fergus Graham, Bart., for permission to draw upon the Graham Papers; to the County Archivist of Hertford-shire for access to the Panshanger Papers; and to the late Mr. Charles Smith of Stockport, who gave me the benefit of his wide knowledge of the history of Chartist activity in the Stockport district, and also permitted me to draw on the typescript copy of his *Stockport in the Age of Reform, 1822–1870*, an unpublished history based on the files of the *Stockport Advertiser*.

I also wish to thank the University of Southampton for generous financial assistance towards the publication of this book.

F. C. M.

CONTENTS

PLATES

CHAPTER I

THE CHALLENGE OF DISORDER

THE first eleven years of Queen Victoria's reign stand out as an era of unusual turbulence, which is often contrasted with the indolent tranquillity of the eighteenth century, and the busy tranquillity of the years 1849–73, when British industrialism had outgrown its growing pains, and "the golden age of British capitalism" had dawned. Looking back from the prosperous mid-Victorian epoch upon his youth and early manhood, Charles Kingsley wrote of the years when "young lads believed (and not so wrongly) that the masses were their natural enemies, and that they might have to fight, any year or any day, for the safety of their property and the honour of their sisters".[1]

Memoirs, diaries and published correspondence relating to this period bear witness to a pronounced dread of mob violence, which a historian of the police force has compared with twentieth-century fears of the overthrow of civilization by the violence of international war.[2] It is recorded in the journal of Lady John Russell that, several days before the Chartist demonstration on Kennington Common on 10 April 1848, Charles Trevelyan, the well-known Secretary of the Treasury, visited the homes of Cabinet Ministers, and frightened their wives by talking of the effect which the sound of cannon fire might have upon them.[3] Shortly after the demonstration had taken place, the Duke of Wellington told the House of Lords that its consequence had been "to place all the inhabitants of the metropolis under alarm, paralysing all trade and business of every description, and driving individuals to seek for safety by arming themselves for the protection

---

[1] Quoted from G. M. Young, *Early Victorian England*, II, 436.
[2] Charles Reith, *Police Principles and the Problem of War*, 48.
[3] *Lady John Russell: A Memoir*, ed. Desmond MacCarthy and Agatha Russell, 97–8.

of the lives of themselves, and of their neighbours, and for the security of their property".[1] Six years earlier, in the summer of 1842, a semi-political strike, which was then convulsing the manufacturing districts, had been described by Lord Melbourne, in a letter to the Queen, as "certainly very near, if not actually, a rebellion".[2] Estimates of this character, made by members of the governing class who had been reared on anti-Jacobin alarm, cannot be accepted uncritically, especially as instances of a more confident outlook may be cited, even from sources which could not be said to be indifferent to the security of property.[3] Nevertheless it is amply evident to the student of the Home Office Papers, and of contemporary newspaper material, that England in the thirties and forties of the nineteenth century faced a serious problem of disorder.

The age in which these disturbances occurred was one of revolutionary economic change. British industrialization, which had been gathering speed in the closing decades of the eighteenth century, attained its greatest momentum in the second quarter of the nineteenth (when production was increasing more rapidly than ever before).[4] The power loom was conquering the weaving branch of the cotton and worsted industries, and in the closing years of the period woolcombing was being revolutionized by the introduction of combing machinery, invented by Heilmann in Germany, and Donisthorpe and Lister in England. Railway building dominated the economic life of the period, and called forth a development of metallurgy and mining which was quite

[1] Quoted from Julius West, *A History of the Chartist Movement*, 249.

[2] *The Letters of Queen Victoria, 1837–61*, ed. Benson and Esher, I, 425.

[3] On 4 May 1839, when Chartism was at its peak, *The Manchester Times*, a middle-class radical newspaper, affirmed: "We never knew a period in the history of Manchester, when there was less pretence to talk of disturbances than the present." *The Manchester Times*, 4 May 1839, p. 2. For further examples of the same attitude see extract from Morley's *Life of Cobden*, quoted by S. Maccoby, *English Radicalism, 1832–52*, 171; also *The Morning Chronicle*'s comment on the elaborate precautions taken by the authorities before the Kennington Common demonstration. E. Halévy, *The Age of Peel and Cobden*, 209, n. 2.

[4] The rate of growth of industrial production was greater than 3 per cent per annum between 1818 and 1855, as compared with less than 2 per cent per annum between 1700 and 1780 and between 1876 and 1913. W. Hoffmann, *British Industry, 1700–1950*, trans. Chaloner and Henderson, 30–3.

without precedent. The mushroom growth of the Scottish iron industry, based on the working of the rich blackband ironstone of Lanarkshire, and the utilization of Neilson's hot-air blast, invented in 1829, was the principal development in metallurgy, but the South Wales industry, which manufactured iron rails, also grew by about 150 per cent. between 1830 and 1847.[1] The output of coal was being raised by the digging of new pits and the carrying of older ones to deeper levels. Railway communications, when they had been constructed, also swelled the tide of continuing migration from the country districts to the towns. Although most of what were to become the largest English towns had reached their maximum rate of growth between 1821 and 1831, the railways worked powerfully on the middle-sized towns, the ports and the iron centres, and rendered an almost indefinite growth of London possible.[2] Meanwhile some of the older industrial centres, notably the clothing towns of the West Country, suffered a loss of inhabitants.

These vast social and economic changes, which both preceded and pervaded the Chartist period, were by no means wholly detrimental to the working classes. The researches of the late Sir John Clapham, Professor T. S. Ashton and other students of economic history emphasize that working-class living standards rose appreciably during the first half of the nineteenth century, and would have risen still further had it not been for the offsetting effect of war and unwise governmental policy. Moreover many of the most pressing working grievances in the new order— irregular employment, truck payments, long hours of labour, bad housing—were legacies from the eighteenth century.[3] And although scholarly reflection has lately stressed the difficulty of measuring statistically changes in the standard of living, especially over long periods of time, there is at least a strong presumption that, as factory production expanded, in the years

[1] Sir J. H. Clapham, *An Economic History of Modern Britain, I, The Early Railway Age, 1820-50*, 426.
[2] The population of towns with upwards of 20,000 inhabitants grew by 1,100,000 between 1821 and 1831, by 1,270,000 between 1831 and 1841, and by 1,800,000 between 1841 and 1851. *Ibid.*, 536
[3] See M. D. George, *England in Transition*.

1790–1850, a large and increasing proportion of the workers came to benefit from it both as producers and consumers.[1]

But the improvement in the standard of life of these British working men in the new industrial order was not a continuous process. There were setbacks and interruptions. The decade which ended in the presentation to Parliament of the second 'National Petition' was one of comparative stagnation of real wages. That this should have been the case in an era of rapidly expanding industrial output was partly due to the growing inability of British agriculture to provide for the needs of the population and to the restrictions imposed by the Corn Laws on the importation of supplies from abroad. But a further important contributory factor was the character of investment expenditure, which in the 1830s was largely directed towards the purchase of United States securities and the financing of export industries, and thus contributed little immediately to the cheapening of goods for the British consumer.[2] Nor could the industrial worker count upon receiving even a static real income, for the depressions which occurred in the course of the trade cycle involved a lowering in the level of wages and employment. 1837 was a year of sharp recession in the export trades. A limited recovery took place in 1838, but in the following year business activity was again depressed, in consequence of an adverse balance of payments, which led to a raising of interest rates. There was a slight improvement in some branches of industry in 1840, but in 1841 and 1842 depression became more widespread and more severe than in 1839. Cotton factories which in the latter year had merely gone over to short-time working now closed their doors completely, and the cessation of the railway building boom of the late thirties dragged down the metallurgical and mining industries. A recovery set in during 1843, and the middle forties were years of prosperity, but business activity afterwards declined to another low point in

---

[1] T. S. Ashton, 'The Standard of Life of the Workers in England, 1790–1830', reprinted in *Capitalism and the Historians*, ed. F. A. Hayek. For a cautious reaffirmation of the old view, that working-class living standards deteriorated between 1790 and the middle 1840s, see E. J. Hobsbawm, 'The British Standard of Living, 1790–1850', *Economic History Review*, 2 Ser., X, 1957.

[2] R. C. O. Matthews, *A Study in Trade-Cycle History*, 222–3.

1848. The periodical downswing of the business cycle brought misery to a wide range of occupational groups, more especially as it coincided, in 1838–9 and in 1847, with a rise in the price of wheat due to bad harvests.

Although its impact was widespread, cyclical depression fell with particular severity upon one section of the working class —the workers in the domestic handicraft industries, which included handloom weaving, framework knitting and wool-combing. These crafts had entered into a chronic state of distress. Even in good times the wages received by those working in them remained miserably low, amounting in some branches to no more than 4s. 6d. per week,[1] and, when a slump came, the handicraftsmen were driven over the edge of misery into desperation. They were usually the first to be turned away from their labour when the need to cut costs was felt, as their discharge, unlike the dismissal of factory operatives, did not compel the employer to lay idle any part of his own expensive machinery. Moreover, when they had lost their livelihood, they had few savings to fall back upon. The permanent depression of these trades, as distinct from its temporary exacerbation by the downward movement of the trade cycle, was partly due to the competition of the new steam-driven machinery—the power loom and the combing machine—which was being installed in the textile factories of Lancashire and the West Riding. But technological unemployment was not the whole story. Silk weaving, which was hardly affected by machine competition, was equally depressed with other branches of handloom weaving, whilst in framework knitting distress was due not to any technological change, but to the fact that too many people had entered the trade in the generation after Waterloo, when it had ceased to expand its markets.[2] It was from the men employed in these poverty-ridden crafts that Chartism with a strong 'physical force'

[1] Clapham, *op. cit.*, 552; *The Life of Thomas Cooper Written by Himself*, 138–9.
[2] The cause of this failure of the supply of labour to adjust itself to the demand for it was to be sought partly in the ease with which framework knitting might be learnt, partly in the stockinger's almost invariable practice of teaching the craft to his children and partly in the habit, common among employers, of spreading the work over as many hands as possible.

flavour drew some of its most devoted supporters.[1] The Leicester-shire hosiery villages, the handloom weaver colonies of Carlisle and of the parts of Northern Lancashire about Colne and Burnley, and the Bradford district of Yorkshire, with its large complement of woolcombers, were veritable storm-centres, where pikes were manufactured for the Chartists, and the 'respectable' inhabitants trembled for their lives and property.

It is thus in the peculiar combination of an unfavourable trend in real wages, cyclical unemployment, bad harvests and the problem of the depressed handicrafts that the explanation of the greater part of the disorder of the Chartist era is to be found. There were some areas where conditions of employment and residence so brutalized the population as to produce a tradition of lawlessness which burst forth into open riot even in prosperous times. The coal mining district of South Wales was one of these,[2] and it has been shown that the rising among the Monmouthshire colliers which earned for Frost, the Chartist, fifteen years' trans-portation occurred when boom conditions reigned in the coal and iron trades.[3] Nevertheless the timing of most of the disturbances of the Chartist period is such as to suggest that grinding poverty lay behind them. Chartism, the stormy mass movement, not the intelligent endeavour of the Lovettite aristocracy of labour, was born of distress. It was, as Carlyle so clearly saw, "a new name for a thing which has had many names".[4] The unrest which pervaded the manufacturing districts in that age of discontent was not the product of any political agitation or combination of agitations, though it was used by several—by Chartism, by the Anti-Corn Law League, and by the Irish Confederates of '48. It was, to resort again to Carlyle's phrase, "the bitter discontent

---

[1] In the support which it received from an economically superseded class Chartism strongly resembles 'Poujadism' in modern France.

[2] Among the special conditions predisposing the inhabitants of the region towards violence was the exceptionally rapid growth of the population, which imparted to the Welsh mining villages many of the characteristics of American frontier settlements, together with the tradition of lawlessness which was associated with them. Long hours of labour and frequent explosions in the mines further brutalized the Welsh miners. David Williams, *John Frost: A Study in Chartism*, 110 et seq.

[3] *Ibid.*, 118.   [4] Thomas Carlyle, *Chartism*, 2.

grown fierce and mad, the wrong condition therefore or the wrong disposition of the Working Classes of England".[1]

But the acute social discontents of the Chartist period were not caused solely by the operation of blind economic forces, which the government either could not, or would not, control. Positive government policy made its contribution to unrest. If Bronterre O'Brien's articles in *The Northern Star* convinced the English workmen that they formed a helot class, deprived of political rights, and, therefore, treated without consideration, it was because their minds had been prepared for the revelation by the conduct of Whig administrations since the passing of the First Reform Act. The upholding of the severe sentences passed on the Dorset labourers in 1834, and on the Glasgow cotton spinners in 1837, fostered the impression that the middle classes were using their new-found power to wage bitter, relentless war on the workers. But the measure which did most to provoke the working classes of England to rebellion was the New Poor Law of 1834. Designed to solve one of the great social problems of the agrarian South, where pauperism was thought to be due to the lax administration of the Poor Laws, this measure had no remedy for poverty but the harsh deterrent workhouse. It seemed, therefore, to carry the implication that poverty was a crime,[2] and to be framed with the intention of forcing down the level of wages by increasing the urgency of employment.[3] Though the manufacturing districts as a whole were free from the abuses which marked the administration of the Poor Laws in the southern counties, there was scarcely a workman in factory or cottage who was unlikely to have to apply for relief in times of commercial depression. The New Poor Law was, therefore, a matter of vital moment for the industrial working class, and, although it was not applied in all its vigour to Lancashire and the West Riding of Yorkshire, the mere threat of it evoked an indomitable spirit of resistance. The Law was construed, not merely as a blow and an insult to

[1] *Ibid.*

[2] "Rightly or wrongly . . . the labourers of England believed that the new poor law was a law to punish Poverty." Alfred, *The History of the Factory Movement*, II, 76.

[3] E. Dolleans, *Le Chartisme* (1831-48), 23.

the working classes, but as an unconstitutional measure, which justified armed resistance.[1] The latter argument was also used against the Whig Proclamations and police measures of 1839, and the disposition to accumulate and parade arms and other weapons, which so frightened the authorities in the year of the first Chartist Petition, was encouraged by a mistaken belief that the government was behaving unconstitutionally.[2]

The causes of distress and resentment which have been touched upon in the preceding pages operated mainly upon the industrial working class. For this reason, the manufacturing and mining districts were the real trouble spots, with London gaining in importance as a centre of disorder towards the close of the period. The rural districts of the South of England lay quiet in the twenty years after the savage repression of 'the Last Labourers' Revolt' of 1830, though frequent burnings of hayricks served as a sombre reminder that all was not well in the English village. Nevertheless the 'Rebecca' Rising of 1842-4, which was localized in the western portions of South Wales, was the only serious agrarian outbreak of the age of the Chartists.

As might have been expected from the nature of their causes, the disturbances were not spread out evenly over the period, but tended to occur in clusters, at times when distress was most severe, when employment fell, and the cost of living soared. Between these main phases of unrest Britain enjoyed an uneasy tranquillity, broken only by an occasional trade dispute, or quarrel between the unruly 'navigators' employed in constructing the numerous lines of railway, and by the disorder which accompanied the holding of a general election. During the period under review

[1] *The Northern Star* pointed out to its readers that the exhortations to acquire arms, addressed to the multitude by Rayner Stephens, the Anti-Poor Law agitator, all had reference to "the principles and practices of the Poor Law Amendment Act", and expressed regret that the government had abandoned its original intention to prosecute him for a conspiracy to resist the Poor Law Amendment Act, as an opportunity to settle the constitutional question by the decision of the court had been missed. *The Northern Star*, 4 May 1839, p. 4.

[2] William Lovett, seconding in the Chartist Convention an address which advised the people to arm, said that he had been converted to this policy by the government's disposition to put down meetings by proclamation, which was not law. *The Northern Star*, 18 May 1839, p. 6.

there were four principal clusters of disorder. The first was from the spring of 1837 to the end of January 1840.[1] The last was from February to August 1848. The second covered the summer months of 1842, from the middle of July to the middle of September, and was followed almost immediately by the third, which began in November 1842, continued unabated until October 1843, and extended on a more limited scale into the following year.

Chartism, the dominant working-class movement of the age, influenced to a greater or lesser extent all these phases of disturbance, but did not monopolize any of them. When the first phase opened, in 1837, the disorder had no unifying theme. Resistance to the New Poor Law, which the Commissioners were starting to apply to the manufacturing counties of Lancaster and York, was the largest single manifestation of discontent, but the peace was also broken by a lengthy trade dispute in Glasgow, a bread riot in Manchester and several serious affrays at Birmingham, Stoke-on-Trent and elsewhere, arising from the general election of the summer. Gradually, however, the agitation for the 'Six Points' of the People's Charter gathered up the threads of unrest, and became the centre of the popular movement in the second half of 1838 and in 1839. In the latter year a Convention consisting of delegates from many parts of the country met in London, and assumed the direction of the 'democratic' campaign. A National Petition calling for universal suffrage and the other Chartist reforms was presented to Parliament on 12 July. The House of Commons declined to consider it, and shortly afterwards the Convention was dissolved, without giving a clear lead to its followers on the subject of 'ulterior measures'. Riots occurred at Birmingham on 15 July, and at Bolton, Manchester, Macclesfield, Hindley and elsewhere about the middle of August. On 4 November a large army of colliers and ironworkers headed by Frost, a former member of the Convention, marched into Newport from the Monmouthshire hills, and challenged the forces of authority

[1] Excitement did not remain at the same level throughout this lengthy period. Within it were intervals of comparative tranquillity (as for example in March 1838 and in September 1839), but, taken together, the years in question constitute a reasonably well-rounded phase of disturbances.

stationed in the Westgate Hotel. But these disturbances were easily put down, and by the middle of the winter of 1839-40 Chartism was under a cloud, discredited by its internal dissensions and by the prosecutions which the government had launched against its leaders.

The movement showed remarkable powers of recovery, and was soon building up for itself a nation-wide organization in the form of the National Charter Association, launched at Manchester in July 1840. But the revival was on 'moral force' lines, and the peace of the country was comparatively undisturbed in 1840 and 1841, except at the time of the general election held in the summer of 1841. The Chartist leaders did not initiate the second phase of disorder, which opened in the early summer of 1842. It began as a strike for higher wages and the removal of certain abuses of a purely economic character (e.g. truck payments), and spread rapidly, accompanied by various acts of violence, until it affected almost the entire industrial area of the North and Midlands and many parts of Scotland. In the later stages a political element crept in. At meeting after meeting the turnouts resolved to remain out of work until the People's Charter became the law of the land, and eventually, after some hesitation, the Chartist Executive, assembled in Manchester, declared for the strike. Soon afterwards the government launched prosecutions against the Chartist and trade union leaders, and the outbreak was brought to an end.

Scarcely had order been restored to the industrial North and Midlands than the third phase of disorder began in a portion of the country which had previously been accounted quiet—the agricultural counties of West Wales, especially Carmarthenshire and Pembrokeshire. These Rebecca Riots, so-called because the rioters dressed themselves up as women, and acted under the command of a leader known as Rebecca,[1] were mainly directed towards the removal of local grievances—vexatious road tolls,

---

[1] In fulfilment of the text from the 24th chapter of Genesis: "And they blessed Rebekah, and said unto her, Thou art our sister, be thou the mother of thousands of millions, and let thy seed possess the gate of those which hate them."

high rents, tithes and heavy poor rates—which pressed upon the impecunious small farmers of the Principality;[1] but Chartism had some connection with the disturbances, especially in their later stages.[2]

Whilst 'Rebecca' kept South Wales in turmoil the manufacturing districts of England entered the tranquil period of the middle forties. During those years Chartism was weak, divided and preoccupied with the land scheme devised by Feargus O'Connor. Losing support among the English working men, whose interest in politics cooled rapidly when they became more prosperous, it turned its attention outwards to a wider world, and forged close links of friendship with continental revolutionaries and Irish rebels.

But the trade depression of 1847 and the political turmoil in Europe in 1848 revived the embers of discontent in England. In the last of the four phases of disorder, which began early in 1848, Chartism was, as in 1839, the focus of the unrest. There was another Convention and another Petition to Parliament. The latter floundered in ridicule when it was discovered how many of its alleged six million signatures were forgeries, but the derisive laughter of the propertied classes did not, as was once supposed, deal an immediate death-blow to the movement. On the contrary the Chartists kept up an alarming agitation for several months,

---

[1] It is worthy of note that what had made the burdens particularly intolerable at this time was the drastic fall in the price of farm produce in the two years prior to 1843. According to J. H. Vivian, M.P. for Swansea, this depreciation was due to the depressed state of the iron and coal trades of Glamorganshire and Monmouthshire, the counties in which the Welsh farmer marketed much of his produce. Vivian also pointed out that the depression in the ironworks caused many of the workmen who had migrated thither from the Carmarthenshire and Pembrokeshire countryside to move back to their parishes of settlement, thus increasing the burden of the poor rates which fell upon the farmer. Hence the Rebecca Riots, like the other great outbreaks of the period, owed their origin partly to the downswing of the business cycle. *The Times*, 28 June 1843, p. 5; 12 December 1843, p. 5.

[2] The attack on the Carmarthen workhouse, which took place on 19 June 1843, was partly attributed by a correspondent of *The Times* to "Chartists and rabble of the town". *Ibid.*, 22 June 1843, p. 5. The researches of Professor David Williams indicate that the connection between the two movements was slight. *The Rebecca Riots: A Study in Agrarian Discontent*, 150–2.

and their efforts were seconded by those of the Young Ireland leaders, who were bent on stirring up the Irish population of the towns and cities of Great Britain in pursuance of their nationalist aims. But these tactics only resulted in arrests, and by the beginning of autumn Chartism had ceased to threaten the public peace.

Viewed in their entirety, the disturbances of the Chartist period were far less destructive than those of a previous generation. If unrest was more widespread than in the comparatively stable, silver age of the eighteenth century, it was also more restrained in character, more restrained also than in the early years of the nineteenth century, when the dislocations caused by the Napoleonic War depressed the living standards of the British working class. The late thirties and forties of the nineteenth century were marked by no orgies of devastation comparable with the Gordon Riots of 1780,

> when the rude rabble's watchword was destroy,
> and blazing London seemed a second Troy,

or even with the Bristol Riots, which had occurred as recently as 1831. There is much truth in the Hammonds' contention that "violence, the most important fact in the Gordon Riots, was the least important fact in the Chartist demonstrations; that unlike the mob, drawn by a strong passion, which spent its inarticulate fury in burning Newgate prison to the ground, the men and women who kept the Chartist movement alive had a steady and responsible quarrel with the conditions of their lives".[1] Machine-breaking, which had been the essence of Luddism, and had raged in the manufacturing districts as late as 1826, was no longer a feature of the popular response to acute distress. This improvement cannot be attributed entirely to police reform, and to the perfecting of methods of repression, as there were times, notably during the Plug-Plot disturbances of August 1842, when the insurgents had whole towns at their mercy, yet refrained from acts of looting and incendiarism. In the main it must be ascribed to the fact that the English industrial working class was on the

[1] J. L. & Barbara Hammond, *The Bleak Age*, 14.

whole better housed, better fed, better educated, and far less degraded than in preceding years.

Nevertheless, although the urge to wanton destruction had been considerably weakened by the time of the Chartist disturbances, it had not been completely banished, and broke through on several occasions. At Todmorden, on the borders of Lancashire and Yorkshire, where feeling ran high against the New Poor Law, and was encouraged by the powerful radical mill-owner, John Fielden, an angry mob toured the dwelling-houses of prominent local magnates on 21 November 1838, setting fire to one, destroying the furniture at another, and breaking the windows, doors and shutters at a further nine.[1] At Birmingham, where for a time the Chartist Convention held its meetings, a large body of rioters, enraged by the steps taken by the magistracy to put down the Chartist agitation, poured into the Bull Ring on the night of 15 July 1839, and proceeded to break open the shops and warehouses which surrounded it. They carried the contents, which included immense rolls of bed ticking, out into the street, where they set fire to them, and then proceeded to convey them blazing back into the buildings from which they had been taken. A two-horse fire engine drove up to extinguish the flames, but was compelled by the mob to withdraw.[2] The actual damage appears to have been limited to the destruction of two shops, but there is every reason to believe that, had it not been for the somewhat belated intervention of the police and the dragoons, Birmingham would have shared the fate which had befallen Bristol in 1831. A month later, on 13 August, a Bolton mob attempted to fire the Town Hall, where the special constables were stationed,[3] and on 15 August 1842 the miners of the North Staffordshire coalfield, whipped up to frenzy by the speeches of the visiting Chartist orator, Thomas Cooper, raided the police stations of the Pottery towns for arms, and visited the houses of the neighbouring gentry, leaving a trail of destruction behind them. The house of the vicar

[1] Todmorden Magistrates to the Home Office dated 23 November 1838. Home Office Papers, 40/38.
[2] Charles Reith, *British Police and the Democratic Ideal*, 234–5.
[3] Winder to H.O. dated 14 August 1839. H.O. 40/44.

of Longton was fired, that of Bayley Rose, the stipendiary magistrate, was sacked. During the night the mob burned to the ground the parsonage at Hanley and the house of a county magistrate, Mr. Parker. On the following day the office of Lord Granville, a prominent local coalowner, was burned down, and so was the house of his agent, Mr. Forrester. On the 17th the house of a Mr. Harding at Handford was fired.[1] These were isolated episodes in the story of English disturbances, but they serve to show that the demon of destruction still lurked beneath the surface of English social life, ready to break loose in times of stress.

The Welsh Rebecca Riots were more systematically destructive, reminiscent to a greater extent of the Luddite outbreak of the Regency period than of any contemporary English disturbances. The rioters proceeded on horseback by night to the various toll gates which lay across the Welsh roads, and demolished each in its turn, often razing the adjoining toll house to its foundations at the same time. Later, when the war against the turnpike trusts had been waged with marked success, the Rebeccaites turned to other acts of destruction. An attempt was made to pull down the Carmarthen workhouse, and the dwelling-houses and hayricks of unpopular magistrates, landlords and tithe owners were singled out for attack. At Gelliwernen House, the home of a Mr. Edwards, the agent of a Carmarthenshire tithe impropriator, the rioters fired repeatedly through the window of the bedroom in which the owner lay sick, and devastated the walled garden adjacent to the house.[2]

Rioting of a limited character occurred more frequently. In this kind of disorder destruction of property was restricted to a minimum, and the amount of violence used by the mob was restricted to what was deemed necessary to coerce or intimidate persons and to influence policy. Thus, for example, the Anti-Poor Law rioters in Bradford, Huddersfield and other parts of

[1] Brothers to Maberley dated 15 and 17 August 1842; Rose to H.O. dated 15 August 1842; Powys to H.O. dated 16 August 1842; Adderley to Dartmouth dated 16 August 1842. H.O. 45/260.
[2] H. Tobit Evans, *Rebecca and her Daughters*, 150-2.

the West Riding in 1837 and 1838 adopted tactics which were clearly designed to prevent the introduction of the New Poor Law into the Riding, by making it impossible for the Boards of Guardians to function. Whenever the latter met to elect a clerk, or to transact some other item of business, a mob collected outside the meeting-place, threw stones at the windows, and assaulted persons going in and coming out.[1] In the disturbances which occurred in the North of England and the Midlands in the summer of 1842, force was employed principally to maintain and extend the strike which was then being conducted first for higher wages and afterwards for the Charter. The strike was communicated from factory to factory and from town to town, by enormous mobs containing several thousand operatives, many of them armed with formidable bludgeons.[2] When they arrived at a cotton or woollen mill, they insisted that its inmates should come out and join them, and, in order to prevent an early resumption of work, they drew the plugs from the factory boilers, thus extinguishing the fires and stopping the engines. From this circumstance the disturbances were known in Lancashire and Yorkshire as the Plug-Plot Riots. The sudden entry of such immense multitudes into towns like Stockport and Bolton, which normally housed about 50,000 people, was in itself an act of disorder, even if no violence was committed, and the strikers did not in fact hesitate to use force when they encountered resistance. Vigorous assaults were made upon those factories which did not immediately yield up their inmates at the approach of the mob, whilst at Todmorden the invaders, having turned out the factories, left behind a warning that, if any of the local operatives resumed work before the entire demands of the mob had been

[1] *Poor Law Commissioners, Third Annual Report* (1837), Appendix A, 7; *Fourth Annual Report* (1838), Appendix A, 8.

[2] Dr. Heginbotham, the historian of Stockport, estimated the size of the turnout mob which entered Stockport on 11 August 1842 at nearly 30,000. H. Heginbotham, *Stockport: Ancient and Modern,* I, 101. This is probably an exaggeration. Most of the estimates of the size of turnout mobs recorded in the Home Office Papers vary from 2,000 to 8,000, though there were some smaller parties. Captain Woodford of the Lancashire County Constabulary put the mob which advanced on Preston on 17 August at 500. Woodford to H.O. dated 17 August 1842. H.O. 45/249A.

complied with throughout the manufacturing district, their properties would be destroyed or burnt.[1] At Castlefield, near Bingley, Yorkshire, the turnouts threatened to set fire to any mill which opened again without their sanction.[2] In the absence of adequate strike funds the need to obtain food gave rise to further violence. In Manchester shops were plundered, and the strikers helped themselves to bread,[3] whilst at Stockport they stormed the workhouse for the purpose of seizing money and provisions.[4] Fierce clashes occurred between the mobs and the small bodies of troops and police sent out to check them, and on several occasions the soldiers were compelled to open fire. These disturbances affected almost simultaneously every important industrial centre in England and Scotland, and were, therefore, unparalleled in magnitude throughout the entire Chartist period, but they were anticipated on a much smaller scale two years earlier, in August 1839, when, in obedience to a recommendation from their leaders, the Chartists had endeavoured to secure abstention from work "for two or three days, in order to devote the whole of that time to solemn processions and solemn meetings". In Bolton, Manchester, Macclesfield and other towns in the same region the workmen had resorted to the device which was to prove so successful in August 1842—that of touring the mills and compelling the operatives to turn out.

Much of the disorder of the period consisted, not of open violence in any form, but of tumultuous demonstration and feverish preparation for a day of deliverance in the future. This was particularly true of the Chartist disturbances of 1838–40 and 1848. During those long periods of agitation riots were surprisingly few, limited in the main to reprisals against the efforts of the local authorities to interfere with demonstrations. The most prominent feature of the popular movement was the succession of large meetings which were held up and down the country, and addressed by O'Connor, O'Brien, Harney and other

---

[1] Crossley and Taylor to H.O. dated 12 August 1842. H.O. 45/249.
[2] Ellis to H.O. dated 16 August 1842. H.O. 45/264.
[3] *Absalom Watkin: Extracts from his Journal, 1814–56*, ed. A. E. Watkin, 216.
[4] Heginbotham, *op. cit.*, I, 102.

champions of the 'democratic' cause. The Chartist leaders and their press hotly contended that these meetings were purely peaceable demonstrations designed to promote discussion of the People's Charter, and that the interference with them, practised by the magistrates, was sheer official tyranny.[1] The reports received by the Home Office tell a very different story, and, although these may be equally biased, their detailed references to particular features of the meetings leave little doubt that the agitation was intended not merely to persuade, but to intimidate, and that, coming at a time of widespread popular distress, it tended to endanger the public peace. This was not true of all Chartist meetings: thus for example at the Whitsuntide demonstrations of May 1839 great care was taken in many places to avoid giving offence to the authorities. Nevertheless, many of the demonstrations organized by the Chartists in that year, and again in 1848, were undoubtedly of an alarming character. The torchlight meetings which were held on the long autumn evenings of 1838 were particularly disturbing, but the same objection extends to many of the meetings which were held by daylight. Language of the most unrestrained character was uttered from the platform to assemblages of several thousand people. A speech by Rayner Stephens at Newcastle in January 1838, attacking the New Poor Law, will serve as an example of the more outrageous kind of 'physical force' tirade delivered at Chartist meetings:

If the people who produce all wealth [declaimed the reverend orator], could not be allowed, according to God's word, to have the kindly fruits of the earth which they had, in obedience to God's word, raised by the sweat of their brow, then war to the knife with their enemies, who were the enemies of God. If the musket and the pistol, the sword and the pike were of no avail, let the woman take the scissors, the child the pin or needle. If all failed, then the firebrand —aye the firebrand—the firebrand, I repeat. The palace shall be in flames.[2]

---

[1] Protesting against the Royal Proclamation of 1839, and the proclamations issued by the magistrates against Chartist meetings, *The Northern Star* advised its readers to "preserve the same unvarying attention to order and peacefulness of conduct which has hitherto characterized them" (i.e. the meetings). *The Northern Star*, 11 May 1839, p. 4.

[2] Maccoby, *op. cit.*, 175.

The meetings at which such language was uttered were frequently preceded or followed by processions through the streets of towns, the processionists hissing and groaning in an ominous fashion as they went.[1] Bludgeons were brandished,[2] and Caps of Liberty and banners bearing the most inflammatory slogans were carried aloft.[3] And, as if these symptoms were not sufficient in themselves to create an atmosphere of alarm, pistol shots were occasionally fired off on the meeting-ground.[4] Even when no acts of violence occurred at them, demonstrations of this kind can only be regarded as disturbances, especially when held repeatedly day after day. Not only did they give grounds for fearing that a breach of the peace was imminent, but their effect, as was seen in London in the spring of 1848, was to frighten nearby shopkeepers into shutting up their shops and removing their stocks to places of safety.[5]

The effect of these campaigns of meetings and processions was heightened in 1839, and to a lesser extent in 1848, by the military preparations undertaken by the Chartists. Training and drilling under the command of old soldiers was reported to be proceeding in many working-class districts in the former year, and in the latter, extremist elements formed themselves into National Guards divided and subdivided in military order.[6] A popular text-book on street warfare written by an Italian revolutionary,

[1] Sheffield Magistrates to H.O. dated 14 August 1839, H.O. 40/51.

[2] See report of a procession and meeting in Newport, Monmouthshire, on Friday, 20 April 1839. H.O. 40/45.

[3] Hyde Magistrates to H.O. dated 16 November 1838. H.O. 40/38.

[4] At a torchlight meeting in Hyde, Cheshire, on 14 November 1838, the speeches were interrupted by frequent discharges of firearms and cries of "We are ready now". *Ibid.* A gun was fired off at a Chartist meeting in Bolton on Friday, 2 August 1839, and was answered by four or five pistol shots from different parts of the meeting-ground. Darbishire to H.O. dated 4 August 1839. H.O. 40/44.

[5] For evidence of the interruption of trade caused by political disturbances see letters to *The Times*, 1 April 1848, p. 8; 7 April 1848, p. 5, and a report in that newspaper of the Trafalgar Square riots, 9 March 1848, p. 5.

[6] The National Guard at Ashton-under-Lyne consisted of six divisions, each under the command of a captain, and each divided into four smaller units of 25 men commanded by a lieutenant. *The Manchester Guardian*, 20 December 1848, p. 7.

Macerone, was said to be in circulation in the disturbed districts in 1839, and from many widely separated districts came reports that arms were being accumulated by the working class, with the encouragement of the Chartist Convention.

It is difficult to obtain an accurate impression of the extent to which the Chartists were arming. No important sale of firearms to the working classes by regular arms dealers took place either in 1839 or in 1848. After carrying out investigations in Birmingham and other towns, Lord John Russell told Parliament on 15 May 1839 that "there had been no very considerable quantity of arms made by the regular manufacturers, and the chief part of the sale which had taken place had been for exportation".[1] A return of arms sold in London during the first six months of 1848, which was compiled by the Metropolitan Police, gives grounds for believing that the London proletariat had not availed itself, to any notable extent, of the contents of gunsmiths' shops.[2] It is clear, however, that firearms, presumably second-hand ones, were being vended to the working classes by hawkers, and that blacksmiths were engaged in grinding pikes for them. *The Stockport Advertiser* noted in April 1839 that "in our Market Place, on Saturday, war like weapons of every description were openly disposed of, by two individuals, after the manner of a Dutch auction".[3] Three months earlier, the same newspaper had alluded to the activities of an individual who was publicly hawking pistols at 3s. a brace in the New Mills district.[4] In April 1839 young Chartists of Llanidloes 'borrowed' muskets from the neighbouring farmers, and severe rioting occurred when the authorities attempted to arrest the ringleaders.[5]

[1] Hansard, *Parliamentary Debates*, 3 Ser., XLVII, 1027.

[2] It ran as follows :—

	Guns	Pistols	Swords	Other Weapons
To Gentlemen, Respectable Tradesmen, Gamekeepers etc.	378	467	71	0
To Mechanics, Labourers etc. who are believed to be, and others known to be, Chartists.	122	162	22	18

Metropolitan Police Memorandum, 3 July 1848. H.O. 45/2410.

[3] *The Stockport Advertiser*, 19 April 1839, p. 2.

[4] *Ibid.*, 18 January 1839, p. 2.   [5] Williams, *John Frost*, 156-7.

Though many of the reports concerning the Chartist armament are certainly exaggerated, there can be little doubt that a considerable quantity of pikes and second-hand muskets and pistols found its way into the hands of the working classes.[1] It cannot, however, be assumed that all, or even the majority of those involved in the disturbances of the period were equipped with such weapons. Of the army of Monmouthshire miners and ironworkers which marched into Newport on 4 November 1839, some undoubtedly carried guns, spears and pikes, but it was observed that others had to make do with hatchets, cleavers, mandrils, rough pieces of iron and scythes.[2] Moreover, according to the professional opinion of General Sir Charles Napier, some of the weapons on which the Chartists relied were of little use. Of their pikes and daggers he wrote to his brother William, a man of military experience: "Oastler's pike was shown to me; it is a half pike with a long springy blade, altogether the worst possible; so are the knives, with which they could not stab, because the blade is curved at the point."[3] Altogether the Chartist armament was not very formidable.

It is also true that despite their frequent training and drilling the Chartists never developed effective tactics of opposition to troops. There seems to have been only one instance during the entire period when an English mob erected a barricade—at

[1] Lord John Russell, as Home Secretary, told the House of Commons in May 1839, that "while he wished on one hand to guard the House against any exaggerated notion of there being large bodies of men regularly armed, on the other hand he believed there were a considerable number of persons in possession of very dangerous and offensive weapons". Hansard, 3 Ser., XLVII, 1025–28. The Mayor of Newcastle on Tyne, who was obviously not an alarmist, as he stated his belief that no serious riot was to be anticipated, affirmed that some of the most ignorant people in the neighbourhood were arming. Russell to Northumberland, dated 4 March 1839. H.O. 41/13. See also Foster to Russell dated 4 May 1839. H.O. 40/43.

[2] Mayor of Newport to H.O. dated 6 November 1839. H.O. 40/45. The Home Office Papers also contain reports that, in the East Midland counties of Leicestershire and Nottinghamshire, the Chartists were drilling with hedge sticks. Inspector Martin to Commissioners of Metropolitan Police dated 28 February 1839. H.O. 40/47.

[3] W. Napier, The Life and Opinions of General Sir Charles James Napier, II, 21.

Stone, Staffordshire, in May 1839.[1] In their clashes with the Queen's troops the angry rioters normally resorted to the straightforward approach of hurling great stones at the soldiery, exposing themselves to heavy retaliation. Regular troops were used with great restraint throughout the period. They did not usually open fire until they were themselves severely assailed by the crowd, but experience was to prove, on more than one occasion during the period, that the largest mobs could not withstand for long the musketry fire of the smallest military detachment. At Newport in November 1839 thirty soldiers, strategically positioned in an upper room of the Westgate Hotel, put to flight two or three thousand miners and ironworkers, some of them equipped with firearms. "At the first shot fired by the soldiers", writes the biographer of John Frost, "the crowd had dropped whatever arms they had, guns, pikes and mandrils, and fled in wild disorder—except apparently one wooden-legged man, who was seen to fire three times at the hotel".[2] At Preston, during the Plug-Plot disturbances, a mob which had belaboured the soldiers with stones stood its ground for a while when the order to fire was given and several of its members were struck, but the shooting of a ringleader, who had stepped out in front of the mob to encourage his followers to continue the assault, put a damper on the proceedings, and caused the crowd to disperse.[3] Clearly the military preparations of the Chartists never succeeded in welding the disaffected elements in English society into a fighting force comparable with the French 'ouvriers'.

The threat to English society in the Chartist period did not in fact arise from the strength of the resistance which the rioters were capable of offering to the forces of the Crown, but from the tendency of disturbances to occur almost simultaneously in different places. This tendency was due in the first place to the widespread economic distress, which turned the manufacturing districts in times of slack trade into a veritable powder magazine, capable of being ignited by the smallest spark. Thus an outbreak in one district quickly spread to its neighbours, and the events of

[1] Ibid., 27. [2] Williams, John Frost, 230.
[3] The Times, 15 August 1842, p. 4.

the summer of 1842 were to demonstrate with what rapidity a strike, beginning in a small tract of territory, situated to the south and east of Manchester, could be spread by roving bands of turn-outs, until it involved the entire industrial area of the North and Midlands. The danger of concurrent outbreaks was increased by the hold which political agitation, notably that of the Chartists, had upon the masses. By convening simultaneous meetings, as at Whitsuntide 1839, and by decreeing demonstrations, such as the 'Two or Three Days Holiday', which was held on 12, 13, and 14 August 1839, the Chartist Convention was able to mobilize, at particular points of time, the unrest latent throughout the country, and to confront the authorities with a serious difficulty in allocating their limited resources. Indeed there is evidence to show that Ernest Jones, one of the leading Chartists of 1848, looked upon the demonstrations in the provinces on the day of the great Kennington Common meeting as a device for preventing the government from concentrating its troops in London.[1]

Whether the Chartists went beyond the convening of demonstrations to the planning of rebellion is a question on which historians are not agreed. Mark Hovell, a leading historian of the movement, believed that the idea of a general rising was mooted early in 1839, postponed, and revived towards the end of the year, when preparations were actually made. According to his view, Frost's outbreak at Newport, Monmouthshire, in November, was the first stage in the realization of this plan.[2] Against this Dr. R. F. Wearmouth asserts that "it is nearer the truth to say that the Chartists never intended, and never planned, a general rising, not even a local one".[3]

Subsequent research has indeed tended to undermine Hovell's assumption that the Newport Rising was part of an integrated national revolt. The theory that the interception of the mail

---

[1] It was resolved in the Convention on 7 April 1848, on the motion of Ernest Jones, that simultaneous meetings should be held all over the country on the following Monday "so that the myrmidons of power in the country might be kept in check by the brave men there". *The Times*, 8 April 1848, p. 7.

[2] Mark Hovell, *The Chartist Movement*, 178.

[3] R. F. Wearmouth, *Some Working-Class Movements of the Nineteenth Century*, 116.

coach at Newport was to act as a signal for insurrection in the Midlands was exposed as ridiculous at the trial of Frost, Williams and Jones, and was specifically contradicted by Frost later in life, when he had nothing to lose by admitting it. Yet it is beyond doubt that Frost, as his biographer admits, was in communication with the Midlands and the North, and even if, as seems probable, no agreement had been reached with these regions to rise on the night of 3–4 November, it is reasonable to suppose that a co-ordinated insurrection was being seriously considered.

Moreover there is a good deal of evidence to suggest that on two subsequent occasions—in the winter of 1839–40, and in the late summer of 1848—the Chartists planned risings which, if not completely general, affected a wide area. The first of these attempts came to a head at Sheffield, Dewsbury and other places in the West Riding on 12 January 1840. The disturbance at Sheffield occurred in the early hours of the morning, when bodies of armed Chartists converging on the Town Hall were dispersed by the dragoons, some prisoners being taken, and a collection of hand grenades and fireballs being found in the house of one of the local leaders. The object was stated to have been the capture of the Town Hall and the Tontine Hotel and, in the event of failure, to 'Moscow' the town.[1] On the same day and at almost the same hour Dewsbury was paraded by more than 100 persons, arranged in military formation, and armed with guns and bludgeons. Headed by a man who called out, "March. Death or Glory! The town's our own", they chased the Deputy Constable over the Gas House wall, and fired off shots in the Market Place.[2] The evidence of witnesses at the trial of the Chartists implicated in the Sheffield rising connects the outbreak with a conference in Dewsbury,[3] and there is independent confirmation of this in Dr. Gammage's *History of the Chartist Movement*. Drawing on the testimony of William Ashton, a Barnsley Chartist, Gammage speaks of a delegate meeting in Dewsbury, which fixed 12 January as the

[1] Clerk of Sheffield Magistrates to H.O. dated 12 January 1840. H.O. 40/57. *The Times*, 16 January 1840, p. 6; 19 March 1840, p. 6.

[2] Deposition of John Hirst enclosed in Hague to H.O. dated 12 January 1840. H.O. 40/57.

[3] *The Times*, 19 March 1840, p. 6.

c

date of a rising.[1] The Sheffield magistrates affirmed that Nottinghamshire was included in the plan,[2] and their evidence receives corroboration from reports in *The Times* that the coaches leaving Sheffield on 11 January were besieged at Barnsley, Bradford, Dewsbury and Nottingham by workmen who inquired eagerly whether the people of Sheffield were up in arms.[3] Perhaps the Yorkshire rising was also intended to produce its echo in the metropolis. Armed meetings were held at the Trades Hall, Bethnal Green, on 14 and 16 January. Writing to Commissioner Rowan of the Metropolitan Police, with reference to the first of these meetings, an anonymous informant, who seemed to enjoy the confidence of the London Chartists, hinted at such a connection. "There has been information received from the country", he wrote, "that the Government prevented the signal for a rise".[4]

The second Chartist attempt at a co-ordinated rising was in August 1848. Lancashire and London were the areas principally affected. In the Manchester district the crisis occurred on the night of 14–15 August. Seventy armed Chartists stole out of the Working Men's Hall in Oldham in the early hours of the morning, and moved off secretly and quietly in the direction of Manchester. According to a report sent to the Home Office by the Oldham magistrates the object of this enterprise was to set fire to the town of Manchester and to shoot its magistrates. It was also affirmed by the Oldham justices that the rising was to be general throughout the kingdom and that Ernest Jones, who was serving a prison sentence for sedition, should be liberated.[5] Ashton-under-Lyne was paraded just before midnight by several bodies of men, armed with pikes and guns, and a policeman was shot dead in the street.[6] At Hyde a mob visited the factories, pulling out the boiler plugs, as in 1842.[7] Thomas Brown, the Constable, who tried

---

[1] R. G. Gammage, *A History of the Chartist Movement*, 264.
[2] H. Parker to H.O. dated 15 January 1840. H.O. 40/57.
[3] *The Times*, 18 January 1840, p. 6.
[4] Anonymous letter to Colonel Rowan dated 14 January 1840. H.O. 61/25.
[5] Mellor and Jones to H.O. dated 15 August 1848. H.O. 45/2410A.
[6] Mayor and Magistrates of Ashton to H.O. dated 15 August 1848. H.O. 45/2410A.
[7] Hibbert and Clarke to H.O. dated 15 August 1848. H.O. 45/2410K.

to interrupt its progress, received the confident assurance: "They're now all out, all over England, Ireland and Scotland, and before this time tomorrow night we'll either make it better or worse."[1] In Manchester the Chartist and Confederate Clubs were in session throughout the night,[2] and the following night extensive arrests were made by the police.[3] In London, on the 16th, the Metropolitan Police rounded up bodies of armed Chartists in the taverns.[4]

The remarkable synchronization of these outbreaks would have been sufficient to arouse the strongest suspicion that they had been co-ordinated in advance, and the evidence which was tendered to the police, and later at the trials of the parties implicated, strengthens the conviction that what occurred in the middle of August 1848 was the working out of a preconceived plan. It is true that most of this evidence is derived from tainted sources, from police spies and persons turning Queen's evidence, and deserves, therefore, to be treated with the greatest reserve; but there are elements in it which corroborate one another, and leave little doubt that conspiracy was afoot. John Latimer, a Chartist who gave evidence against his fellows, deposed that a man named Milligan attended a conference in Manchester on behalf of the Ashton Chartists, and brought back news from it, on the afternoon of 14 August, that the rising was to be that night.[5] Powell, the notorious informer against the London Chartists, described in the witness-box a meeting of delegates from various district branches at the Lord Denman beer shop in Webber Street, on 15 August, when Lacey, who had been as a delegate to Manchester, gave a report, which led to the fixing of the rising in London for the next day.[6] And the Ashton informant expressly confirmed that London had been represented at the Manchester Conference. "Milligan", he deposed, "said that every town in England would

[1] Deposition of Thomas Brown. H.O. 48/40.
[2] Mayor of Manchester to H.O. dated 15 August 1848. H.O. 45/2410A.
[3] Telegraph Message from Superintendent of Intelligence Dept. to H.O. dated 16 August 1848. H.O. 45/2410A.
[4] The Northern Star, 19 August 1848, p. 5.
[5] Deposition of John Latimer dated 8 September 1848. H.O. 48/40.
[6] The Northern Star, 26 August 1848, p. 8; 30 September 1848, p. 6.

rise at the same time, and that the delegate from London, whose name I do not remember, had stated to him that he had 200,000 men under him, well organized and armed, ready for action."[1] The 200,000 armed men existed only in the London delegate's imagination, but the evidence of the several accomplices called as witnesses at the trials of the Chartist prisoners agrees in establishing that a small sub-committee of five members had been meeting in the capital prior to 16 August, and that plans for an outbreak were laid on the preceding evening.[2]

It is true that these insurrections were not typical of Chartism as a whole: they form two comparatively brief episodes in its long history, and it is not without significance that, both in 1839-40 and in 1848, the outbreaks occurred when the Chartist agitations of those years had passed its peak, when popular support had fallen away, and when many of the leading figures in the movement were serving prison sentences. The numbers involved in them were ridiculously small, and conclusive evidence implicating the first-rank leaders of the Chartist movement is not to be obtained.

The danger confronting the government in the age of the Chartists was not so much from 'sedition, privy conspiracy and rebellion', as from spontaneous tumult. To some extent that danger could indeed have been averted had governments pursued a more enlightened social policy in the years before it became acute, and had they known how to employ financial policy to minimize trade depressions. But statesmen can hardly be blamed for failing to be Keynesians a century before Keynes. It is true that the teachings of the latter were in some measure anticipated in the currency theories of Thomas Attwood, the Birmingham banker who presented the first 'National Petition' to Parliament, but Attwood was regarded by his contemporaries as a crank. The Chartists themselves, however much they admired him as a political reformer, did not share his views as to the desirability

---

[1] Deposition of John Latimer dated 8 September 1848, H.O. 48/40.

[2] Evidence of Thomas Powell (*The Northern Star*, 26 August 1848, p. 8) and of George Davis (*ibid.*, 30 September 1848, p. 7). For a note on the credibility of the evidence of these two witnesses, see below, p. 214 n. 5. The point made there is also applicable to their testimony in this particular.

of increasing the quantity of paper money. Moreover, even if governments had been able to draw upon the more refined theory of a later generation, it is doubtful whether effective steps could have been taken, in the state of economic organization and resources existing at the time, to free the working classes from the grinding poverty which drove them towards revolt.

It is also to be remembered that the rulers of Britain in the thirties and forties of the nineteenth century were not indifferent to the sufferings of the poor. Most of them were held back from too ready an acceptance of the remedies which were urged upon them from below by the sincere conviction that the interests of the whole nation, including its poorest members, could best be promoted by the operation of a free economy, unimpeded by government interference. But in spite of the limitations of their outlook, some statesmen of the first rank strove, according to their lights, to mitigate distress. Sceptical of the benefits to be derived from legislative action with regard to miners' grievances, Sir Robert Peel was sufficiently convinced of the justice of the demands put forward by the Staffordshire colliers in the summer of 1842 to institute an official inquiry. In a letter to Graham, his Home Secretary, he unfolded his motive: "I think it would be found", he wrote, "that there are practical grievances—possibly not to be redressed by law—of which the employed have just reason to complain. What law cannot effect exposure might." [1]

When rioting occurred the authorities had no option but to put it down unless they were prepared to abdicate from their responsibilities and deliver the destinies of the nation into the hands of a mob. The amount of severity justified on such occasions was the amount necessary for the purpose of restoring public order: no more, but also no less. Moreover, the surest

---

[1] C. S. Parker, *Sir Robert Peel from his Private Papers*, II, 543. Graham shared Peel's views, for he told the Lord Lieutenant of Staffordshire in August 1842 that the latter would "faithfully represent the Government by marking a kind sympathy with the feelings and just claims of the workmen". Graham to Talbot, dated 25 August 1842. H.O. 79/4. On the opposite benches Lord John Russell took a keen interest in the education of the masses. He was vice-president of the British and Foreign School Society from 1824 to 1861. Spencer Walpole, *The Life of Lord John Russell*, I, 329 n. 1.

way to minimize human suffering and loss was to intervene with the necessary force as soon as it became clear that a disturbance was probably imminent instead of waiting until acts of violence had been committed. It is in the light of its ability not merely to suppress, but also to prevent, outrage that the machinery of public order must be judged.

CHAPTER II

CHAPTER II

THE LADDER OF AUTHORITY

IN the ensuing analysis of the machinery of public order a distinction has been drawn between the authorities charged with the maintenance of the public peace, which are described in the present chapter, and the instruments for enforcing their commands, which are treated in the four subsequent chapters. Blurred though it is, by the lack of correspondence between legal and constitutional fictions and nineteenth-century facts, this division will yet serve as a convenient basis of treatment.[1]

The task of maintaining or restoring public order in the early years of Queen Victoria's reign rested upon an imposing hierarchy of authorities arranged in descending order as on the rungs of a ladder. At the head stood Parliament and the executive government. Parliament's function was of a twofold character—to strengthen by legislative action the hands of the central and local authorities, and to control the exercise of power by those organs of government, by putting questions to the ministers of the Crown, by receiving petitions against official and magisterial mismanagement and by authorizing inquiries into such delinquencies.

In general, Parliament shunned the second of these functions. It acted upon the still widely accepted assumption that the routine management of disturbances was no concern of the legislature, and might be left to government alone until such time as a scandal provided the opposition with ammunition to fire at the administration. In the light of the extreme excitement which prevailed in many places and on many occasions during the Chartist period, the references to disturbance in the records of parliamentary debates are surprisingly few. In December 1837 John Fielden, one of the representatives in Parliament of the opposition to the New Poor Law, accused the reformed House of Commons

[1] For the difficulty of classifying the Constable, see below, pp. 73-4.

of neglecting to inquire into the circumstances of the recent
Anti-Poor Law riots in Bradford. Neither the member for the
borough nor the members for the West Riding had previously
brought the matter before Parliament.[1] During the spring of 1839,
when alarm prevailed in the manufacturing districts of the North
on account of the military preparations of the Chartists, the subject of disturbances was raised only four times in the House
of Commons,[2] and the initiative in bringing it forward seems
to have come from one or two persons whose opinions were
probably not at all representative—notably from Colonel Sib-
thorp, the arch-reactionary of English politics, and from Viscount
Dungannon. On each occasion the House showed no desire to
prolong discussion of the matter. When Williams Wynn protested against the rashness of adjourning Parliament at a time
when the Chartist Whitsuntide demonstrations lay in the immediate future, and cast a shadow of impending disorder, his protest
was ignored.[3]

After the burning of the shops in the Birmingham Bull Ring
in the middle of July the interest of Parliament suddenly
quickened, and for three or four nights the situation in Birmingham was very fully debated in both Houses, leading members
of the government and the opposition taking part in the discussion. It is to be noted, however, that even then Parliament did
not take it upon itself to suggest a policy for combating the disturbances. The debates merely reflected the desire of certain prominent Conservatives to investigate the conduct of the liberal magistrates of Birmingham, with the object of discrediting both
them and the Whig government which had nominated them to
the bench.[4]

Three years later, at the time of the Plug-Plot disturbances,
Parliament maintained its attitude of non-intervention. On
12 August, when the rioting was at its height, the legislature was
prorogued without reference being made to the state of the

[1] Hans., 3 Ser., XXXIX, 948 et seq.
[2] On 8 April, 30 April, 15 May and 6 June.
[3] Hans., 3 Ser., XLVII, 1025 et seq.
[4] *Ibid.*, XLIX, 370, 408, 438 and 586.

country in the speeches of either the Queen or the Speaker of the House of Commons. The Rebecca Rising, which spread terror and confusion over a large area of South Wales in the following session, was not discussed at all in Parliament.

Parliament's neglect of internal disturbances was due not only to the assumption that they were the proper responsibility of the executive, but also to the remoteness of the disturbed areas from the seat of government. Disorders in the capital were much more urgently considered. In the year 1848, when riots in Manchester, Bradford, Liverpool and Ashton escaped the notice of Parliament, the unsettled state of the metropolis received attention in debate on no fewer than ten occasions between 8 March and 8 June.

Turning to the other function of Parliament in the machinery of public order, we find that the executive was reluctant to seek its assistance in the form of legislation. Admitting this in reply to a suggestion by Mr. Williams Wynn, on 15 May 1839, the Home Secretary, Lord John Russell, supplied the reasons for this attitude. The first was that the Chartist agitators were so clearly mischievous that they easily placed themselves within reach of the penalties of the existing law. The second and more convincing reason was that, as soon as Parliament was approached for new powers, there was aroused in that body a certain sympathy and jealousy with regard to the constitution.[1] The first point weighed only against acts restricting the rights of citizens (such as the proposed disarming bill, which was the occasion of Russell's remark), but the second applied equally to measures for improving the efficiency of the forces of order. For the House contained a determined band of radicals headed by John Fielden of Todmorden, Thomas Wakley and Thomas Slingsby Duncombe, ready to proclaim the threat of a standing army whenever a reform of the police system was in contemplation. These men would undoubtedly make a great show of their opposition in debate, and, as Russell might well have added, they would undoubtedly be joined by members of the more moderate opposition who were not prepared to deny the government the powers which it requested, but revelled in the opportunity of criticizing the

[1] *Ibid.*, XLVII, 1026.

administration. With the exception of a few extremists like Disraeli the Tory party supported the Whig Police Bills of 1839, but Peel did not allow the occasion to pass without condemning the government for bringing up the proposals late in the session, and accusing the Birmingham magistracy, believed to be a liberal preserve, of gross political partiality.[1] What the government feared was not defeat, which was unlikely, but a public washing of political dirty linen, which was extremely probable. Hence it was the policy of governments to defer appeal to Parliament until extended powers could no longer be dispensed with. The bills for the reform of the police of Manchester, Birmingham and Bolton and for the inception of a professional constabulary in the counties were all introduced late in the session of 1839, and the Enrolled Pensioners Bill was brought forward a fortnight before the end of that of 1843. Waiting conferred upon government the added advantage of being able to rush unpopular measures through an empty House, for it was the practice of many members, in that age of immature party discipline, to withdraw from parliamentary business well before the end of the session. Only fifty-seven members registered their votes at the second reading of the Enrolled Pensioners Bill, and Duncombe, a radical critic of the government, complained of "the deserted benches both behind and in front of the right honourable Baronet" (Sir Robert Peel).[2]

When Parliament was required to strengthen the hand of the executive, it was asked to do so in a manner very different from that of the age of Pitt and the age of Sidmouth. Not by tightening up the law, not by introducing new offences, not by taking away civil liberties was the threat of disorder met, but by improving the means of enforcing the existing law: the formation of a police force rather than the suspension of Habeas Corpus was the action sought from the legislature. It is not without significance that whereas Luddism was countered by an act making frame-breaking punishable by death, a suggestion that the law was not

[1] Hans., 3 Ser., XLIX, 700–4, 942–7.
[2] Ibid., LXXI, 644–5. Voting on the Birmingham Police Bill fell from 147 on 23 July 1839 to 46 on 13 August; on the Rural Police Bill, from 99 on 7 August to 58 on 15 August. The session ended on 27 August.

sufficiently penal in the case of the Welsh gate-wreckers of 1843 was spurned by the Home Office.[1] During the spring of 1848 the government appeared to revert to the older methods of repression by obtaining from Parliament a more stringent Aliens Act and a measure introducing the new crime of Treason-Felony, but these were devised to deal not with Chartism or any English disturbance, but with the threat of Irish rebellion.[2] Coercion in Ireland was a very different problem from the maintenance of order in Great Britain. Nineteenth-century statesmen did not confuse the two.

It was to the executive government that the citizens of this country, inside Parliament and without, looked for the preservation of the public peace. The existence of a Secretary of State charged with the oversight of the Home Department did not relieve the other organs of this executive from responsibility for public order. The Crown was still sufficiently engaged in the actual task of government to have views on the subject and to urge them upon its ministers. The weight of Queen Victoria's influence was thrown on the side of energetic repression. During the Great Strike of 1842, she was in constant communication with both the Prime Minister and the Home Secretary on matters concerning the riots. Somewhat acidly she wrote to Peel on 17 August 1842, in a letter which does not appear in the authorized selection:

The Queen has just been writing to Sir James Graham (and repeats the same to Sir Robert Peel) that she is surprised at the little (or no) opposition to the dreadful riots in the Potteries . . . and at the passiveness of the troops. It is all very well to send troops down in numbers, and to publish Proclamations forbidding these meetings, but then they ought to act, and these meetings should be prevented. The Queen

---

[1] Pugh to H.O. dated 15 July 1843. H.O. 45/454 I.

[2] In a letter from Lord Campbell to the Prime Minister the proposal to introduce a Treason-Felony Act is discussed with reference solely to the Irish situation. Campbell to Russell dated Saturday night, April 1848. Russell Papers, P.R.O. 30/22/7. Lansdowne's speeches in the House of Lords suggest that Young Ireland's intrigue abroad was the deciding factor in causing the government to introduce the Aliens Act. Hans., 3 Ser., XCVIII, 137 and 265–6. Halévy is misleading on this point. *The Age of Peel and Cobden*, 210.

thinks everything should be done to apprehend this Cooper, and all the Delegates at Manchester. The magistrates in many places seem to act very laxly. . . .[1]

The Queen adopted the same tone during the Rebecca Riots,[2] and when, in May 1848, the Chartists and Irish Repealers embarked upon a campaign of meetings and processions in London she was again active, urging the Whig government to prevent the processions and to take up some of the leaders.[3] It is impossible to assess how far her representations affected government policy, as they usually coincided with other powerful influences working in the same direction. It is clear, however, that the Home Secretaries of the period took care to keep her well informed of what was going on. Sir James Graham wrote full and regular reports to her during the Plug-Plot disturbances,[4] and Sir George Grey sent her a copy of the plan of the organization of the National Charter Association which the Commissioners of the Metropolitan Police had obtained in June 1848.[5]

Even the Privy Council had its place in the machinery of public order, in that it was required to assemble for the promulgation of a Royal Proclamation calling upon the magistrates to enforce the law. The rôle of the Cabinet was less formal. Speaking in Parliament on 15 May 1839, Lord John Russell stated that he had frequently brought the question of disturbances before the Cabinet.[6] A special meeting of the Cabinet, which lasted for two hours, was hastily convened in August 1842, when the Plug Riots threatened to overturn all order in the manufacturing districts.[7] It was at a Cabinet meeting, augmented by the attendance of other prominent figures in the machinery of public order, such as the Commander-in-Chief and the heads of the Metropolitan

[1] The Queen to Sir R. Peel dated 17 August 1842. *Peel Papers*, Brit. Mus. Add. MSS. 40,434.

[2] *The Letters of Queen Victoria, 1837–61*, ed. Benson and Esher, I, 483.

[3] Correspondence of Queen Victoria with Lord John Russell. Royal Archives, Windsor Castle, C.8.

[4] *Queen Victoria's Letters, 1837–61*, I, 423–7.

[5] Grey to the Queen dated 4 June 1848. Royal Archives, Windsor Castle, C.56.

[6] Hans., 3 Ser., XLVII, 1026.

[7] *The Manchester Guardian*, 17 August 1842, p. 1.

Police, that the plans for the defence of London on 10 April 1848 were discussed and approved.[1]

Nor did questions of public order escape the eye of the Prime Minister during this period. The Whigs regarded the Home Office as 'always more immediately' under the Prime Minister's control,[2] and Melbourne, who had filled the office of Secretary of State for the Home Department in the days of the Reform Bill Riots, was able to pass on to his own Home Secretaries, Russell and Normanby, the benefit of his experience. The former consulted him frequently on questions of public order, sending him letters and reports from the disturbed districts, and the treatment of disturbances by the Whig government was influenced by him at several points. Melbourne's approach to the social conflicts of his age was one of gravity which bordered on fear,[3] and his influence was usually cast on the side of alertness and energy in the maintenance of public order. Sometimes he advocated un-mitigated severity, as when, early in 1840, he argued that Frost should pay for the Newport Rising with his life.[4] But Melbourne was restrained from extravagant repression by the prudence in his make-up. He feared the excesses of an over-zealous Tory magistracy hardly less than those of the mob,[5] and hesitated to order political prosecutions from fear of legal difficulties.[6] It was on his advice, too, that Lord John Russell opposed the plan (advanced by General Napier in April–May 1839) to put the Yeomanry on permanent duty.[7]

Melbourne's successor, Peel, whose reputation for controlling

---

[1] Earl Russell, *Recollections and Suggestions, 1813–73*, 253.

[2] Spencer Walpole, *The Life of Lord John Russell*, I, 335–6.

[3] There are good grounds for thinking that Queen Victoria's strong reaction to the Plug-Plot disturbances and the Rebecca Riots owed much to Melbourne's endeavours to instil his own fears into his sovereign. Melbourne to Queen Victoria dated 17 August 1842 and 22 June 1843, *Queen Victoria's Letters, 1837–61*, I, 425, 483.

[4] Williams, *op. cit.*, 290, 293.

[5] " I have no doubt the magistrates are now alarmed ", he wrote to Russell on 7 March 1839, "but alarm produces danger." Melbourne to Russell dated 7 March 1839. The Panshanger Papers, File No. 15.

[6] Melbourne to Russell dated 27 November and 1 December 1838. *Ibid.*

[7] Melbourne to Russell dated 30 April 1839. *Ibid.*; Napier, *op. cit.*, II, 20 and 32.

every department of state with an intensity now impossible is established, made no exception in the case of the Home Office, notwithstanding the fact that it was held by Graham, his trusty lieutenant and 'second self'. During the riots of August 1842, he spent the whole morning, on at least one occasion, going through all the correspondence from the country with his Home Secretary.[1] But the government's responsibility in matters of public order was carried in the main by the Home Secretary. His was an office which received a tremendous accession of business through the steady accumulation, in the second quarter of the nineteenth century, of social legislation involving the administrative control of a central authority. Even before our period closed a former Home Secretary was to be heard complaining that a multitude of other duties interfered with the Secretary of State's powers of concentration upon those of his functions which related to public order. Speaking in the House of Commons in 1847, on a proposal to extend the responsibility of the Home Office for Poor Law administration, Lord John Russell remarked:

The Home Secretary of State is a person who is responsible for the peace of the country, and for the due administration of the criminal law of the country, so far as the prerogative of the Crown is concerned, as advised by the Administration of the day. . . . . But if you impose upon him other duties; if you tell him that he must devote one portion of his time to the superintendence of the working of the Factory Bill, and another portion of his time to regulation of the dietary of a workhouse; and if you require other portions of his time to be occupied by the details of other Bills, which have been passed within the last few years, you must necessarily thereby diminish his power to give attention to those great objects which are, by virtue of his office, solely committed to his care.[2]

Certainly the post was no sinecure. "I have not been one day absent from this office since February," wrote Graham, who was always conscientious, in August 1842.[3]

On the public order side alone the functions of the Home

---

[1] *Queen Victoria's Letters, 1837–61,* I, 424.
[2] W. C. Costin & J. Steven Watson, *The Law and Working of the Constitution: Documents, 1660–1914,* II, 175.
[3] C. S. Parker, *Life and Letters of Sir James Graham, 1792–1861,* I, 324.

Secretary were numerous enough. Some of them were of a routine character. For example, he possessed certain rights of patronage over the subordinate ranks of the machinery of public order, recommending to the Crown appointments to the office of Lord Lieutenant, appointing the Deputy Lieutenants on the recommendation of the Lords Lieutenant, advising the Crown in the appointment of the London Police Court magistrates, and—a power acquired under the Municipal Reform Act of 1835—nominating the magistrates of the corporate towns. He also exercised an administrative control varying in degree over the various police forces of the country. In the Metropolitan Police district, where control was the tightest, the Commissioners were his nominees, but in the municipalities of the provinces, Home Office direction was limited to the receipt of a quarterly report of the numbers and equipment and a copy of the rules made by the Watch Committee for the guidance of constables.

In times of disturbance, the Home Secretary assumed the task of controlling and co-ordinating the activities of magistrates throughout the country. He urged them to make provision for the defence of their own localities and favoured them with opinions on points of law after consultation with the Law Officers of the Crown through the medium of the Solicitor of the Treasury. This advice was normally made available to the magistrates in response to their individual queries, but in times of great emergency the Home Office attempted to ensure a uniform policy by issuing Proclamations or by despatching circular letters to the Lords Lieutenant, mayors, justices of the peace, etc.[1] In Scotland the power of advising the local authorities was shared with the Lord Advocate and Solicitor General of Scotland and, in their absence, with the Lord Justice Clerk.[2] In London the responsibility of the Secretary of State extended beyond the giving of advice to the planning of arrangements to preserve the public peace. The

[1] E.g. the Circular to Lords Lieutenant urging the formation of armed associations in May 1839.

[2] John Hope to James Graham dated 25 September 1842. H.O. 45/266. Sometimes the policy of the Lord Advocate conflicted with that of the Home Office, as in the matter of offering rewards for information. Alison to Graham dated 16 August 1842. H.O. 45/266.

City authorities had to be approached with deference,[1] but the Metropolitan Police and magistrates of the London Police Courts were at the direct disposal of the Home Secretary.[2] It was on the authority of the latter that Chartist meetings and processions were banned in London, and the final arrangements for the defence of the capital on 10 April 1848 were made at a meeting held in the Home Office on the 9th.[3] In the country at large co-ordination implied more than an attempt to promote a uniform magisterial policy. It meant linking up official activities in one area with those in another, as when, in the spring of 1839, the Home Secretary, having heard from the Lord Lieutenant of Monmouthshire that arms from Birmingham had been delivered in his county, possibly for the use of the Chartists, asked the mayor of Birmingham to ascertain privately the sales of the firm which had supplied them.[4]

In addition to its purely advisory functions the Home Office shouldered the duty of assisting the local authorities, when they had exhausted their local resources, with the vast reserves of money, men and authority which rested at its command. On the authority of the Secretary of State for the Home Department, Metropolitan Policemen might be loaned to the provincial justices, regular troops quartered in a disturbed area, Enrolled Pensioners called out, Yeomanry corps diverted from their own county to a neighbouring one, arms issued by the Board of Ordnance to the special constables. With his recommendation, the Treasury would reimburse the magistrates for expenses incurred in collecting information, providing temporary barracks for the accommodation of the troops or conducting prosecutions. Alternatively he might relieve the magistrates of all responsibility for prosecutions by ordering the Treasury Solicitor to take charge

[1] Graham to Lord Mayor of London dated 21 August 1842. H.O. 45/252.
[2] H.O. to Hall dated 21 August 1842. H.O. 45/252. H.O. to Commissioners of Police dated 8 and 10 April 1848. H.O. 65/16.
[3] *The Northern Star*, 15 April 1848, pp. 6–7. The meeting was attended by the Commissioners of the Metropolitan Police, the Lord Mayor, the City of London Police Commissioner and the Home Secretary.
[4] H.O. to Mayor of Birmingham dated 2 April 1839. H.O. 41/13; C. H. Leigh to H.O. dated 25 March 1839. H.O. 40/45.

of them. The Home Secretary could also draw upon the royal prerogative of mercy to supplement the offer of rewards for information with that of pardons for accomplices willing to betray their fellow conspirators. His warrant was sufficient authority for obtaining information by the opening of letters at the Post Office.

Finally, as a parliamentarian, the Home Secretary was responsible for piloting bills dealing with questions of public order through the House of Commons, and for defending the actions of his department in that chamber. When, as during the tenure of office of Lord Normanby, the Secretary of State sat in the House of Lords, these duties fell to the parliamentary Under-Secretary.

When the Chartist period opened, the office of Home Secretary was held by Lord John Russell, a Whig politician of the first rank, who was to be twice Prime Minister of England. Whatever else may be said in his favour, Russell's excellence did not lie in the mastery of the details of administration. In the autumn of 1838, when the manufacturing districts were ringing with the fiery oratory of Stephens and Oastler, he did not even trouble to have accurate reports of the speeches of those two demagogues taken down and filed at the Home Office.[1] His private papers contain very few references to Chartism, and those are indicative of no great grasp of detail.[2] When Napier interviewed him early in 1839, he found him "very ignorant of what is going on".[3] Russell was, in fact, far too completely absorbed in high matters of state—leading a House of Commons where the government's majority was precarious, and advising the Prime Minister on Cabinet changes—to give much of his time to running an office.

[1] Melbourne to Russell dated 23 November 1838. Panshanger Papers, No. 15.

[2] The following extract from a letter to Lord Melbourne will serve as an example of his vagueness. "The Chartists", he wrote, "have some new plan in contemplation which they keep quite secret. Much will depend on the Warwickshire trials." Russell to Melbourne dated 31 July 1839. Russell Papers: P.R.O. 30/23/3.

[3] Napier, *op. cit.*, II, 6. It is also a sign of Russell's habitual slackness in matters of internal disturbance that Melbourne found it necessary to write to him immediately after the Bull Ring riot of 15 July: "You will of course have this affair at Birmingham closely looked into." Melbourne to Russell dated 17 July 1839. Panshanger Papers, No. 15.

D

Moreover, temperament as well as necessity led him to prefer legislation and high politics to administration.

But Russell's conduct of the Home Office is redeemed by the fact that he had a cool head and behaved with restraint towards the Chartists. Julius West asserted that "the Home Secretary was in fear and trembling of a Chartist insurrection", but this claim is scarcely substantiated by the evidence which West himself uses.[1] Who can doubt that the "affliction" which Napier noted in Russell, and which West tacitly equated with fear, was a compound of the death of his wife which left him "stunned by the immensity of his loss",[2] and failing health which made him appear, at a dinner at Buckingham Palace in the spring of 1839, "so thin and worn and sad" that it made a fellow guest "unhappy to see him"?[3] Russell's chief offence, if it is an offence, was that he thought little of Chartism, not that he feared it. Sharing with Melbourne the view that the insurrectionary movement of the age was largely, if not entirely, the handiwork of agitators, he yet differed from his chief in assuming that the appeal of these demagogues was of necessity limited, that "the good sense and virtue of the people of England would be fatal to their schemes and objects".[4] Cognizant of the existence of distress he belittled it, and could not imagine that consequences seriously prejudicial to good order would arise from it. And as he was contemptuous of the Chartist leaders, he was unwilling to resort to an immediate curtailment of civil liberties in order to crush them. The following extract from his letter to Lord Harewood shows how far he was prepared to go in the direction of tolerating even physical force Chartism:

My Lord—I was much obliged to your Lordship for sending me Mr. Oastler's letters. As far as I can perceive, this gentleman's exhortation to the people to arm is not likely to induce them to lay out their money on muskets or pistols. So long as mere violence of language is employed without effect, it is better, I believe, not to add to the importance of these mob leaders by prosecutions. I should for the same

---

[1] West, *op. cit.*, 128–9.
[2] Spencer Walpole, *op. cit.*, I, 311. Lady John had died on 1 November 1838.
[3] *Ibid.*, 316 n. 2.
[4] Debate on the first National Petition. *The Times*, dated 13 July 1839, p. 4.

reason wish the great meetings for universal suffrage and the like to be uninterrupted, care being taken to guard against a breach of the peace by civil force—or if necessary by military aid.

The matter would assume a different complexion if from discontent at the Poor Law, the high price of bread, or any other cause, combinations formed for the purpose of intimidating by physical force should be organized. . . .[1]

The same nonchalance made him at first unwilling to countenance an increase in the military force to deal with Chartism in the winter of 1838–9, though in this, as in other matters, he was later to modify his attitude.[2]

On the debit side, it must be admitted that Russell displayed a certain temerity which led him into courses inconsistent with his general policy of good-humoured toleration of Chartism and prejudicial to the government's position. The removal of Frost from the Newport magistracy for a crime amounting to no more than the use of truculent language furnished the Chartists with valuable propaganda, and removed Frost's incentive to work for peace in South Wales. Russell would have meted out the same treatment to Fielden of Todmorden after the latter had discharged his workmen as a protest against the election of a Board of Guardians. Fortunately, however, there were those among his ministerial colleagues who saw the danger as well as the injustice lurking in such a step, more especially as Fielden, unlike Frost, had a seat in Parliament.[3] Furthermore, Russell falls under suspicion of jobbery—the besetting sin of the Whigs. For it is tempting to connect the mission to Bradford of the interfering Colonel Angelo, which so exasperated General Napier in August 1839,[4] with a letter received by Russell a few weeks earlier from

[1] Draft of this letter dated 18 September 1838. H.O. 52/38.

[2] He wrote to Melbourne on 2 December 1838: ". . . there is nothing in the state of Great Britain or Ireland to require more troops. . . . In England if we cannot do with our present force, we cannot do at all." Russell Papers: P.R.O. 30/22/3. A fortnight later, however, a cavalry regiment was ordered up from Ireland. Jackson to H.O. dated 17 December 1838. H.O. 40/39.

[3] There is a long letter from Lord Holland written in 1838 with the object of dissuading Russell from this course. Russell Papers: P.R.O. 30/22/3 1838 (undated).

[4] Napier, *op. cit.*, II, 76.

his brother, Lord Tavistock, soliciting a post for one Angelo, who had been "three years waiting in London for the chance of employment, without seeing his family in France".[1]

Whatever Russell's defects, the replacement of him by Normanby at the end of August 1839 was the supercession of ability by mediocrity. Constantine Henry Phipps, first Marquis of Normanby, was the least distinguished of the Home Secretaries of the period. Russell, who had himself suggested that he and Normanby should exchange offices, made no pretence that the change would be good for the Home Office.[2] The plain fact was that Normanby had proved unequal to the task of managing the Colonial Office at a time of peculiar difficulty in colonial affairs. In the view of Torrens, "he had neither the knowledge requisite nor the industry to acquire it, the calmness of judgment or the comprehensiveness of view". He was in fact "a mere man of fashion".[3] That such an exchange could occur, in the year of the first Chartist Petition, is an indication that Chartism was the least of the worries of the Whig Cabinet in 1839. During his tenure of the Home Office the comparatively few minutes on official correspondence which can be definitely attributed to him indicate hesitancy and unwillingness (or inability) to take decisions.[4] The only major question of policy in the field of public order to arise during his term of office—viz., the fate of the Newport rebels— was taken out of his hands and discussed at Cabinet level.[5] It seems probable that Melbourne's influence imprinted itself more firmly on the Home Office during this phase, for we know that the Prime Minister stressed to the President of the Council, when Normanby took office, the need to "keep him up and assist him to the best of our power".[6]

---

[1] Tavistock to Russell dated 25 July 1839. Russell Papers: P.R.O. 30/22/3.

[2] Walpole, *op. cit.*, I, 335–6.

[3] W. M. Torrens, *Memoirs of Lord Melbourne*, II, 311. Greville thought more highly of Normanby's ability, but Greville was a personal friend. *A Journal of the Reign of Queen Victoria, from 1837 to 1852*, I, 164.

[4] E.g. J. W. Leach to H.O. dated 25 September 1839. H.O. 40/41; Correspondence arising out of the Newtown election riot. H.O. 45/54.

[5] D. Williams, *op. cit.*, 293 et seq.

[6] Torrens, *op. cit.*, II, 312. Russell also hinted that the watchful eye of Melbourne might save the situation. Walpole, *op. cit.*, I, 335-6.

When Lord Melbourne's ministry gave place to that of Sir Robert Peel, in September 1841, the spirit of the leisurely Whig oligarchs fled the Home Office. The new Home Secretary, Sir James Graham, was a born administrator and indefatigable worker. His grasp of detail and decisive leadership are evidenced by the Home Secretary's minutes on official correspondence, which became far more numerous than they had previously been. He laboured to infuse efficiency into the whole machinery of public order, urging the magistrates to improve their police forces,[1] pursuing a thorough and relentless inquiry into their misconduct during the Great Strike of 1842,[2] lending support to a proposal to employ Assistant Barristers in aid of the unpaid magistracy,[3] and planning the organization of the Chelsea Pensioners as an auxiliary armed force.[4]

In his approach to problems of public order, however, Graham was a pessimist. He had none of Lord John Russell's faith in "the good sense and virtue of the people of England". According to his view there was something inherent in an industrial society which disposed men to riot.[5] His was the nature which anticipated disturbances,[6] and placed the most serious construction upon them when they occurred.[7] In consequence, he was a little disposed to wield a sledgehammer for the purpose of cracking a nut. During the Plug-Plot disturbances he courted a reputation for severity by urging upon the magistrates that if the troops were required to act against the mob they should "act with vigour and without a parley",[8] and by advocating the suppression of large public meetings regardless of their character.[9] Twelve months later he was prepared to contemplate a charge of high treason against the

[1] Parker, *Graham: Life and Letters*, I, 323-4.
[2] E.g. H.O. to Derby dated 24 December 1842; H.O. to Stamford & Warrington dated 24 December 1842. H.O. 41/17.
[3] Parker, *Graham: Life and Letters*, I, 333 et seq.
[4] C. S. Parker, *Sir Robert Peel from his Private Papers*, II, 546-7.
[5] Parker, *Graham: Life and Letters*, I, 328-9.
[6] A. B. Erickson, *The Public Career of Sir James Graham*, 160.
[7] Witness his readiness to attribute the strikes of August 1842 to conspiracy and centralized direction. Parker, *Graham: Life and Letters*, I, 321-2.
[8] H.O. to Huddersfield Magistrates dated 17 August 1842. H.O. 41/17.
[9] H.O. to Lyttelton dated 19 August 1842. H.O. 41/17.

gate breakers of South Wales.[1] But the same pessimism rendered him more eager than most of his contemporaries to inquire into the causes of the sinister disposition which he perceived among the people of England. It was not so much that he regarded redress of grievances as a substitute for force in maintaining order (though in South Wales, where the superficial causes of the Rebecca Riots, at least, were obvious, he was prepared to concede that "a kind consideration of the wants and feelings" of the populace and "for the fair reward of honest industry" would be "more effectual than the terror of punishment in conciliating the good will of the community and in restoring peace" [2]). On the contrary, he embraced the view that the insurrectionary fever of the British working class was beyond the power of legislation or education to cure—at any rate for the present—and that therefore "the law and civil rights must be upheld by power".[3] But for the future, he held that the severe and inflammable discontent might at least be mitigated by removing the taxes from essential food-stuffs, by fostering popular education and by inquiring into frauds practised by masters upon their workpeople. The Plug-Plot disturbances turned his mind the more surely towards these measures.[4]

When the Whigs returned to Downing Street in the summer of 1846, the Home Office was given to Sir George Grey, nephew of the Reform Bill premier. Interested rather in the practical application of accepted principles than in the enunciation of new ones, Grey was more exclusively an administrator than Graham. He was renowned as a "cool and clear headed official",[5] and succeeded, during his long tenure of power, in making the Home Office peculiarly his own. Sharing with Russell, now Prime Minister, a marked confidence in "the good sense of the working classes",[6] he was able to meet the Chartist disturbance of 1848

---

[1] See minute signed by Graham on Jenkin to Maule dated 12 September 1843. H.O. 45/454 II.

[2] Draft of Circular to Lords Lieutenant of disturbed counties dated 15 September 1843. H.O. 45/454 II.

[3] Parker, *Graham: Life and Letters*, I, 329.

[4] Parker, *Sir Robert Peel*, II, 546–7.

[5] Mandell Creighton, *Memoir of Sir George Grey, Bart., G.C.B.*, 37.

[6] *Ibid.*, 47.

with "a clear cool head . . . and an admirable perception of the temper of the people".[1] As a parliamentary orator Grey was much inferior to the epigrammatic Graham, but in one important respect, touching the parliamentary duties of the Home Secretary, he was Graham's surpasser. A cold unsympathetic character, Graham, despite his rhetorical skill, was prone to antagonize the House, as in the debates on the opening of letters at the Post Office. Grey, by contrast, inspired general confidence, spoke without bitterness, never invited opposition or exposed himself readily to attack. And after all, no less a figure than Lord Melbourne had written, with respect to the duties of the Home Secretary, that "more is to be done by personal influence and being on good terms with the members of the House than by ability and eloquence".[2]

In the performance of his numerous and growing duties the Secretary of State had the assistance of a permanent Under-Secretary, an Under-Secretary who usually[3] sat in Parliament and changed with changing administrations, and a private secretary. The parliamentary Under-Secretary shared with his chief the Home Office business in the House of Commons, and the permanent Under-Secretary normally handled the correspondence. Most of the letters to magistrates, military commanders and others, relative to disturbances, were, in fact, sent out over the latter's signature rather than the Home Secretary's. Samuel March Phillipps, who occupied the position of permanent Under-Secretary throughout the Chartist period until the spring of 1848, must have exerted a considerable influence upon affairs, for he had wide experience, having held the office since 1827, and was a recognized authority on legal matters. His *Treatise on the Law of Evidence*, published in 1814, was a standard text-book in its day.[4]

---

[1] *Ibid.*, 65–6.

[2] *Ibid.*, 101.

[3] But not invariably. Sir Denis Le Marchant, who held the post from July 1847 to May 1848, had no seat in the Parliament elected in 1847. In using the terms permanent and parliamentary Under-Secretary to describe these officers it must, therefore, be recognized that the distinction between them was not as sharp as it has since become.

[4] *Dictionary of National Biography*, XLV, 192.

When Phillipps was on leave, however, his duties were undertaken by the parliamentary Under-Secretary. Henry Manners Sutton, parliamentary Under-Secretary to Sir James Graham, had to take his turn at administration when the Plug-Plot disturbances and the Rebecca Rising were at their height. And when the government was making its preparations to preserve order at the Chartist demonstration of 10 April 1848, it was another parliamentary Under-Secretary, Sir Denis Le Marchant, who carried, under Sir George Grey's superintendence, the burden of the arrangements at the Home Office. He was the officer who interviewed a deputation from the Chartist Convention prior to the demonstration.[1]

The Law Officers of the Crown, the Attorney General and the Solicitor General, occupied an important position in the central government in matters of public order. They assisted in framing royal proclamations, advised on the prosecution of Chartist leaders and newspapers and personally conducted the more important legal proceedings. In their advisory capacity, the Law Officers were not limited to giving an opinion on points of law, but made recommendations on the expediency of instituting prosecutions. In December 1837 the Whig Law Officers, John (later Baron) Campbell and Sir Robert Rolfe, advised the Home Secretary not to prosecute *The Northern Star* for printing seditious articles and reports of speeches "unless any real practical evil has been found to result from the circulation of that paper".[2] Fifteen months later, when consulted about speeches delivered by Feargus O'Connor, Oastler and others at the Crown and Anchor tavern in the Strand, they gave an opinion that, although parts of those speeches were technically illegal, a prosecution should not be undertaken, as it would involve an appearance of harshness and a risk of acquittal.[3] In a less lenient government the Attorney General was to be found working out a positive strategy of prosecutions designed to ensure the greatest possible effect. With the

[1] Gammage, *op. cit.*, 311.

[2] Frankland Lewis, Lefevre and Nicholls to Russell dated 4 January 1838. H.O. 73/54.

[3] Opinion of Law Officers on speeches delivered at the Crown and Anchor tavern on 19 March 1839. H.O. 48/33.

object of pinning responsibility for the Plug-Plot disturbances (which were, in fact, mainly spontaneous) on the Chartists, the Anti-Corn Law League and the trade unions, Sir J. F. Pollock, Attorney General under Peel, cunningly clubbed together in a single indictment Feargus O'Connor and the Chartist and trade union delegates who had met in Manchester during the strike, on the one hand, and the actual leaders of the mobs which had turned out the factories, on the other.[1] To drive home the lesson, he would have treated the defendants to the pomp and circumstance of a trial at Bar in the Court of Queen's Bench,[2] but this proposal, though seriously considered by the government, was eventually rejected as inexpedient.

The county being a vital unit in British local administration, its officers, the Lord Lieutenant and the High Sheriff, carried, immediately below the central government, a responsibility for the suppression of disorder. In the English counties, however, the Sheriff's rôle was almost negligible. Once "the governor of the shire, the captain of its forces, the president of its court, a distinctively royal officer",[3] he had gradually lost his functions and status. A decision of the Law Officers of the Crown in 1810 had denied him the right "to interfere in the disposition of troops, or to control the magistrates in suppressing civil tumult".[4] The force which it was his special prerogative to command, the 'posse comitatus', the *levée en masse* of the adult male population of the county, was not practical politics in an age when many adult males were among the disaffected. Moreover, the Sheriff's social position in no way fitted him for leadership in the county, as he usually belonged to the gentry class from which the ordinary magistrates were drawn.[5] Nor could he lead by virtue of experience, for his office was an annual one. In these circumstances it is not surprising to find little mention of High Sheriffs in the correspondence of the period relating to disturbances. The High

[1] Pollock to Graham dated 9 October 1842. Graham Papers, Bundle 54A.
[2] Pollock to Graham dated 12 October 1842. *Ibid.*
[3] Pollock & Maitland, *History of English Law*, I, 533.
[4] S. & B. Webb, *English Local Government*, I, 489 n. 4.
[5] *Ibid.*, 377 n. 2.

Sheriff of Cheshire was reported active in putting down begging bands in August 1842, but in this he was merely acting along with the county magistrates.[1]

Very different was the rôle of the Scottish sheriff, who performed extensive administrative duties in addition to the judicial functions which he retains to this day. In effect, there were three different orders of sheriff in nineteenth-century Scotland. The first was the Sheriff Principal, usually a great nobleman like the Duke of Buccleugh or the Marquess of Queensberry, who held his office simultaneously with that of Lord Lieutenant, in which capacity we must principally regard him. The second was the Sheriff Deputy, generally known quite simply as the Sheriff. He was a salaried official—an advocate of three years' standing—charged with the performance of certain regular duties, but the intervals between these duties were usually long enough to enable him to reside away from his county, an act of 1838 having granted him permission to do so.[2] The third category of sheriff was the Sheriff Substitute, also a paid official, but required to reside in his sheriffdom.

The Sheriff Deputy played a considerable part in the suppression of riots and tumults. He was not always non-resident. The Sheriff Deputy of Lanarkshire was a hard-working official, tied to his county by a heavy routine, and therefore always on the spot when danger threatened. The post was held during the Chartist period by Archibald Alison, a man of tremendous energy, who handled the Glasgow spinners' strike in 1837, and laboured for a whole week, in August 1842, to put down plunder by the Lanarkshire colliers in the rural districts of the county, without the assistance of a single magistrate save the Vice-Lieutenant.[3] The possession of a continuously resident professional administrator responsible for the peace of the county as a whole gave Lanarkshire an advantage enjoyed by no English shire; and even where the Sheriff Deputy had become non-resident he was usually ordered back to his shrievalty to direct the magistrates when

---

[1] Stringer to H.O. dated 16 August 1842. H.O. 45/242.
[2] 1 & 2 Vict., c. 119.
[3] Alison to H.O. dated 11 August 1842. H.O. 45/266.

disturbances occurred.[1] James L'Amy, Sheriff Deputy of Forfar, proceeded to his county at the behest of the Solicitor General of Scotland in June 1839, and arrested seven of the Kirriemuir rioters in their beds;[2] he returned to it again in August 1842, and in concert with the magistrates made preparation which led to a repulse of the mob from the mills of Dundee.[3]

In both the English and the Scottish counties, however, it was the Lord Lieutenant who took precedence. His leadership was derived partly from the powers of the two great offices of Lieutenant of the County and Custos Rotulorum, which he held simultaneously. The appointment of county magistrates and Deputy Lieutenants rested at his disposal, and with it the right to supervise and control them. The county yeomanry force was also directly under his jurisdiction. He signed the commissions in it: his authority was required for calling it out. But the authority of the Lord Lieutenant stemmed also from his social position, for such an office appealed to men already exalted above the rank and file of the county bench—to the greater nobility of the land. There was a large sprinkling of earls among the Lords Lieutenant of the English counties during the Chartist period, whilst Shropshire, Nottinghamshire and Leicestershire had dukes at their heads.

Men of such distinction were frequently non-resident, living either in London or on their estates in other parts of the country. They were not laden with the burden of much routine work of county administration, having ceased to preside at general sessions of the peace with any degree of regularity.[4] The outbreak of disturbances, however, furnished them with the opportunity to give a lead to their counties. Their response to the challenge was

---

[1] On 21 May 1839 the Home Office drafted a letter to the Scottish Solicitor General suggesting that, in all cases of Chartist demonstrations, the Sheriff Principal should be desired to return to his post. It seems fairly clear that, in this instance, the officer indicated is the Sheriff Deputy, not the Lord Lieutenant. H.O. 40/52.

[2] L'Amy to Lord John Russell dated 19 June 1839. H.O. 40/52.

[3] L'Amy to Airlie dated 24 August 1842. H.O. 45/266.

[4] Webb, op. cit., I, 287.

extremely uneven. Some were content to remain at a distance, promulgating to the magistrates by letter the instructions contained in Home Office Circulars, passing on to the Home Office requests received from the magistrates and giving their formal consent to the use of the Yeomanry. Of such a character was the contribution, in 1839 and 1842, of the Lords Lieutenant of Lancashire, Cheshire, and the West Riding, three of the most important areas of unrest. Age was a limiting factor upon the activities of the Earl of Stamford and Warrington, Lord Lieutenant of Cheshire, who was seventy-seven at the time of the strikes in 1842, and to a scarcely less extent upon those of Lord Harewood, whose lieutenancy was the West Riding, and who reached the age of seventy-two in 1839. The same excuse cannot be pleaded on behalf of the Duke of Sutherland, a man in his fifties, who held in plurality the lieutenancies of Shropshire and the Scottish county from which he took his title. He was absent from the latter when riots broke out in September 1841,[1] and absent from the former during the disturbed days of August 1842.[2]

Other Lords Lieutenant took their responsibilities seriously in times of disturbance. Lord Lyttelton, the Lord Lieutenant of Worcestershire, a young man of twenty-five years of age, having been ordered to his county by the Home Secretary towards the end of July 1842, proceeded without delay to Dudley, the centre of disaffection. During his stay in the coal-mining area he persuaded the magistrates to make provision for their own defence,[3] reorganized the Yeomanry in such a way as to enable them to be kept out on permanent duty,[4] and used every exertion to procure accurate evidence of language used at Chartist meetings.[5] Even more active was the Earl of Powis, who distinguished himself by the vigour with which he suppressed the Chartist disturbances in Montgomeryshire in 1839.[6] In August 1842 he handled the

---

[1] Sutherland to H.O. dated 10 October 1841. H.O. 45/57.
[2] Sutherland to H.O. dated 23 August 1842. H.O. 45/258.
[3] Lyttelton to H.O. dated 1, 8 and 13 August 1842. H.O. 45/263.
[4] Lyttelton to H.O. dated 13 August 1842. H.O. 45/263.
[5] Lyttelton to H.O. dated 16 August 1842. H.O. 45/263.
[6] *Dictionary of National Biography*, XXVI, 184.

situation not only in his own lieutenancy, Montgomeryshire,[1] but in the neighbouring county of Shropshire, whose lieutenant was away in Scotland.[2] Lord Londonderry, the sixty-six-years-old Lord Lieutenant of Durham, hastened home from Paris when the news of the colliers' strike of 1844 reached him, though in this case personal interest reinforced public duty, for he was an extensive coalowner.[3] Other Lords Lieutenant personally active in suppressing disorder were Lord Talbot of Staffordshire and Capel Hanbury Leigh of Monmouthshire. The latter made himself conspicuous by his zeal in collecting information about Chartist activities,[4] searching packages suspected of containing arms[5] and warring against unstamped newspapers.[6] His credulity in the matter of the reports of worthless spies sometimes laid him open to ridicule.[7]

Where the Lord Lieutenant was inactive or incapacitated leadership was sometimes assumed by the Vice-Lieutenant. Indeed some of the most strenuous exertion on behalf of public order during the period under review was displayed by Vice-Lieutenants. In this capacity George Rice Trevor, son of Lord Dynevor, took charge of his father's lieutenancy, Carmarthenshire, during the Rebecca Riots, arranging the disposition of the Metropolitan Policemen sent down to the county,[8] and even accompanying the military in pursuit of parties of gate-breakers.[9] As Vice-Lieutenant of Staffordshire in 1842, Lord Dartmouth settled with the military authorities the distribution of the armed force in his county,[10] and superintended in person the arrangements to preserve the peace on the occasion of a great Chartist

[1] Powis to H.O. dated 24 August 1842. H.O. 45/258.
[2] Powis to H.O. dated 22, 23, 24 August and 6 September 1842. H.O. 45/258.
[3] Londonderry to H.O. dated 15 April 1844. H.O. 45/644.
[4] Copy of L. Brown of Newport to Lord Fitzroy dated 8 November 1840. H.O. 40/55.
[5] C. H. Leigh to H.O. dated 25 March 1839. H.O. 40/45.
[6] C.H. Leigh to H.O. dated 28 November and 3 December 1839. H.O. 40/45.
[7] Brown to Fitzroy Somerset dated 8 November 1840. H.O. 40/55.
[8] Rice Trevor to H.O. dated 16 September 1843. H.O. 45/347A.
[9] Rice Trevor to H.O. dated 22 July 1843. H.O. 45/454.
[10] Dartmouth to H.O. dated 13 July and 27 July 1842. H.O. 45/260.

meeting at West Bromwich on 1 August 1842.[1] Very similar were the activities of Lord Aylesford when the great strike movement reached the Warwickshire coalfield on 13 August 1842. He proceeded to the spot, made preparations to safeguard the peace, and headed the coalowners (who were also magistrates) in their negotiations with their men.[2] But no energetic Vice-Lieutenant compensated for the inactivity of the Lords Lieutenant in Lancashire, Cheshire and the West Riding. In southern Lancashire the gap was partly filled by the exertions of John Frederick Foster, the salaried Chairman of the Salford Quarter Sessions, who brought the magistrates of the Manchester area to an intended consistency of action in May 1839,[3] but the civil power undoubtedly suffered from a want of leadership.

Descending still further the ladder of authority, we reach the two great collective jurisdictions of the county—the Lieutenancy, which embraced the Deputy Lieutenants of the county, and the general sessions of the county magistrates. The former was of negligible importance by this time. It does not appear to have functioned during the Chartist period except in conjunction with the general sessions of the magistrates, as in Staffordshire early in September 1842.[4] The office of Deputy Lieutenant was by now usually held by men who were already Justices of the Peace,[5] so that a meeting of the latter was in effect a meeting of the former. The magistrate who was also a Deputy Lieutenant enjoyed a mere social distinction from his brothers of the Bench, and did not incur a heavier responsibility.

The general sessions of the magistrates, however, had an important part to play in the machinery of public order. The county justices met regularly in quarter sessions, which were held either

[1] Dartmouth to H.O. dated 31 July 1842. H.O. 45/260.

[2] Aylesford to H.O. dated 15 and 17 August 1842. H.O. 45/261A.

[3] Napier, *op. cit.*, II, 34.

[4] Resolutions passed at a meeting of the magistrates and Deputy Lieutenants of the County of Staffordshire convened by the Lord Lieutenant at the Shire Hall on 5 September 1842. H.O. 45/260.

[5] The Webbs estimate that in 1843, of the 3,012 Deputy Lieutenants for the whole of England and Wales, 2,545 were also Justices of the Peace. *Op. cit.*, I, 287 n. 4.

in the county town or (in the case of large counties like Lancashire and the West Riding) in different towns situated in various parts of the county in turn. In addition to the purely routine duties of administration and patronage which it exercised in relation to the constabulary of the county (appointing the High Constable of the Hundred, where there was one, or receiving reports on the rural police force), quarter sessions also had much responsibility for augmenting the forces of order in an emergency. It might call out the Yeomanry, adopt the Rural Police Acts of 1839-40, appoint superintending constables, under an act of 1842, to supervise the parish constables, or set in motion over a wide area defensive operations based on the use of civilian volunteers. Because the regular sittings did not always coincide with the times of the greatest unrest, it was often the case that the collective authority of the county magistrates could only be brought to bear on disturbances if special meetings were convened for the purpose. There was a meeting of the Cheshire magistrates at Nether Knutsford on 22 August 1842, at which it was decided to institute a system of horse patrols, manned by volunteers, to convey information to the authorities of sudden attacks on property; a similar meeting of the Staffordshire bench in the Shire Hall a fortnight later adopted measures of a like character.[1]

Like all collective bodies, however, the general sessions needed a strenuous individual to energize them, and as such a person was often lacking there was usually considerable delay before the machinery was set in motion. Sir Henry Bunbury, a retired general and former Under-Secretary of State for War, wrote to Lord John Russell: "If fires and riots grow alarming the Justices of the Peace wait for the Lord Lieutenant. He may be an aged or an inactive man, or he may not be resident in the county; but till the Lord Lieutenant comes forward the Justices do nothing collectively." [2] Furthermore, even when assembled, the general sessions of the peace displayed, as might have been expected, all

---

[1] Potts to H.O. dated 24 August 1842. H.O. 45/242. Resolutions of Staffordshire Magistrates dated 5 September 1842. H.O. 45/260.

[2] Bunbury to Russell dated 24 December 1838. Russell Papers: P.R.O. 30/22/3.

the parsimony, all the prejudice, all the incompetence, of the individual magistrates of whom they were composed. They showed the utmost reluctance to employ the only resource at their disposal which could have placed public order on a firm basis— viz., the power to establish a professional police force.

In the first instance, it was the individual justice (or group of justices forming a petty sessional division) who had to shoulder the burden of the conflict with disorder. When riots broke out in a particular locality it was the clear duty of the local magistrates to muster a sufficient local force, to lead it in person to the scene of disorder, to read the Riot Act to the mob and, if necessary, to give the order to fire. If the regular police force was inadequate, any two or more justices had power to swear in special constables. Should these prove insufficient, they might call out on their own authority the local troop of Yeomanry, or requisition a regular military force from the nearest barracks. Towards the end of the period they acquired the additional power to summon a corps of Enrolled Military Pensioners, afterwards applying to the Home Office for a warrant legalizing their action. They might forbid meetings likely to prejudice the public peace. They might also issue warrants for the arrest of rioters and, in default of sureties for their good behaviour, commit them to prison to take their trial at the Assizes or Quarter Sessions. Their warrants would also enable Chartist arms, private papers and unstamped periodicals to be seized. Finally, if all these measures failed to restore the peace, it was up to the local magistrates to move the Lord Lieutenant or the government to send further aid in the shape of regular troops, Yeomanry, Metropolitan Policemen, or hard cash. Their regular control over the machinery of public order extended to the swearing in of parish constables and, universally after 1842, to the appointment of the same.

Who, then were these men upon whom so much depended? The answer is that they were largely "the principal landed proprietors within the county, whose fathers and grandfathers had held their estates before them; nearly all men of high standing and personal honour according to their own social code, but narrowly

conventional in opinions and prejudices".[1] The minimum qualification for the county bench was still, as fixed by an act of 1744,
"an estate of freehold, copyhold, or customary tenure in fee, for
life or a given term, of the yearly value of £100", and the prejudices of Lords Lieutenant rendered the selection even more
exclusive. Lord Talbot, whose lieutenancy was the important
industrial county of Staffordshire, rejected the candidature of a
powder blue manufacturer, "according to the rule, laid down and
strictly conformed to by me", excluding persons "engaged in the
manufacture or trade of the district".[2] Snobbery was not the sole
determinant of this attitude. Behind it lay also a sincere reaction
against the venality of the infamous trading justices of the
eighteenth century. "They are in the habit of hearing the case
over the counter before they come into Court", wrote a Home
Office correspondent concerning retail tradesmen in the office of
magistrate, "and when they come they bring the counter with
them."[3] Opinions no less than social status furnished grounds for
exclusion. The Tory Lord Lieutenant of Nottinghamshire, the
Duke of Newcastle, was deprived of his office by the Whig
government at the beginning of May 1839 for pressing with more
energy than discretion his objections to the appointment of a
Mr. Paget to the county bench. The Duke objected to Mr. Paget
"first, because he was a man of violent political opinions; and,
secondly, because he was a Dissenter".[4] A Home Office correspondent attributed the shortage of active magistrates in the
Hinckley district of Leicestershire in February 1839 not to any
want of potential magistrates, but to the Lord Lieutenant's habit
of using the commission of the peace as a political prize.[5] The
Duke of Portland's correspondence with the Home Office over

[1] Webb, *op. cit.*, I, 386.

[2] Talbot to Williams dated 25 January 1839. H.O. 52/43.

[3] Simpson to Normanby dated 29 November 1839. H.O. 52/41.

[4] C. C. F. Greville, *A Journal of the Reign of Queen Victoria, 1837–52*, I, 195.
Contrary to established custom, which left the recommendation to magisterial
posts to the Lord Lieutenant, the Lord Chancellor had on this occasion selected
Paget and one other for appointment to the Nottinghamshire county bench.
See Brougham's pronouncement on recommendations by the Lord Lieutenant.
Hans., 3 Ser., XVIII, 161 et seq.

[5] W. S. Darkin to Phillipps dated 2 February 1839. H.O. 52/41.

the Middlesex commission reveals, on the part of the former, a distinct reluctance to recommend reformers.[1]

Notwithstanding the prejudices of Lords Lieutenant, a certain number of persons drawn from the employing and mill-owning class found their way into the commission of the peace for the manufacturing counties. John Howard, a Cheshire county magistrate who resided at Brereton Hall, owned a mill at Hyde.[2] Jowett, the owner of a factory at Ashton-under-Lyne, was also a magistrate[3] and, if the complaints of the aggrieved powder blue manufacturer are worthy of credence, the Lord Lieutenant of Staffordshire sometimes departed from his rule against commercials. The complainant affirmed that William Taylor Copeland, a porcelain manufacturer of Stoke-on-Trent, who had been lord mayor of London in 1835, acted as a magistrate at Stoke, and that others connected with the collieries had held the office.[4] Three of the magistrates of Ashton-under-Lyne in 1842—Messrs. Wright, Lord and Buckley—and one named Cheetham of Stalybridge, were reported as members of the Anti-Corn Law League.[5]

Clerical justices were still numerous, though their appointment was discouraged—by reforming ecclesiastics like Bishop Blomfield who feared that the priest would be swallowed up in the magistrate, by Whig statesmen who disliked their uncompromising Toryism, and by Lords Lieutenant who suspected their inclination towards collective regulation of morality. From Derbyshire, Kent and Sussex they were regularly excluded,[6] but the Duke of Portland in his capacity of Lord Lieutenant of Middlesex was still doing battle royal with the Whig Home Office on their behalf in 1839 and 1840.[7] Occasionally the government relented, and clergymen were appointed.

[1] See H.O. minute on Portland to Normanby dated 30 October 1840. H.O. 52/47.
[2] Howard to Stamford and Warrington dated 3 January 1843. H.O. 45/347.
[3] Ashton Magistrates to H.O. dated 10 December 1838. H.O. 40/38.
[4] J. Meigh to Williams dated 30 January 1839. H.O. 52/43.
[5] Report of Lieutenant-Colonel Martin to Sir Thomas Arbuthnot dated 24 September 1842. H.O. 45/268.
[6] Webb, op. cit., I, 384.
[7] Scott-Portland to Normanby dated 27 September 1839. H.O. 52/43; dated 30 October 1840. H.O. 52/47. The Home Office was consulted under a

The exclusiveness of the basis of selection contributed to a deficiency in the quantity of magistrates, which impeded the operation of the machinery of public order during the Chartist period. This was especially marked in the industrial areas where few resident gentry were to be found. The large and disorderly Leicestershire village of Rothley was without a magistrate in 1839 because the only person of education and fortune in the parish happened to be a clergyman.[1] Indeed, the exclusion of the clergy from the commission of the peace was particularly inconvenient, since, as the Duke of Portland pointed out, clergymen, unlike so many of the squirearchy, were normally resident. "I may add", he asserted, "that it has long been a rule in Derbyshire to exclude clergymen from the commission, and the consequence is that it is often very difficult to find a magistrate. I live within a mile of the borders of that county, and when I am from home, parties are sometimes obliged to go twelve or thirteen miles to get their business done." [2] A marked example of the numerical deficiency of magistrates comes from Wigton in Cumberland, where, on the outbreak of rioting in August 1842, the only resident magistrate was an infirm old gentleman hardly equal to patrolling the streets before a mob, and seldom in fact active.[3] But it is not unique. Three years earlier, in August 1839, when Chartist disturbances were hourly expected in Middleton, the nearest magistrates were to be found at Manchester, Bury, Oldham and Ashton-under-Lyne, six, six, four and seven miles distant from Middleton respectively. It was impossible to adopt precautionary measures, for special constables could not be appointed for want of someone to swear them in.[4] Furthermore, in the portions of South Wales

special agreement between Portland and Lord John Russell relative to the commission of the peace for Middlesex and Westminster. Scott-Portland to Normanby dated 12 September 1839. H.O. 52/43. It is clear from the correspondence which took place that Normanby claimed an equal right with the Duke of Portland to nominate to the Middlesex bench, and equally clear that Portland did not recognize that right. Scott-Portland to Normanby dated 19 October 1839 and H.O. Minute. H.O. 52/43.

[1] William Acworth to H.O. dated 22 July 1839. H.O. 40/44.
[2] Scott-Portland to Normanby dated 27 September 1839. H.O. 52/43.
[3] Fitzroy Somerset to H.O. dated 27 August 1842. H.O. 45/243.
[4] Helsall to H.O. dated 15 August 1839. H.O. 40/37.

affected by the Rebecca Riots, large stretches of country were without a resident J.P., and the operations against the rioters were so hampered by the difficulty of procuring the services of a magistrate to direct the troops,[1] that the Vice-Lieutenant of Carmarthenshire began to prepare the mind of the Home Secretary for the proclamation of martial law in the region.[2] It was in the nature of things that landed gentry should be particularly scarce in the industrial areas, where the problem of disorder was especially acute, and whilst society continued to look mainly to that class for its magistrates there was bound to be an acute local shortage.

But the defects of the magisterial bench were not of quantity alone. Of its quality Sir Henry Bunbury wrote in his letter to Lord John Russell: "In their respective neighbourhoods some [magistrates] will be found timid, foolish or lazy, while others may be doing more harm than good by rashness and want of temper. Half the squires (and nobles too) will be crying out for horse and foot, each wanting a troop or a company for the defence of his particular house."[3] Bunbury's brother-in-law, General Napier, was even more scathing. "The county magistrates", he wrote, "are a miserable set generally; they insult the people, are hated, and on every alarm grow frightened. The magistrates of the towns have a little more pluck, but the county magistrates bully them, finally inoculate them with their own fears, and then pour in calls for troops."[4]

Such sweeping condemnations, of which many examples could without difficulty be furnished, cannot, of course, be taken literally. Strong prejudices against political opponents coloured so many contemporary criticisms of the magistrates, and every

[1] Hugh Owen to H.O. dated 20 September 1843. H.O. 45/454 II.
[2] Rice Trevor to H.O. dated 13 September 1843. H.O. 45/454 II.
[3] Bunbury to Russell dated 24 December 1838. Russell Papers: P.R.O. 30/22/3.
[4] Napier, *op. cit.*, II, 63. It is not easy to reconcile this with his judgment expressed on a subsequent occasion: "The Tory magistrates are bold, violent, irritating and uncompromising; the Whig magistrates sneaking and base, always ready to call for troops, and yet truckling to the mob." *Ibid.*, 153. For the county benches were largely Tory, whilst the Whig-Radicals were strongly entrenched in many of the towns.

allowance must be made for such bias in assessing complaints of their conduct which were tendered to the Home Secretary. It is undeniable that charges of gross neglect of duty, arising from fear or indolence, may be sustained against some of the magistrates of the county bench. General Napier had reason to complain of magistrates who went grouse shooting at the height of the Chartist disturbances of 1839,[1] and the Rochdale magistrates did not even trouble to send to the Home Office a report of an important Chartist meeting in November 1838 which lasted from 7 p.m. to 11 p.m., and was addressed by O'Connor, Stephens, Fletcher, Taylor and Greenwood.[2] Several instances may be cited where magistrates disappeared from the scene of disorder when troops had been requisitioned, leaving the field clear for the soldiers. Some of these may be accounted for by bad timing or lack of co-ordination between magistrates, but it is hardly possible to place so benevolent an interpretation on the action of the magistrates of Leigh who were only with difficulty persuaded to remain in the town, whilst the troops were rendering aid to the civil power.[3] Old age and infirmity incapacitated not a few members of the magisterial bench, whilst one, a Mr. Henry Ashworth of Bolton, explained as follows his absence from a meeting of the Lancashire county magistrates convened during the Plug-Plot disturbances: "There are military considerations involved, and as I am well known to entertain religious scruples, on those grounds I did not suppose that my brother magistrates would have seen any advantage from calling for my presence, when it is even possible that I might rather embarrass than aid them." [4]

[1] *Ibid.*, 79.
[2] Unsigned and undated letter enclosing a copy of *The Manchester Guardian* dated 22 December 1838. H.O. 40/37. H.O. to Rochdale Magistrates dated 22 December 1838. H.O. 41/13.
[3] Napier to H.O. dated 16 August 1839. H.O. 40/53. But the Wolverhampton magistrates excused their failure to meet a company of the 12th Foot which had been ordered into the town in July 1842 by stating that they did not expect it. Hill to H.O. dated 31 July 1842. H.O. 45/260. This may well be true as Lord Dartmouth, the Vice-Lieutenant, and not the magistrates of Wolverhampton had made the application for troops. Dartmouth to H.O. dated 27 July 1842. H.O. 45/260.
[4] Copy of H.O. to Derby dated 22 August 1842. H.O. 45/249.

On the other hand there were magistrates who showed a certain over-hastiness, a want of good temper and discretion, in their dealings with the people. The Rev. G. A. Evors, a clerical justice, of Newtown, Montgomeryshire, is reported to have said to one of the mob who had grossly insulted him on polling day at the general election of 1841: "If you don't quit the streets I will order the soldiers to shoot you." [1] On the very same day the magistrates of Ashton-under-Lyne provided a similar example of irresponsible temerity by ordering the county police to attack a peaceable assemblage gathered round the hustings and by taunting them with cowardice when they remonstrated.[2]

These, no doubt, are extreme cases, and may be matched by instances of outstanding bravery and exceptional competence. Charles March Phillipps, the Whig squire of Garendon Park near Loughborough and brother of the permanent Under-Secretary at the Home Office, went to the large, unruly village of Sheepshead on the night of 16 August 1842 to put down a riotous assemblage occasioned by a violent attack on a policeman in the execution of his duty. He read the Riot Act to the people from the upper window of a building, to the accompaniment of a volley of stones from below, and was besieged in the building for three hours until a troop of horse from Loughborough arrived to rescue him.[3] Thomas Powys of Burslem, a magistrate and Deputy Lieutenant of Staffordshire, who had at one time served in the foot guards, saved the Potteries from even greater devastation than actually occurred, by his exertions on 15 and 16 August 1842. His spies must have ranged far afield, for on 15 August he went to Leek, having ascertained correctly that turnout parties from Congleton and Macclesfield intended to visit the town that day.[4] When, early on the following morning, the mob took the road again, this time for the Potteries, Powys was ready for them. He had assembled over 100 Chelsea out-pensioners at Newcastle, and had drawn up a troop of cavalry in the square at Burslem to await the

---

[1] The correspondence relating to this incident appears in H.O. 45/54.
[2] Captain Woodford's Report dated 5 July 1841. H.O. 45/46.
[3] Phillipps to H.O. dated 18 August 1842. H.O. 45/250.
[4] Powys to H.O. dated 15 August 1842. H.O. 45/260.

arrival of the mob from Leek and another mob from Hanley. The result was that, when the multitudinous invaders reached Burslem, the troops opened fire upon them on Powys' instructions, and put them to flight. In all he did, Powys was nothing daunted by the knowledge that the mob had spent the night of the 15th burning the houses of magistrates who had made themselves unpopular. He was soon to hear that after the affair at Burslem about 500 rioters had proceeded to his own house, Westwood, for the purpose of burning it to the ground.[1] During the Rebecca Riots the Llanelly bench contained three magistrates— William Chambers, life-tenant of the Llanelly estate and chairman of the petty sessions, his son William Chambers Junior, a young man of good education and decidedly liberal opinions, and R. J. Nevill, the proprietor of large copper works in the Llanelly district—whose zeal in eliciting information about nocturnal outrages could hardly have been excelled.[2] As a direct consequence, the Chambers farms at Mansant, Tynywern and Gelliglynog fell victims to incendiaries.[3] Many other examples could be quoted, did but space permit, to demonstrate both the zeal of individual justices of the peace and the almost insuperable difficulties with which they had to grapple.

But the average English county magistrate was neither superlatively conscientious nor utterly lacking in sense of responsibility; he was not a genius, neither was he an imbecile. Though subject to all the weaknesses of human nature, he honestly desired the preservation of the public peace, and contended for it to the best of his limited ability. It is nevertheless possible to distinguish certain attitudes arising partly from present circumstances, partly from historical experience, and partly from ingrained class prejudices, which may be said to have been characteristic of the county bench during the period under review, and which militated against the efficient functioning of the machinery of public order.

[1] Powys to H.O. dated 16 August 1842. H.O. 45/260.

[2] Chambers to H.O. dated 5 August 1843. H.O. 45/454 I; Love to Phillipps dated 7 September 1843. H.O. 45/453; *The Times*, 16 January 1844, p. 5. See also numerous references to Nevill and the two Chambers in David Williams, *The Rebecca Riots: A Study in Agrarian Discontent.*

[3] Tobit Evans, *op. cit.*, 176.

The first was a lack of local self-reliance. "Your gentry," wrote Bunbury to Lord John Russell, "putting their political prejudices out of the question, are likewise sadly helpless, and whether under the present government or that of 20 years ago I have always found them inclined to flock with an 'esprit moutonnier' b ind the hurdles which they expect the state to interpose between them and the wolf rather than make exertions for themselves." [1] The courses of self-help open to the county magistrates were briefly summed up by the Conservative Home Secretary, Sir James Graham, in 1842: "The magistrates may have a rural police, and charge the expenses on the county rate. Parishes and townships may have constables, and pay them out of poor rate. Special constables may be sworn by the magistrates and paid out of county rate. Gentlemen and millowners by local arrangement may form watch and ward, may arm their servants and retainers, may patrol on horseback, and command the strong arm of the law, which is on their side." [2] They vastly preferred, however, to clamour to government for new laws which would make it easier to seize Chartist arms, or deter the Rebeccaites by imposing heavier penalties for the destruction of turnpike gates and tollhouses, and to strengthen the force at their disposal by requisitioning troops for their localities. Behind this attitude lay a bewildering complexity of motives. Among them was a trust in the deterrent effect of harsh penal laws, a preference which had been abandoned by the more advanced legal reformers of the period, but lingered on in the minds of country squires. Coupled with this was a want of confidence in the efficiency of civilian defence arrangements, which, except in the case of county police forces, did not lack justification, and a feeling that disorder was in any case sporadic, and that, therefore, an outlay on a large permanent police establishment was unnecessary.[3] Indeed financial considerations loomed large as determinants of the conduct, or rather the inactivity, of the magistrates. Graham wrote in 1842, after outlining as above

[1] Bunbury to Lord John Russell dated 24 December 1838. Russell Papers: P.R.O. 30/22/3.
[2] Parker, *Graham: Life and Letters* I, 323–4.
[3] See below, pp. 130–1.

the courses of action available to the magistrates: "But they must take some trouble, they must spend some money, they must incur some risk." [1] It was cheaper simply to call for troops and to billet them without regard for their safety or comfort on the inn-keepers, who were constitutionally obliged to accommodate them.

Secondly, as Bunbury noted in the letter before quoted, many magistrates proved incapable of taking a large view of disturbances. General Napier referred to the same error, when he wrote in August 1839: "With respect to Colonel Angelo's memorandum, I have to observe that he has been misled as to Bradford being the 'focus of Chartism'. The magistrates and inhabitants of every town and village in the neighbourhood will tell him the same story that their town or village is the 'focus of Chartism', whereas it is only the focus of their own fears." [2] Preferring private interests to the public good, or perhaps blinded by the former to the latter, they were prepared to weaken the general disposable military force by demanding garrisons for their own districts, and occasionally, if hostile critics are to be believed, for their own residences.[3]

A third characteristic of the county bench was its predisposition to run to excesses in dealing with disturbances. This showed itself in a tendency to call for the services of troops when none were required, to use force unnecessarily in dispersing crowds which had not reached the state of riot, and might, if left alone, separate of their own accord, to arrest seditious speakers at the height of public meetings and, above all, to ride roughshod over civil liberties. It was, in fact, the 'Peterloo' touch.

Even in times of comparative tranquillity, when the prospect of disorder was remote, the county magistrates were liable to issue their proscription of Chartist meetings. Thus, for example, in December 1842, the Oldham magistrates headed by the Rev. Thomas Mills forbade a meeting which had no more sinister purpose than the election of delegates to the Complete Suffrage

---

[1] Parker, *Graham: Life and Letters*, I, 323–4.
[2] Napier to H.O. dated 22 August 1839. H.O. 40/53.
[3] Walters to H.O. dated 23 March 1844. H.O. 45/642; Bunbury to Russell dated 24 December 1838. Russell Papers: P.R.O. 30/22/3.

Conference. This they did against the expressed wishes of the Home Secretary, who saw "no reason to interfere".[1] Three years earlier, the magistrates of Clitheroe had unsuccessfully pressed upon the Home Secretary the introduction of a statute which would make possible a more thorough attack on public meetings than was permitted by the Common Law.[2] Fear and a lack of sympathy between classes so far apart on the social ladder as the landed gentry and the industrial proletariat prompted this severity, though a common hatred of master manufacturers sometimes created an artificial bond between gentleman and artisan, causing the former to behave with unusual indulgence towards the latter. The aforementioned bond was especially strong in the West Riding of Yorkshire, and undoubtedly had much to do with the manifest failure of the Yorkshire magistrates to do their duty during the Anti-Poor Law disturbances. Sympathy with the workers was even more widespread among Tory county magistrates in the closing stages of the Plug-Plot disturbances of 1842, when it was widely believed that the Anti-Corn Law League manufacturers had driven their men to strike, in order to embarrass the Tory government. Mr. Orford, a Cheshire magistrate residing near Stockport, told the master manufacturers of that town that, unless they would exert themselves to keep their men at work, they need not apply to him for military assistance.[3]

The defects of the county bench received some attention from government during the period. Himself a former county magistrate, Sir James Graham was especially active as Home Secretary in instigating thorough inquiry into the conduct of the justices who had failed in their duty during the strike of 1842.[4] Gaps in the magistracy were filled, during the Rebecca Riots, by spurring the Lords Lieutenant to look into the matter,[5] and by sending

---

[1] The Rev. T. S. Mills to H.O. dated 13 December 1842; Hibbert, Mellor and Lees to H.O. dated 18 December 1842. H.O. 45/249.

[2] Russell to Foot, Aspinall, Garnett, Abbott and Thomson dated 6 August 1839. H.O. 41/14.

[3] Orford to H.O. dated 24 August 1842. H.O. 45/242.

[4] H.O. 45/347 and 350.

[5] H.O. to Powell, Rice Trevor and Owen dated 3 October 1843. H.O. 41/18.

down to the disturbed areas a person of experience who would serve as a justice in a temporary capacity.[1] Any government, not least Peel's second ministry, needed to exercise caution, however, in tampering with the county magistracy. Graham's scheme for employing salaried Assistant Barristers in aid of Quarter Sessions was shelved because it would have the effect of "depriving the gentry of property and education of their influence in the several counties in which they reside".[2]

A partial exemption from the jurisdiction of the county authorities and local magisterial benches was enjoyed by the boroughs. After the sweeping reforms of 1835 these retained the management of their own police forces, and in the majority of cases possessed a separate commission of the peace, though (except in Quarter Sessions boroughs exempted by long usage or by a non-intromittent clause) the county magistrates had the right to exercise concurrent jurisdiction within the borough.

In the age of Chartist unrest boroughs remained badly represented in the new industrial districts which were the seat of disorder. The characteristic municipality was a sleepy market town of the agricultural South, whilst the urban aggregations of the new industrial districts rested under the sway of manorial lord and county magistrate. In 1837 Liverpool, Wigan and Preston were the sole corporate towns of Lancashire south of the Ribble; the West Riding boasted only three—Leeds, Pontefract and Doncaster; the tangled knot of Pottery towns none save nearby Newcastle under Lyme; whilst Walsall alone of the cumulations to the north-west and south-west of Birmingham possessed a charter of incorporation. Birmingham, Bolton and Manchester were added to the list of boroughs in 1838, but not until 1844 and after was any substantial progress made in the direction of incorporating the centres of industry. Salford, Warrington, Ashton-under-Lyne, Bradford, Wakefield, Halifax and Wolverhampton then obtained charters in rapid succession between 1844 and 1848.

The functions of the municipality relating to public order were

[1] See below, p. 74 n. 1.   [2] Parker, *Graham: Life and Letters*, I, 335.

shared between the corporation which, through its Watch Committee, managed the police and the bench of borough magistrates. The latter consisted of the mayor and other parties selected officially by the Home Secretary, but the feeling was strong among the radical town councillors that magistrates should be appointed democratically,[1] and although this principle had not been adopted by the legislators of 1835 Lord John Russell had given an assurance in Parliament, that "with regard to the nomination of magistrates in corporate towns, the recommendation of the respective town councils would have great weight with the advisers of the Crown".[2] This principle was largely followed out by Whig Home Secretaries in the late thirties,[3] and the majority parties in the town councils were, therefore, able to use the magistracy as a political prize, and to exclude from it their political opponents. The Town Clerk of Lichfield was perfectly frank about the situation prevailing in his borough: "The Council", he wrote, "with its present majority will not select anyone of the political party opposed to them, because they do not think it safe in the present state of affairs to entrust those persons with an office of local power and moral influence to be employed by them in infusing their political hostility through every accessible avenue and channel of social life." [4] Complaints of a similar exclusive principle were received at the Home Office from Great Yarmouth and Lyme Regis in 1839,[5] and the Earl of Warwick, no doubt a prejudiced observer, instanced Warwick, Coventry and Stratford on Avon as examples of exclusive boroughs with magistracies composed of radicals alone.[6]

This political exclusiveness both enhanced the difficulties of

---

[1] The Council of the borough of Wells carried a resolution in 1839 to the effect that its own members were the most eligible people to become magistrates "because they were elected by the burgesses at large to guard their rights—and by a parity of reasoning may be best to punish their wrongdoings". Proctor to Russell dated 22 March 1839. H.O. 52/43.

[2] Hans., 3 Ser., XLIX, 411–12.

[3] Greville, *op. cit.*, I, 250.

[4] Simpson to Normanby dated 29 November 1839. H.O. 52/41.

[5] Preston to Normanby dated 7 November 1839. H.O. 52/43; Farnall to H.O. dated 29 November 1839. H.O. 52/41.

[6] Warwick to the Secretary of State dated 9 January 1839. H.O. 52/43.

filling magisterial vacancies, and detracted from the respect due
to the magistrates as impartial conservators of the peace, and in
some of the larger towns, where the problems of disorder loomed
large, a disposition to modify it in the interests of public security
was manifested. Philip Muntz, the Birmingham reformer, who
became the second mayor of that town, is reported to have said:
"Good magistrates they must have. He cared not from what
party. They should not be selected from any class or party."[1]
This did not prevent the Birmingham corporation from giving
15 out of 21 places in the list of recommendations to the borough
bench which they sent up to the Home Office to Liberals, mainly
members of the Council, but they did include in their list the
names of six townsmen who were already county justices, and
Lord John Russell so far departed from his practice of accepting
the recommendations of councils without demur as to strike out
three names from the Birmingham list, and to add those of four
Conservatives and three Whigs.[2] The Home Secretary was also
inclined to interfere in the matter of the Liverpool bench. When
in February 1838 the mayor wrote in, recommending five additions to the commission of the peace, his letter was minuted:
"Ask Mr. Hall [the stipendiary magistrate] of Liverpool as to
these gentlemen—and it is desirable they should not be all of the
same politicks."[3] Nevertheless, in the early years of our period
at least, the magistracies of industrial boroughs were largely composed of Liberals, virtually nominated by the Liberal town
councils. The agitators of '32 had become the conservators of the
peace of '39. Later, however, the balance was somewhat redressed by the action of Peel's second ministry which seized the
opportunity soon after its accession to power in 1841 to nominate
a number of Conservatives borough magistrates.[4]

[1] *Ibid.*   [2] Conrad Gill and Asa Briggs, *History of Birmingham*, I, 234.

[3] Mayor of Liverpool to H.O. dated 21 February 1838. H.O. 52/37.

[4] In December 1841 the town council of Leicester carried a motion of protest
against the action of the government in creating eight new Tory magistrates
without consulting the Town Clerk. *The Leicester Chronicle*, 18 December 1841.
For this reference I am indebted to my colleague Mr. A. T. Patterson. Five
Tory magistrates were added to the Stockport bench in November 1841, on
the initiative of the Home Secretary. *The Stockport Chronicle*, 19 November
1841, p. 2.

Exempt from the real property qualifications of the county bench, and the patronage of aristocratic Lords Lieutenant, the borough magistracies lay open to the successful business man and industrialist though there was a prejudice against shopkeepers.[1] In the year 1838 the Leeds magistracy consisted of one physician, one surgeon, one printer, two spinners, one woolstapler, one cloth merchant and manufacturer, one stuff merchant, one tobacco manufacturer, one banker, one solicitor, four merchants and six persons designated 'esquire'.[2] Four manufacturers and one corn merchant were inserted in the Stockport commission in November 1841; Birmingham found vacancies for two bleachers in 1845 and a coal merchant in January 1848; the Stafford bench was increased by a chemist, a surgeon and a banker in January 1842 and a shoe manufacturer in 1846.[3]

In the larger boroughs, at least, the machinery of government functioned more efficiently in relation to the problem of disorder than in the extra-municipal areas. The borough magistrates were generally readier than their equivalents in the county to meet constantly and regularly during riots,[4] and to assume as individuals fixed responsibilities for the performance of this or that duty.[5] No doubt the common membership of the corporation, which most of them shared, gave them a team spirit which the county justices lacked, whilst the commanding position of the mayor on the borough bench ensured that leadership would not be found wanting. Other incentives to regular meetings of the magistrates were the possession of a Public Office, Police Office or Court House, in which the meetings might be held, and the concentration of magistrates' houses within a limited geographical area.

[1] Simpson to Normanby dated 29 November 1839. H.O. 52/41.
[2] Tottie to Russell dated 11 October 1838. H.O. 52/38.   [3] H.O. 90.
[4] Pendlebury to H.O. dated 24 July 1839. H.O. 40/41; at Stockport during the latter half of July 1839 the magistrates were holding daily meetings with reference to Chartist proceedings.
[5] At Leeds during the Plug-Plot riots a special meeting of the borough magistrates fixed the duties of certain magistrates in the event of the outbreak of disorder. Mayor of Leeds to H.O. dated 17 August 1842. H.O. 45/264; the Coventry magistrates, at a special meeting on 17 August 1842, made arrangements for two of their number to be in constant attendance at the Police Office. Mayor of Coventry to H.O. dated 17 August 1842. H.O. 45/261A.

During the Plug-Plot Riots it was in the corporate towns of Lancashire—Bolton, Wigan and Preston—that the stand against the turnout mobs was first taken, in obedience to the Home Office Circular, and throughout those disturbances the boroughs maintained a higher standard of orderliness than the extra-municipal areas. Leeds remained practically free from disturbances whilst Bradford, Halifax and Huddersfield fell into the hands of unruly mobs. Newcastle under Lyme remained quiet whilst the nearby Pottery towns were in uproar. Of course, the boroughs often enjoyed the benefit of a superior police force and a military garrison too, but some credit must be allowed to the energy and discretion of their magistrates in accounting for their more effective resistance to disorder.

It was, however, an energy tempered by a greater measure of restraint than was known to the county magistrates. Though the merchants and manufacturers who ruled the corporate towns were capable of acting with vigour against mobs, their conduct as magistrates was dominated to a less extent than that of the country gentlemen by fear of the people and lack of sympathy with their aspirations. Roworth, the mayor of Nottingham, drew the praises of General Napier by his efforts to raise a fund for the relief of the poor during the winter of 1839–40.[1] The Derby magistrates prevented a strike in August 1842 by visiting the mills, together with the masters, and reasoning with the men.[2] The mayor of Bolton stipulated during the riots of August 1839 that the troops should not fire except in case of urgent necessity.[3] The magistrates of Manchester, Birmingham, Nottingham, Stockport and Bolton showed reluctance to interfere with public meetings, and had to be bullied into suppressing them by wealthy townsmen, neighbouring county magistrates, the government and the military authorities. It is true that the Birmingham magistrates provoked the riot of 4 July by using Metropolitan Policemen to break up a Chartist meeting in the Bull Ring, but it must always be remembered that two months earlier Charles Tindal of the Birmingham

[1] Napier, *op. cit.*, II, 111.
[2] Bainbridge to Maberley dated 23 August 1842. H.O. 45/244.
[3] Mayor of Bolton to H.O. dated 16 August 1839. H.O. 40/44.

branch of the Bank of England had charged them with carelessness and neglect in failing to put down Chartist assemblages,[1]
and that the Home Office had repeatedly exhorted them, in
the strongest terms, to take action against such meetings.[2] As to
demonstrations in Manchester at the time of the Plug-Plot disturbances, Sir William Warre, the military commander, wrote:
"I had some difficulty in persuading the magistrates to issue proclamations and notices forbidding them, in the then excited state
of the town, within the limits of the borough, and to disperse
such meetings by force when assembled." [3] Many instances may
be cited where the borough authorities offered the Chartists the
use of their town halls and court rooms, in the hope of turning
them from the holding of outdoor meetings.[4]

Sometimes, however, the administration of law and order in
the corporate towns was hamstrung by the clash of rival authorities. One aspect of this was the conflict between the county
magistrates and the corporations of the boroughs within the
county, a struggle which frequently assumed a political complexion, as the former were largely Conservative and the latter
Liberal. Mr. Orford, the Cheshire magistrate of High Lane near
Stockport, spoke the mind of many of his class when he wrote:
"The greatest nuisance and the greatest curse ever inflicted on this
country, but more especially during these parlous times, is the
borough and Whig magistrates, they paralyse everything within
their power." [5] Always an impediment to the efficient working of the machinery of public order, this hostility, for which
the county magistrates were usually far more to blame than the
borough,[6] became especially dangerous when, as in the case

---

[1] Governor of Bank of England to H.O. dated 8 May 1839 and enclosure.
H.O. 40/50.
[2] Phillipps to Mayor of Birmingham dated 9 and 11 May 1839. H.O. 41/14.
[3] Warre to Arbuthnot dated 31 August 1839. H.O. 45/268.
[4] Lord Francis Egerton to H.O. dated 6 August 1839. H.O. 40/44; Burgess
to H.O. dated 2 March 1842. H.O. 45/261.
[5] Orford to H.O. dated 24 August 1842. H.O. 45/242.
[6] The borough magistrates often manifested the greatest willingness to
co-operate with the county authorities in the preservation of order. Woodcock
to H.O. dated 20 August 1839. H.O. 40/37; Potts to H.O. dated 9 August
1839. H.O. 40/41; Aylesford to H.O. dated 24 August 1842. H.O. 45/261A.

of boroughs not possessing a separate commission of the peace, the county magistrates exercised *de facto* jurisdiction within the borough.

Tenby in Pembrokeshire furnishes an example of the discord to which this could lead. It was the privilege of the chief citizen of a borough lacking a separate commission to take his place at the petty sessions beside the county justices of the division. Now William Richards, mayor of Tenby, was a noted reformer and opponent of the powerful interest of Sir John Owen in Pembrokeshire, and among the county magistrates who served with him on the bench were some of his most implacable enemies. A crisis was reached in March 1839, when a dispute concerning the enclosure of some land belonging to the burgesses produced a violent altercation at the close of the petty sessions, resulting in a duel between the mayor and another magistrate, in which the former was severely wounded.[1] Such occurrences inevitably degraded the magistracy, and it is not surprising to learn from the pen of the rector of Tenby that "the lower orders appeal (as in the present instance they do) to these very dissentions and breaches of the peace as an excuse for their own delinquencies".[2]

Scarcely less injurious to the public safety was the warfare which was waged in Manchester, Birmingham and Bolton to prevent the newly-formed corporations from establishing their authority. The three towns all received charters of incorporation in 1838, and in each case legal doubts were raised as to the validity of the charter of incorporation. The opportunity was thus given to the existing institutions of local government to resist the transference of their authority to the new borough councils. In Manchester the borough-reeve and constables, officers of the Court Leet, and the Police Commissioners, clung jealously to their powers. And when the great Chartist demonstrations occurred in the spring of 1839 the citizens were treated to the extremely unedifying spectacle of rival authorities, the mayor and the borough-reeve, the borough magistrates and the justices of the

---

[1] Richards to Russell dated 16 September 1839. H.O. 52/43; Norris to H.O. dated 4 July 1839. H.O. 52/43.
[2] J. H. Humphreys to Russell dated 10 July 1839. H.O. 52/43.

surrounding county, making separate preparations to combat disorder within the confines of a single town,[1] whilst the general in command of the troops set himself the well-nigh impossible task of bringing them together.[2] At Bolton the collision was even sharper, for the county justices declared openly against the borough bench. On 22 July 1839, when Chartist excitement was rising, the magistrates of the Bolton division of the hundred of Salford consulted the Home Office as to whether they had concurrent jurisdiction with the borough magistrates within the borough of Bolton. The law, as it then stood, gave such rights to county justices in all boroughs not possessing a separate court of Quarter Sessions, and, having consulted the Attorney General, Lord John Russell replied in the affirmative, being careful to add that "the magistrates of the borough are immediately responsible for the peace of the borough, and are well warranted in exercising the functions of magistrates under the Charter of Incorporation".[3] Soon afterwards the following placard was put out from a bookseller in the town:

Borough of Bolton: Whereas a number of would be gentlemen, presumptuously calling themselves Borough Magistrates, are in the habit of holding a Court over the Tap Room and Stables in Bowker's Row, and at which Court they are granting Summonses and Warrants, by those means obtaining funds to support their so called Corporation: This is to give notice to the Inhabitants of the Borough of Bolton that by applying at the said Court for Summonses and Warrants they are assisting the so called Corporation to keep up their expensive farce of Mayor, Aldermen and Council-men.

The Inhabitants of the Borough are therefore requested to apply at the Old Police Office for all Summonses and Warrants as heretofore, it having been decided by the highest Legal Authority that the County Magistrates have jurisdiction within the Borough.[4]

A few days later, when the Bolton Riots of August 1839 had

---

[1] On Saturday, 4 May 1839, the borough magistrates met at the York Hotel and the county magistrates also held a meeting. The two meetings issued public notices, practically identical in character, setting forth the illegality of certain Chartist proceedings, and both notices were posted in the town. *The Times*, 9 May 1839, p. 5.

[2] Napier, *op. cit.*, II, 36.

[3] Joseph Ridgway to H.O. dated 22 July 1839 and Minute. H.O. 40/44.

[4] Darbishire to H.O. dated 9 August 1839. H.O. 40/44.

broken out, two of the county magistrates came into the borough with offers of assistance. Whether they came with the firm intention of creating mischief, or whether it was simply that their animosity to the borough magistrates made smooth co-operation impossible, is rather uncertain, but the fact remains that the failure of one of these two county justices to carry out the duty assigned to him almost led to the destruction of the Bolton Town Hall by an angry mob.[1]

In certain of the larger centres of population salaried magistrates had been appointed to supplement the work of the unpaid justices of county and borough. Such functionaries presided over the Metropolitan Police Offices. These were trained lawyers described by the Webbs as " 'a set of quiet, gentlemanlike persons'; perhaps the 'failures' of their profession; concentrating their attention on trying the ordinary cases of a London police court; entirely divorced from County Business . . ."[2] Their functions were not, however, entirely judicial, for they extended to the swearing in of special constables, and even to the task of accompanying military detachments, as on 10 April 1848. Stipendiary magistrates were also to be found in the provinces, at Manchester and Stoke-on-Trent in particular. They were usually appointed as a result of petitions from localities which found themselves deficient in unpaid justices, and the right of appointment lay with the Crown acting on the advice of the Home Office. These stipendiary magistrates were the confidential agents of the Home Secretary in their localities.[3]

The two lowest ranks in the machinery of public order were those of High and Petty Constable. Though in the works of seventeenth-century legal writers like Sir Matthew Hale these appeared as executive officers taking their place next to the sheriff and justice of the peace,[4] by the second quarter of the nineteenth

[1] Darbishire to H.O. dated 16 August 1839. H.O. 40/44.

[2] Webb, *op. cit.*, I, 580.

[3] H.O. to Maude dated 7 December 1838 (Confidential). H.O. 41/13.

[4] H. B. Simpson, 'The Office of Constable', *English Historical Review*, X (1895).

century they had become little more than incompetent policemen attendant upon the magistrates. It is as such that we shall have occasion to treat them in the succeeding chapter.

Of such a character, then, was the ladder of authorities responsible for the preservation of the peace. On the middle and lower rungs of it were undoubted deficiencies both of quantity and quality, so that the civil power was frequently inactive and wanting in leadership. These defects were partially overcome by the exertions of energetic magistrates and Lords Lieutenant who functioned outside their usual jurisdictions in the place of their absent neighbours, and by the action of the Home Office which bestirred the local authorities with circulars and occasionally sent London police court magistrates and other responsible persons to assist them in their duties.[1] Nevertheless, although the civil power never broke down completely, and martial law was not proclaimed, the efficiency of the machinery of public order depended, to an unhealthy degree, on the leadership and energy shown by senior officers who commanded the troops in the disturbed districts. The prominent part they played in directing operations against disorder mirrors the ineffectiveness of English civil administration.

[1] Mr. Henry, a London police magistrate, was sent to Manchester in August 1842 to help the two local stipendiary magistrates to carry out the arrest of the leaders of the Plug-Plot. Graham to Warre dated 17 August 1842. Graham Papers, Bundle 52A; Colonel Hankey was despatched to South Wales in October 1843 to assist the resident magistrates in organizing and directing the movements of the civil force and in accompanying military patrols. He was to be made a magistrate of the disturbed counties for the purpose. H.O. to Rice Trevor dated 16 October 1843. H.O. 41/18.

CHAPTER III

THE CIVIL FORCE. (I) THE OLD POLICE

T̲URNING from the authorities responsible for the public peace to the resources at their disposal, we find that there was widespread agreement, among the leading figures in the government and in the army, as to the order in which those resources should be drawn upon. Lord John Russell and the Duke of Wellington, General Charles Napier and Sir James Graham, notwithstanding their varied political outlooks, stood united in the belief (which they all held firmly and dogmatically) that the suppression of riot was, in the first place, the task of the civil force, and that the troops should be held in reserve, to be used, if necessary, in aid of the civil power, but not as a substitute for it. It is the purpose of this chapter, and the ensuing one, to describe the civil force available for the maintenance of public order in the age of the Chartists.

Over most of rural[1] England at the beginning of our period, and some of it even at the end, the only permanent police force in existence was that furnished by the High Constable of the Hundred and the petty constables of the parishes and townships. The former was a salaried official, appointed and removed by Quarter Sessions, except where a franchise kept the hundred court alive. He had the oversight of the petty constables within his hundred, but his control had become so irregular as to be purely nominal.[2] The petty constables were not, therefore, a united

---

[1] This adjective is used (as it was in the popular phrase, 'the Rural Police Acts') to denote everything lying outside the corporate towns. It includes, therefore, not just the placid agricultural districts, but restless manufacturing and mining villages, and larger communities which were towns in everything except municipal organization.

[2] In the Aveland Hundred of Lincolnshire the High (or Chief) Constable, who received a salary of £24 p/a, paid out of the County Rate, came into

force but scattered, uncontrolled local officers, each responsible for his own parish or township and no more. Needless to say they were not even adequate to maintain law and order in their localities. March Phillipps, the squire of Garendon Park, Leicester-shire, situated betwixt the disturbed town of Loughborough and the large hosiery village of Sheepshead, where poverty, ignorance and riotousness prevailed, wrote to the Home Office in 1839 stating that in his parish there was but one constable, a joiner with a large family, afraid to do his duty.[1]

Not only were there too few constables to be effective. The quality of those who served the office left much to be desired. The right of appointment rested with the Court Leet or where this had lapsed, as was more usually the case, with the justices of the peace, who acted on the nominations of the parish vestries. It is difficult to generalize about the character of Courts Leet and vestries. The Webbs tell us that the juries which nominated the constables in the Courts Leet consisted of "two or three dozen of the more respectable and substantial householders".[2] Parish vestries showed a baffling diversity of origin, powers and social composition. The close vestries of Northumberland and Durham which had existed by immemorial custom for three centuries comprised "the principal occupiers of land in the various town-ships", and were known collectively as the "gentlemen of the four-and-twenty".[3] If the 1834 Poor Law Report is to be believed, however, open vestries in the rural districts consisted of farmers and tradespeople,[4] whilst those in some of the larger towns were occasionally invaded by mobs consisting of several thousand people. In the latter case, however, it became customary to decide important issues, including the election of parish officers, by a referendum which gave weight to persons of property by a

contact with the petty constables once a year and on such other occasions when they chose to come to him for advice. *Select Committee on the Expediency of Adopting a More Uniform System of Police in England, Wales and Scotland,* 2nd Report, Mins. of Evidence, pp. 68–9; 1852–3 (715), XXXVI.

[1] C. March Phillipps to H.O. dated 30 January 1839. H.O. 40/44.

[2] Webb, *op. cit.,* II, 23.   [3] Webb, *op. cit.,* I, 179.

[4] *Report of the Royal Commission on the Administration and Practical Operation of the Poor Laws,* p. 62; 1834 (44) XXVII.

system of plural voting sanctioned by the Sturges-Bourne Act of 1818.[1] On the balance, power rested with the propertied classes, though the smaller type of property often predominated.

One might, therefore, have expected care to be taken in the appointment of conservators of the peace. On the contrary, however, it was frequently the practice, as noted by a Lincolnshire police officer, that "persons in the middle class of life at the vestry appoint, in different parishes, persons who are not so proper as otherwise".[2] The explanation of this anomaly lies in the extreme unpopularity of the office, which involved heavy and unpleasant duties, but carried neither status nor reasonable remuneration. Persons of respectability shunned the office, allowing it to fall into the hands of "such as prefer earning a shilling or two by serving a warrant or a summons rather than by attending to their work".[3] Illiteracy was a common fault among petty constables, whilst a Leicestershire Copyhold Court elected for three successive years the most drunken man in the village to serve as constable.[4] Where persons of low social status were chosen, political disaffection unavoidably crept in. At Middleton in 1839 five of the six Court Leet constables were reported to be Chartists.[5] Constables of low character were also tempted to abet breaches of the peace and other offences, since their only remuneration was by fees and allowances arising from legal proceedings.

If, on the other hand, respectable tradesmen were chosen, as was the case in Staffordshire and parts of Lincolnshire,[6] they shirked their responsibilities, either because they could ill spare the time from their business, or because they feared to undertake duties which would bring them into collision with their customers. The Chartist weapon of exclusive dealing was greatly feared by this type of constable.

---

[1] Webb, *op. cit.*, I, 166 et seq.

[2] *S.C. on Police, 1852–3*, 2nd Report, Mins. of Evidence, p. 63.

[3] *Royal Commission on the Establishment of a Constabulary Force in the Counties of England and Wales*, 1st Report, p. 101; 1839 (169) XIX.

[4] March Phillipps to H.O. dated 30 January 1839. H.O. 40/44.

[5] Helsall to H.O. dated 15 August 1839. H.O. 40/37.

[6] *S.C. on Police*, 1st Report, Mins. of Evidence, p. 73; 1852–3 (603) XXXVI; 2nd Report, Mins. of Evidence, pp. 11 and 68.

Some attempt had been, and was still being, made to improve the petty constable system without changing its fundamental character. The Watching and Lighting Act of 1833 [1] had provided for the payment of constables, who were still to be appointed on a parochial basis, from a rate levied by the overseers of the poor. The Act was unfortunately permissive, and required a two-thirds majority in the parish vestry before the paid constable could be engaged. In the large and disorderly village of Rothley in Leicestershire such an officer was appointed with singularly good effect, but only because the need for a two-thirds majority vote was not generally known.[2] In 1842, Parliament passed an Act which not only extended the facilities for appointing salaried petty constables, but made available a new method of infusing discipline into these local officers—viz., by setting Superintending Constables, trained in professional police forces, over them. These new powers were quickly adopted by many of the counties which had not by that time established forces of a more modern character.[3]

Such reforms did not, however, eradicate the evils inherent in the system. The parish was, as a unit, too small for successful operation against disturbers of the peace. Moreover, the appointment of Superintending Constables did not render the unpaid parish constables efficient. The former were appointed to districts too large to permit of adequate supervision,[4] and were given no

[1] 3 & 4 W. IV, c. 90.
[2] Acworth to H.O. dated 22 July 1839. H.O. 40/44; Acworth to H.O. dated 28 December 1838. H.O. 52/37.
[3] By 1846, 15 out of 23 counties having no Rural Police Force had appointed paid constables. By 1853, 14 of those 23 counties had Superintending Constables. These calculations are based on *An Abstract of a Return of those Parishes etc. that have adopted the System of Paid Constables*; 1846 (715) XXXIV. Also on *A Return Showing the Several Counties etc. in which Superintending Constables have been Appointed*; 1852-3 (675) LXXVIII. Cheshire, Middlesex and Surrey have been ignored, the first because it had an inefficient police act of its own, passed in 1829, and the two latter because they were partly included in the metropolitan police district.
[4] A Superintending Constable of Kent had 32 parishes in his division: *S.C. on Police, 1852-3*: 1st Report, Mins. of Evidence, p. 119. An Oxfordshire counterpart had 30, with 60 or 70 parish constables. *Ibid.*: 2nd Report, Mins. of Evidence, p. 88.

effective disciplinary powers. In Oxfordshire they were able to do no more than to lay information of cases of neglect of duty before a magistrate at the time of the annual re-election of constables.[1] At the best the superintendents shouldered the responsibility which should have fallen upon their subordinates.[2] At the worst the superior officers, from being themselves virtually uncontrolled, fell into the bad habits of their inferiors.[3] Meanwhile the salaried petty constables took up supplementary jobs, since their remuneration was insufficient for a comfortable livelihood.[4]

In those aggregations of industrial population which were large enough to deserve the title of town, but possessed none of the institutions of municipal government, the police establishment was sometimes a little better, but varied considerably from place to place. It was common in such places for the elected constables to allow their duties to devolve upon paid deputies, the office of constable becoming, as in Manchester, a mark of social distinction. The deputy constable might, or might not, have the management of a police force, and there might be a corps of night watchmen provided either by private subscription or by a body of Improvement Commissioners established by Act of Parliament. Manchester was comparatively well off even before the incorporation of the borough. In April 1837 there were about 30 regular constables in the town and a night watch of about 150 under the Police Commissioners,[5] though the quality of the day police seems to have left much to be desired.[6] Halifax, however, in December 1838, could muster no more than two constables, two deputy constables and a nightly watch.[7] Wakefield had one constable, appointed annually, two deputies and watchmen

---

[1] *Ibid.*, 89. [2] *Ibid.*, 97.

[3] A West Riding Superintending Constable bungled through drunkenness the arrest of some Chartist ringleaders in May 1848. Milligan, Wickham, Tempest and Pollard to H.O. dated 29 May 1848. H.O. 45/2410AC.

[4] *S.C. on Police, 1852–3*: 2nd Report, Mins. of Evidence, p. 66.

[5] Wemyss to Jackson dated 18 April 1837. H.O. 40/35. In December 1838 Sir Frederick Roe spoke of 36 paid men and 150 watchmen. Roe to H.O. dated 17 December 1839. H.O. 61/21.

[6] A. Redford and I. S. Russell, *The History of Local Government in Manchester*, I, 82–92.

[7] Jackson to H.O. dated 5 December 1838. H.O. 40/39.

varying from six to sixteen in number "according to the season of the year".[1] Dewsbury had "no local establishment beyond . . . the solitary constable who according to the practice of the North of England is chosen annually for every township of each parish, this constable serving gratuitously and nominating Deputies who are remunerated by fees for serving processes of law".[2] Bradford with a population of 90,000 had a Chief Constable, his two assistants and a constable for every township.[3] Over the Pennines in Lancashire the situation was just as ludicrous. At Burnley, in close proximity to the "numerous and . . . mischievously inclined" population of Colne, the civil force consisted of one constable, one captain of the watch and eight watchmen.[4] Blackburn had one constable and two assistants;[5] Rochdale one constable, two beadles and thirteen watchmen.[6] At Stalybridge the number of constables, excluding specials, was six, at Ashton four, at Hyde two, at Dukinfield three.[7] Yet all these were already thickly populated manufacturing towns.

So obviously inadequate was the civil force over much of England outside the corporate towns that attempts were made to supplement it by private enterprise. Industrial concerns which employed large bodies of unruly workmen resorted to the expedient of establishing their own police. The railway companies in particular employed a private police force to maintain order among the burly Irish navigators whilst the work of construction was proceeding.[8] A similar force rested at the disposal of the iron-masters of the Tredegar Works in Monmouthshire,[9] and of their counterparts in Lanarkshire.[10]

In effect, the petty constable system only becomes intelligible

---

[1] Jackson to H.O. dated 9 December 1838. H.O. 40/39.   [2] *Ibid.*
[3] Angelo to H.O. dated 19 August 1839. H.O. 40/51.
[4] Jackson to H.O. dated 9 December 1838. H.O. 40/39.
[5] *Ibid.*   [6] *Ibid.*
[7] Jackson to H.O. dated 19 December 1838. H.O. 40/39.
[8] H. O. Fitzwilliam dated 19 October 1838. H.O. 41/13. Clerk of Rugby Petty Sessions to H.O. dated 27 August 1838. H.O. 40/39.
[9] Bute to H.O. dated 1 October 1840. H.O. 40/57.
[10] Alison to Graham dated 19 August 1842. H.O. 45/266.

as a method of preserving order in the light of a general obligation resting upon the whole community to assist the peace officers in the event of disturbance. The age was past when the entire active male force of the county would assemble at the behest of the Sheriff. The Sheriff of Lanarkshire, it is true, issued during the strikes of August 1842 a proclamation calling upon "the Posse Comitatus of the County, to come forward to the support of the Public Peace",[1] yet the results of the appeal did but demonstrate that "these boasted securities of self-government amounted to nothing".[2] Nevertheless the tradition of collective responsibility for personal service in the repression of disturbances was kept alive during the Chartist period by the employment of special constables and the formation of armed associations. These were the resources from which the primitive police organization of so much of early Victorian England was supplemented in time of riot.

Special constables had long been used to preserve the peace, but in the decade immediately preceding the Chartist riots the mode of employing them had been reduced to a system by legislation.[3] On receipt of information taken upon oath that disturbances existed, or were apprehended and that the civil force was inadequate, any two justices of the peace were empowered to swear in special constables, compelling service if necessary. Expenses incurred in equipping these special constables with staves, or in remunerating them for trouble and loss of time, were chargeable to the County Rate (or in a corporate town to the Borough Rate), except in the case of appointments rendered necessary by disputes between railway labourers, when the burden was shifted to the railway company.

Normally special constables were not armed beyond the constable's staff. In 1839, however, it was government policy to offer weapons of a more lethal character—cutlasses and pistols—

---

[1] Proclamation dated 8 August 1842. H.O. 45/266.
[2] A. Alison, *Some Account of My Life and Writings*, I, 488.
[3] Acts regulating the appointment of special constables were passed in October 1831 and August 1838, whilst the Municipal Corporations Act of 1835 contained an important provision respecting them.

to the magistrates for the purpose of equipping the specials.[1] This course of action was attended by the danger of incurring a charge of arming class against class, and by that of placing arms in private houses and other places where they could not be properly guarded. In consequence, Sir Robert Peel's government reacted strongly against the policy of its predecessors, even advising the magistrates to call for troops rather than arm the specials.[2]

Needless to say the principal reserve for the recruitment of special constables was the middle class. At Wigan in 1839 the magistrates despatched a circular appealing for special constables to the parliamentary electors only.[3] At Bolton also, in 1842, the magisterial summons was directed to the electoral body.[4] Stockport in May 1839 called upon its Burgesses.[5] It is true that working-class special constables were enrolled in large numbers, especially in 1848, often at the instigation not of the magistrates, but of their employers, who did not scruple to hold the threat of dismissal over the heads of those who refused to be sworn.[6] In these cases, however, it was frequently stipulated that the obligation of the workmen should not extend beyond the protection of the works in which they were employed.[7] It seems probable that the motive in appointing them was to ensure their good behaviour rather than to use them for police purposes. Certainly the Dewsbury magistrates in August 1842 swore in the workmen of

[1] *Copy of Lord John Russell's Letter to Magistrates in Sessions, to Mayors of Boroughs in certain counties directing them how to proceed for the preservation of the peace in disturbed districts.* 1839 (299) XXXVIII.

[2] H.O. to Still dated 31 August 1842. H.O. 41/17.

[3] Part of H.O. dated 6 August 1839. H.O. 40/37.

[4] Winder to H.O. dated 15 August 1842. H.O. 45/249.

[5] Coppock to H.O. dated 11 May 1839. H.O. 40/41.

[6] Railway companies were notorious in this respect. See F. C. Mather, 'The Railways, the Electric Telegraph and Public Order during the Chartist Period, 1837–48', *History*, XXXVIII (1953); also *The Northern Star*, 25 March 1848, p. 2. Five hundred workmen employed in the Liverpool docks were dismissed for refusing to be sworn. Many of them subsequently capitulated. Arbuthnot to H.O. dated 2 August 1848; Warre to Assistant Adjutant General dated 1 August 1848. H.O. 45/2410AB.

[7] Eight hundred operatives were appointed special constables at Warrington in August 1842 for the protection of the manufactories in which they worked. Warrington Magistrates to H.O. dated 19 August 1842. H.O. 45/249.

the various mills with no other intention than that of "placing those sworn in on the side of order".[1]

Reliance upon the middle class for the effective part of the special constabulary force rendered it extremely difficult to recruit such a body where its services were most in demand. For the most turbulent parts of the manufacturing districts were often those where no substantial middle class existed. Twenty years after the bogey of Chartism had been laid, James Bryce described, as follows, the social structure of industrial Lancashire outside the great towns of Liverpool and Manchester: "What is called the middle class is but small, there being few professional men, since neither a doctor's nor a lawyer's practice is lucrative in such places, and few rich shopkeepers, since all the better people do their shopping in Manchester or Liverpool, buying nothing but groceries and such like in the local store".[2] From Barnoldswick in Yorkshire,[3] from the Shropshire[4] and Warwickshire[5] coalfields, came protests from the magistrates, during the Chartist period, that the class structure of their localities would not permit the formation of a substantial force of special constables.

In regions such as these, such middle-class persons as there were felt so isolated and so dependent upon their neighbours of the working class that they were reluctant to offer their services. At Barnsley, in 1839, exclusive dealing was practised to such an extent by the Chartists that it was impossible to prevail on any persons engaged in trade to come forward voluntarily as special constables.[6] Nor was it only for their businesses that the middle classes feared. The shopkeepers of Colne told the magistrates in May 1839 that their lives and properties would be in danger if they came forward voluntarily as special constables.[7] Three years later, during the Plug-Plot disturbances, the Lord Lieutenant of

[1] Greenwood to H.O. dated 18 August 1842. H.O. 45/264.
[2] *Schools Inquiry Commission*, General Reports, Vol. IX, pp. 750-1; 1867/8 [C 3966, VIII] XXVIII.
[3] Ingham to H.O. dated 17 June 1842. H.O. 45/264.
[4] Eyton to H.O. dated 19 August 1842. H.O. 45/258.
[5] Aylesford to H.O. dated 22 August 1842. H.O. 45/261A.
[6] Cooke to H.O. dated 8 May 1839. H.O. 40/51.
[7] Bolton to H.O. dated 18 May 1839. H.O. 40/37.

Lancashire ascribed the backwardness shown by the inhabitants of his county in offering their services to a desire "to feel secure before they enter upon this duty, that in case of difficulty and disturbance they should meet with support which in many places it would be impossible for them to expect from such a distance as Manchester before the case which required it was at an end".[1] It is not surprising, therefore, that the recruitment of special constables was most disappointing precisely when the need for it was greatest—viz., when the civil power was otherwise weak.

To the extent that it arose from the unwillingness of certain middle-class persons to mark themselves out from their fellows (and thus become targets for private vengeance), reluctance to serve the office of special constable could be overcome if the magistrates would exercise the power granted to them by the Special Constables Acts, to conscript whole classes of people, as indeed they did, after some delay, at Atherton and Colne in 1839 and at Bolton in 1842.[2] But the magistrates usually preferred to exhaust the possibilities of voluntary service first, and the enrolment of special constables was thus a very slow procedure, full of delays and hesitations.

Difficulties of recruitment belong largely to the early years of the period. There was a remarkable change in the situation in 1848. The almost legendary muster of 170,000 special constables[3] in the London area was matched throughout the provinces. In March, Manchester had 10,974,[4] whilst in Liverpool on St. Patrick's day some 3,000–4,000, selected from the principal inhabitants, assembled in and about the Exchange Buildings.[5] In the Pottery towns the magistrates had more volunteers than they required, but did not like to refuse appointment.[6] Three Rugby

[1] Derby to H.O. dated 18 August 1842. H.O. 45/249.
[2] Bolton to H.O. dated 18 May 1839. H.O. 40/37; Atherton Magistrates to H.O. dated 22 May 1839. H.O. 40/37. Winder to H.O. dated 15 August 1842. H.O. 45/249. To assist them in making a compulsory levy the magistrates had at hand the lists of parliamentary electors, which provided a useful register of persons suitable for enrolment as special constables.
[3] Hovell, op. cit., 290.
[4] Maude and Gladstone to H.O. dated 9 March 1848. H.O. 45/2410A.
[5] Rushton to H.O. dated 17 March 1848. H.O. 45/2410A.
[6] Rose to H.O. dated 30 March 1848. H.O. 45/2410Y.

schoolboys wrote to the Home Office offering to assemble 60 boys all over 17 years of age, for the service of the government as special constables.[1] Of the large towns, only in Leicester, where great sympathy existed between the middle and working classes,[2] and in Birmingham, where industrialization had not yet created a marked social cleavage between capital and labour,[3] was the response poor. The propertied classes were in the grip of a hysteria, induced by developments on the continent rather than by the actual situation at home, but it was a hysteria of assertion, not, as on previous occasions, of despair and inaction. The increased supply of special constables at the later date reflects the growth both in the size[4] and in the self-confidence of the English middle class, and also the rise of an efficient police machine which won doubters to the side of law and order.

To raise a levy of shopkeepers and warehousemen, to equip them with truncheons and to place black and white cockades in their hats is not, however, to create an effective constabulary force. Without organization, discipline, exercise, a force of special constables would be, what the Stafford magistrates wrote of the men they had appointed, "little, if anything, better than a disorganized body to oppose a riotous and armed mob".[5] Some attempt was made during the period to organize the specials, but this was mainly confined to the corporate towns, where the police was better, where the authorities were more active and where the division into wards furnished a natural basis for organization. At Congleton in April 1848 the special constables, amounting to almost 600, were arranged under the aldermen of each ward.[6]

---

[1] Three Rugby Schoolboys to H.O. dated 11 April 1848. H.O. 45/2410.

[2] Mayor of Leicester to H.O. dated 9 April 1848. H.O. 45/2410R.

[3] Arbuthnot to H.O. dated 9 April 1848. H.O. 45/2410AB.

[4] Five or six hundred warehouse clerks enlisted as specials in Manchester in April 1848. Maude to H.O. dated 19 April 1848. H.O. 45/2410A. This group was a section of the lower middle class thrown up by the transformation of Manchester from a manufacturing town into the commercial metropolis of a vast manufacturing district.

[5] Stafford Magistrates to H.O. dated 22 August 1842. H.O. 45/260.

[6] Wilson to H.O. dated 19 April 1848. H.O. 45/2410K. For other examples see Report of D. Dundas. H.O. 40/49; Heard to H.O. dated 1 April 1848— Enclosed Regulations. H.O. 45/2410S.

The training and drilling of special constables was beset by many difficulties. Public opinion was all too ready to denounce anything savouring of military display,[1] the Home Office would not afford the magistrates unqualified support in imposing it,[2] the specials themselves sometimes objected to it,[3] and unless a good regular police force was in existence it was not easy to find persons competent to carry out the instruction.[4] In any case, a hastily summoned force of special constables was unlikely to prove of much value unless it was used in conjunction with a well-organized permanent police, which would both inspire it with confidence and endue it with direction. During an election riot at Newtown, Montgomeryshire, in 1841, 240 specials acting under the rural police kept the mob at bay until the arrival of troops,[5] whilst at Colne in Lancashire the special constables put up a brave show under the County Constabulary.[6] By themselves, however, the special constables proved useless, the magistrates not daring to bring them into conflict with the mob.[7] At Huddersfield in 1837[8] and at Dewsbury in the following year[9] the specials actually fled from the rioters even though, on these occasions, detachments of the Metropolitan Police were present with them. In brief, the experience of the Chartist disturbances confirms the observation made by General Jackson in 1838 that "in many of the large towns such as Hull, Leeds, Manchester, Newcastle-on-Tyne, Derby, etc., a good system of internal police being as you

[1] Maude to H.O. dated 19 April 1848. H.O. 45/2410A.

[2] In 1848 the Home Secretary forbade any species of drill or military training in the metropolis, and training to the use of arms in the provinces. H.O. to Fen dated 19 April 1848. H.O. 65/16. H.O. to Mayor of Liverpool dated 19 July 1848. H.O. 41/19.

[3] Black to May dated 20 March 1839. H.O. 40/44.

[4] Metropolitan Police officers sometimes had to be detached to the provinces for the purpose. Black to May dated 20 March 1839. H.O. 40/44.

[5] Chief Constable's Report. H.O. 45/54.

[6] Bolton to H.O. dated 11 August 1840. H.O. 40/54.

[7] Over 100 specials were sworn at Holmfirth in August 1842, but these merely followed a mob of strikers from place to place, not daring to interfere. Kidd to H.O. dated 17 August 1842. H.O. 45/264. For a similar case at Bingley in 1848 see Ferrand to H.O. dated 27 May 1848. H.O. 45/2410AC.

[8] C. Reith, *British Police and the Democratic Ideal*, 209.

[9] *S.C. on Police, 1852–3*: 2nd Report, p. 91.

are aware well established, the subsidiary aid of 'Special Constables' etc., can be required only in case of emergency, when
such aid is likely to prove most valuable and efficient—but without something to form upon, a 'Constabulary Force' (if by that
term be meant Special Constables) is, I fear, but little to be
depended on".[1]

The difficulty of obtaining an adequate supply of special
constables in the manufacturing districts led to the employment
in that capacity of the army out-pensioners of the Chelsea and
Greenwich Hospitals resident within the area. These veterans at
least had the advantage over civilian special constables of having
received a military training, and could be effectively coerced into
service by the threat of withdrawing their pensions. The suggestion that they might be useful came initially from Manchester,
where a meeting of the borough-reeve, constables and several
gentlemen on 23 April 1839 decided to seek government sanction
for their employment, pleading as a precedent the Reform Bill
unrest of December 1830.[2] This idea appealed to the authorities
at the Home Office, since great difficulty had been encountered
in obtaining the services of the respectable classes as special
constables, and the military commander of the Northern District
showed reluctance to supply regular troops to protect the property
of those who would do nothing to defend themselves. In effect,
the Whig government adopted the Manchester plan as its own,
and proceeded to urge it upon the rest of the country. The
Commissioners of Chelsea Hospital were ordered to issue a
notice to all out-pensioners requiring and commanding them to
hold themselves in readiness to act as special constables at the
behest of the magistrates of their locality.[3] Meanwhile the Home
Secretary advised the local authorities to swear in Chelsea pensioners as an alternative to receiving a military detachment.[4]

[1] Jackson to H.O. dated 9 December 1838. H.O. 40/39.
[2] Maude to H.O. dated 25 April 1839 and minute. H.O. 40/43.
[3] H.O. to Mayor of Carlisle dated 11 May 1839. H.O. 41/14.
[4] H.O. to Harewood dated 3 May 1839; H.O. to Evans dated 6 May 1839.
H.O. 41/13.

G

The strength of the force thus placed at the disposal of the civil power varied from place to place. At Monmouth at the time of the committal of Vincent and his fellow-Chartists the pensioners were reported to be very few,[1] whilst in a circle of five miles around the borough of Leicester there were only 50.[2] More than 1,200, however, were resident in Manchester, but of these 1,200 it was estimated that only 200 or 300 would be fit for service.[3] Everywhere a large section of the pensioners would be found incapacitated by age and infirmity, whilst immoderate habits claimed a toll of many others. Nevertheless Birmingham raised a force of 500–700 in the spring of 1839.[4]

The pensioners were in fact employed extensively against the Chartists in 1839, and during the disturbances of the summer of 1842. They were used for example in dispersing Chartist meetings in Birmingham,[5] in ensuring the peace of Pontypool on the occasion of the Newport Rising,[6] and in patrolling the streets of Manchester in August 1842.[7] The correct procedure was to swear them in as special constables, and to pay them an allowance from the rates over and above their pensions for the period during which they were out in aid of the civil power.[8] Service was enforced by threatening recalcitrants with the loss of their pensions.[9] Arms were supplied by the government freely in 1839,[10] but with greater caution in 1842.[11]

Experience, however, soon revealed the defects inherent in the employment of pensioners as special constables. Living, as they

---

[1] Dyke to H.O. dated 11 May 1839. H.O. 40/45.

[2] Heyrick to H.O. dated 16 February 1840. H.O. 40/55.

[3] Maude to H.O. dated 25 April 1839. H.O. 40/43.

[4] Scholefield to H.O. dated 10 May 1839. H.O. 40/50.

[5] Thorn to H.O. dated 2 July 1839. H.O. 40/53.

[6] Leigh to H.O. dated 6 November 1839. H.O. 40/45.

[7] Supt. Beswick's Report to Mayor of Manchester. H.O. 45/268.

[8] Minute on Maude to H.O. dated 25 April 1839. H.O. 40/43.

[9] H.O. to Lyttelton dated 12 August 1842. H.O. 41/16.

[10] *Copy, Russell's Letter on preservation of peace in disturbed districts*; 1839 (299) XXXVIII.

[11] Arms were sent to Manchester, where strong barrack accommodation and a large military force would guarantee their safety. H.O. to Warre dated 15 August 1842. H.O. 41/16. An application from Halifax was rejected. H.O. to Pollard dated 18 August 1842. H.O. 41/17.

did, in their own homes and moving in working-class circles, the old soldiers were connected by innumerable ties of consanguinity and acquaintance with the disaffected—a circumstance which might, as General Napier noted, render them excellent spies, but which might equally well diminish their reliability in the event of disturbance.[1] Further, the very mode of employment prevented the pensioners from deriving any real benefit from their military background. Deprived of martial discipline, and operating as a mere civil force under the command of a magistrate, they showed themselves scarcely less inefficient than any other body of special constables. In Manchester, during the Plug-Plot disturbances, their defects proved so glaring that they had to be withdrawn from patrol duty, the mayor claiming that they had fled on the approach of a mob, leaving the police to sustain serious injury.[2] Yet another difficulty was that of obtaining from the parsimonious magistrates the payment to which the pensioners were entitled by virtue of the services they had rendered. The riots of August 1842 were followed by a series of acrid disputes over claims to remuneration.[3]

The problems were eventually solved by transforming the pensioners from a civil into an auxiliary military force, properly trained and exercised, subject to military discipline and paid by order of the Secretary-at-War. The transformation was effected by Acts of Parliament in 1843 and 1846. With the new force as it eventually emerged this chapter has no concern. It will be dealt with later when the military arm is reviewed. It should be noted, however, that the new organization was to some extent foreshadowed during the Plug-Plot disturbances, in a plan devised by the Duke of Wellington to meet the emergency. Believing,

[1] John Hindes of Shoreham was deprived of his pension for acting as chairman at a Chartist meeting. Barrow to H.O. dated 30 April 1841 and minute. H.O. 45/140. Old soldiers were also reported to be drilling the Chartists. Harewood to H.O. dated 1 May 1839 and enclosure. H.O. 40/51. Maude to H.O. dated 5 May 1839. H.O. 40/43.

[2] Supt. Beswick's report to Mayor of Manchester. H.O. 45/268. Nield to H.O. dated 14 August 1842. H.O. 45/249C.

[3] Wilbraham to H.O. dated 3 December 1842. H.O. 45/268; Hardinge to H.O. dated 23 January 1843. H.O. 45/350; H.O. to Arbuthnot dated 23 August and 1 September 1842. H.O. 41/17.

as he told Sir James Graham, that "as special constables these pensioners were a rabble", but that "under military control of officers they might be trusted with untold gold", the Duke suggested a scheme for arming the pensioners serving as special constables at Glasgow, Birmingham and Manchester, and for placing them under the command of half-pay officers, who might only control them, however, by virtue of authority delegated by the magistrates.[1]

Three half-pay officers and one from the retired list were employed in fashioning these pensioners into an efficient force.[2] Lieutenant-Colonel Angelo selected 600 of the Manchester pensioners, whom the magistrates had dismissed after their previous defection, formed them into divisions each under an N.C.O., drilled them and fostered their military pride by keeping them distinct from police and civilian specials.[3] At Birmingham, where Captain F. Unett took charge of the operation, the plan was to arrange the pensioners in companies, in accordance with the regiments in which they had served, thus appealing to their *esprit de corps*.[4] It was from such beginnings that the later re-organization sprang.

The obligation resting upon the private citizen to succour the forces of law and order in cases of emergency was discharged not only in the enrolment of special constables, but also in the formation of voluntary associations. It had long been customary for farmers and local tradesmen to associate in societies for the prosecution of felons, and when Chartism threatened, in the spring of 1839, the government sought to stimulate local defensive arrangements by extending this principle to the field of public order. A Home Office Circular to the Lords Lieutenant of certain counties, which was issued early in May, promised to supply arms to such of "the principal inhabitants of a disturbed district"

[1] Graham to Wellington dated 20 August 1842. Wellington to Graham dated 21 August 1842. Graham Papers, Bundle 52B.

[2] Fitzroy Somerset to H.O. dated 7 October 1842. H.O. 45/268.

[3] Angelo to H.O. dated 27 August 1842. H.O. 45/249C.

[4] Thorn to H.O. dated 22 August 1842. H.O. 45/270.

as "should be desirous of forming an association for the protection of life and property".[1]

This Circular bore little fruit. A return of associations formed and armed, which was made to Parliament in August 1839, mentioned only two, at Monmouth and at Pontypool, and an abortive one at Mansfield.[2] The Home Office Papers show that an association of tenant farmers acting under landed gentry also started to form in the Christchurch division of Monmouthshire and helped to preserve the peace on the day when Henry Vincent, the Chartist orator, was committed to Monmouth gaol;[3] they also reveal that two associations were contemplated at Loughborough in May[4] and that one of these reached the stage of drilling, having received arms from the government.[5] From the same source also it appears that negotiations were going forward in Bradford, in July and August 1839, for the formation of an association consisting of manufacturers, tradesmen and professional people.[6] On the whole, however, the results of the government's offer were unimpressive.

No doubt fear, especially fear of being marked out for private vengeance by the Chartists, contributed materially to the failure of the project, but it was not the only reason. After some initial delay, during which the propertied classes gathered confidence, numerous offers to form associations were received at the Home Office in the second half of May and the early part of June 1839.[7] The volunteers were quickly discouraged, however, by the treatment which they received at the government's hands.

They found themselves stinted of arms. At Loughborough, as we have seen, two associations were formed in May 1839, one

---

[1] *Copy of Lord John Russell's Letter to Lords Lieutenant of certain counties suggesting formation of associations for protection of life and property etc.* 1839 (299) XXXVIII.

[2] *Return of all associations formed and armed.* 1839 (559) XXXVIII.

[3] C. H. Leigh to H.O. dated 14 May 1839. H.O. 40/45; Blewitt to H.O. dated 6 November 1839. H.O. 40/45.

[4] B. Brock to H.O. dated 21 May 1839. H.O. 40/44.

[5] B. Brock to H.O. dated 26 July 1839. H.O. 40/44.

[6] Memorial of Certain Inhabitants of Bradford to the Lord Lieutenant of the West Riding. H.O. 40/51.

[7] See replies to these offers. H.O. 41/14.

by the members of the Conservative Society and another by
those who did not belong to that body. Application was made to
the Home Secretary for arms for 150 men—the combined strength
of the two associations—but Lord John Russell would not agree
to send more than 90. The Conservative association with 100
members had to make do with 50 cutlasses and 50 brace of
pistols.[1] This it succeeded in doing by issuing cutlasses to one
half of its members and pistols to the other half,[2] but the 40 sets
of arms issued to the other association had to be used for equipping the pensioners and, although this fact was reported to the
Home Secretary, the latter refused to replace them.[3]

There was also much disagreement between the government
and those who wished to form associations as to the form which
the associations should take. It is clear that the country gentlemen
who came forward with their tenants and neighbouring freeholders to respond to Lord John's Circular, did so in the belief
that they were being encouraged to form new companies of
Volunteers and troops of Yeomanry, a project which held out
to them the prospect of acquiring added social prestige and local
influence by getting themselves appointed to the command of
these new corps. It is equally clear that the Whig government,
which had only just carried out a substantial reduction of the
Yeomanry, envisaged nothing more than a civil force of high-
class special constables appearing armed only upon express orders
from one of Her Majesty's justices of the peace but serving, unlike
special constables, without remuneration. Several of the early
attempts to get up associations came to grief in consequence of
this disagreement as to their character. Members of the Christchurch (Monmouthshire) Association became disgusted when
they discovered that the government intended them to be no more
than an association, and one of the moving spirits, Mr. William
Phillips of Whitston, was compelled to retire to the continent
"for protection against the sneers which some of his neighbours

---

[1] Brock to H.O. dated 21 May 1839; Parker to H.O. dated 21 May 1839.
H.O. 40/44; H.O. to Parker dated 22 May 1839. H.O. 41/14.

[2] Brock to H.O. dated 26 July 1839. H.O. 40/44 .

[3] Brock to H.O. dated 23 May 1839. H.O. 40/44; H.O. to Brock dated
24 May 1839. H.O. 41/14.

and the populace very liberally dispensed towards him, in consequence of his failure to be invested with the title of Major-Commandant to which he had been elected".[1] On 20 May 1839 the officers and privates of an extinct Yeomanry Corps in the North Riding of Yorkshire seized the excuse of Lord John Russell's Circular to petition for reinstatement.[2] The Home Secretary declined politely, stating that he "did not intend by the Circular Letter . . . to suggest the forming of associations of a military character".[3] He also refused to sanction the formation of an association at Cockermouth called "The Derwentside Volunteer or Rifle Corps",[4] and a fortnight later, on 13 June, rejected the offer of 60 principal tradesmen of Welshpool to form a Volunteer Rifle Corps.[5]

Not only was the policy of forming armed associations unsuccessful. It was open to the same objections as the arming of special constables. There was no guarantee that the arms sent down by government would be securely guarded, and the class struggle was intensified by the placing of arms in the hands not of an impartial police force, but of the sections of the community which the Chartists regarded as their avowed enemies. The exponents of physical-force Chartism were furnished with an excuse for advising their supporters to procure arms, and a useful addition to their armoury of arguments against the government. Had the Home Secretary offered to arm the "principal inhabitants" or middle classes?; then let the working men arm if only in self-defence. Had the "shopocracy" conspired "to put down Chartism by physical force"?[6] then let the toiling masses sustain it by physical force. Moreover, if the proposal was not to arm class against class, why had the government turned down or ignored the offers of the Salford Radical Association[7] and the Stockport

---

[1] Blewitt to H.O. dated 6 November 1839. H.O. 40/45.
[2] Memorial signed by a Quartermaster of the Richmond Troop on behalf of himself, the N.C.O.s and privates of the late North Yorkshire Yeomanry. H.O. 40/51.
[3] H.O. to Dundas dated 28 May 1839. H.O. 41/14.
[4] Russell to Lonsdale dated 31 May 1839. H.O. 41/14.
[5] Russell to Powis dated 13 June 1839. H.O. 41/14.
[6] The Northern Star, 19 October 1839, p. 6.
[7] Derby to H.O. dated 16 May 1839 and enclosure. H.O. 40/37.

Working Man's Association,[1] to respond to the appeal of the Home Office Circular? And if it was illegal for the Chartists to arm and drill, was it not equally unlawful for the middle class to assume a martial demeanour in their exertions against Chartism?[2]

Three years later the Chartists delivered their *quid pro quo* in the form of a memorial to the Home Secretary which ran as follows:

Your memorialists, having proved themselves by their peaceable conduct friendly to Peace, Law and Order, and who are for the sake of themselves and country willing to [do] all they can to prevent any outbreak of violence on the peaceable subjects of the realm. Your memorialtists, being apprehensive that the parties calling themselves members of the Anti-Corn Law League—manufacturers, shopkeepers and publicans—who because they cannot obtain such large profits from a starving people, are about to resort to every means possible to excite the people to a breach of the peace, by declaring against paying the income tax and other assessed taxes, by stopping the supplies and by also stopping their mills. . . . and as they, the middle classes, manufacturers, shopkeepers, publicans and other Whig members of the Anti-Corn Law League were called upon by Lord John Russell in the year 1839 to form themselves into associations, and Government would furnish them with arms for the protection of life and property, your memorialists call upon you to send us immediately 10,000 stand of arms in order that we may protect the lives, property, peace and liberty of ourselves and fellow countrymen from the threatened violence of the before mentioned parties.[3]

After 1839 the government made no further attempt to encourage the formation of armed associations. During the great strike of 1842 the Home Secretary declined to send arms to the provinces

[1] Memorial to H.O. dated 7 June 1839. H.O. 40/41.

[2] The Barnsley radicals got up a charge against a bank clerk, a warehouseman, a shopkeeper and a pattern weaver for training and drilling in contravention of the Six Acts. After examination before the magistrates, at which R. B. B. Cobbett of Manchester, son of William Cobbett, appeared as prosecuting solicitor, the accused were given bail to appear at Rotherham Assizes. The incident was recorded in *The Northern Star* under the caption: "Conviction of Four of Lord John Russell's 'Respectable' Peace Preservation Physical-Force Men". *The Northern Star*, 8 June 1839, p. 1.

[3] Memorial of National Charter Association, 18 July 1842. H.O. 45/249C.

except for the use of certain of the pensioners,[1] though the spirit of voluntary association was extensively tapped in the establishment of volunteer horse patrols,[2] and that with the government's blessing.[3] In 1848 the suggestion of a Skipton magistrate that some armed force should be set up to aid the special constables was firmly rejected by the Whig Home Office:

It does not appear to me to be expedient under present circumstances [came the reply] to encourage the formation of armed volunteer corps for the purpose of repressing internal disturbance. I think our first reliance should be on a well organized police force, which will be supported in any case of emergency by special constables, and in the event of any serious disturbance of the public peace being apprehended, military assistance may be obtained to support the civil power should the necessity arise. A better organization of special constables would be very desirable and I shall be happy to afford any assistance in effecting this object if the inhabitants of any district desire it.[4]

It is thus evident that emergency policing by shopkeepers, gentlemen's sons and army pensioners did not suffice to render the parish constable system efficient. There may be ground for thinking that an earlier and more energetic implementation of these measures by the magistrates would have produced better results, but the system was itself at fault. Special constables and voluntary associations were, at the best, useful supplements to a properly organized regular police force; they were no substitute for it. But the era of police reforms had begun some nine years before the formulation of the People's Charter with the act with which the name of Peel will ever be associated, and professional police forces of the modern type already existed in England at the beginning of the Chartist period, and were to become more numerous during it. It is to the newer system that our attention must now be turned.

[1] Graham to Peel dated 15 August 1842. *Peel Papers*, Brit. Mus. Add. MSS. 40,447.

[2] In Staffordshire: Talbot to H.O. dated 25 August 1842. H.O. 45/260; In Cheshire: Potts to H.O. dated 24 August 1842 and enclosure. H.O. 45/242; In Manchester: *The Manchester Guardian*, 17 August 1842, p. 2.

[3] Graham to H. Townley Parker dated 24 August 1842: Parker, *Graham: Life and Letters, 1792–1861*, I, 324.

[4] Draft of reply to Harewood to H.O. dated 12 April 1848. H.O. 45/2410AC.

CHAPTER IV

THE CIVIL FORCE. (II) THE NEW POLICE

T HE oldest and the most successful of the modern establishments was the Metropolitan Police, tested, when our
period opened, by the experience of eight years' bitter
hostility. In its direct subordination to the Home Office,[1] not to
any organ of local government, the force which ranged itself
under the command of the two Commissioners at Scotland Yard,
Colonel Charles Rowan and Mr. Richard Mayne, occupied, as
indeed it still does, a unique position in the British police system.[2]
In other respects, however, it served, and deservedly so, as a
model for the rising civil forces of the provinces.

Its excellence rested on the twin pillars of professional efficiency
and unity of control. The former was only achieved with difficulty, and at the cost of much vigilance by the Commissioners. It
is true that jobbery and influence were rigidly excluded from the
determination of promotions. Lord John Russell told the Count
de Ludolf, who had recommended a police sergeant for promo-
tion, that he had "laid down an invariable rule to make promotions in the Metropolitan Police only on the recommendation
by the Commissioners of those men they consider most meri-
torious".[3] But the inadequate pay[4] and the absence, before 1839,

---

[1] A control which extended to the approval of all orders and regulations,
the appointment of constables and superior officers, and the right to "allow"
the Receiver's expenditure.

[2] Except for the forces operating in Manchester, Birmingham and Bolton
between 1839 and 1842.

[3] Lord John Russell to the Count de Ludolf dated 5 February 1838. H.O.
65/12.

[4] Even under the revised scales of 1839 constables were paid at 3s., 2s. 9d.
and 2s. 6d. per day respectively according to their class. Sergeants drew 3s. 6d.
per day. Russell to Commissioners dated 2 September 1839, H.O. 65/13.
A Staffordshire miner averaged 4s. 3d. for the decade 1830–40. Clapham, *op. cit.*,
I, 559.

of even a superannuation fund, rendered it difficult to attract the right kind of recruit to the force. Only by a continual sifting of unsuitable applicants, and by the immediate expulsion of unworthy constables, was the high professional efficiency of the London Police attained. A study of the figures for removals from the Metropolitan Force given in the Home Office Papers reveals that in the years 1834-8, inclusive, out of a total strength of 3,389 of all ranks, the 1833 figure, the average annual withdrawal from the force amounted to no fewer than 1,064, giving almost a 33⅓ per cent turnover. Of these 1,064, 32·2 died, 709·6 resigned (an indication of the severity of the discipline), 172·2 were discharged for drunkenness, 91·6 for neglect of duty and disobedience, 8·2 on account of criminal charges, 0·2 for assault (the reflection in the average of a single case in 1834), 14 because of conviction by the magistrates for an offence which may have preceded appointment, 2 for absconding with police clothing and 34 for other unspecified misconduct.[1]

Unity of control was very imperfectly realized before 1839. The Metropolitan Police district covered but a fraction of its present area, extending to a range of between four and seven miles from Charing Cross, but excluding the City of London, which jealously preserved its own police force. Even within that area the Commissioners shared control of the police with the magistrates of the London police courts, and with statutory bodies of Improvement Commissioners, such as those responsible for the watching of Westminster Bridge.[2] The Metropolitan Police Act of 1839, however, brought the ideal much nearer to realization by authorizing the extension of the district to parishes within a radius of fifteen miles of Charing Cross, by substituting the Thames Division of the Metropolitan Police for the old independent Marine Police, and by abolishing the Bow Street Runners and the constables attached to the stipendiary magistrates' courts.

The ability of the new force to preserve order in the streets of London was severely tested during the Chartist period. Chartism

---

[1] Calculated from figures given in the Appendix of H.O. 65/12: Metropolitan Police Correspondence.
[2] Mayne to H.O. dated 24 April 1839. H.O. 61/22.

did not present too great a problem in the metropolis in 1839, but in August 1842 the disorder in the provinces touched off a sequence of demonstrations designed to keep the capital in a state of continuous alarm. Nightly meetings were organized on Clerkenwell Green, Kennington Common and other open spaces, and a mob moved in procession through the City of London an hour before midnight. Similar scenes were witnessed in 1848, but for a longer period. Hooligan elements mingled with the demonstrators, smashed the windows of shops, and threw stones at the police when the latter intervened.

In dealing with these disturbances the police were evolving a new technique of controlling disorderly crowds, one which minimized the use of sheer brute force against mobs by combining it with an element of science. Except for a period in the summer of 1848, when cutlasses were issued,[1] the constables were armed with nothing more lethal than the truncheon, and even that was used sparingly for the most part. If nothing else could be said in favour of police action, it was unquestionably more humane than the use of troops, which resulted, as at Peterloo, in serious injury and loss of life for members of the crowd which was being dispersed. To make possible this economy in physical force a science of crowd control, involving knowledge of the behaviour of human beings in the mass, was being formulated and put into practice for the first time in British history.

It could not be said that the new methods had yet triumphed decisively in the conflict with disorder, even in London. There is no doubt that the Metropolitan Police were ultimately victorious in all their encounters with the London mob, and that without recourse to active military assistance. But the struggle was often long and bitter, and the Commissioners made mistakes. The strength of their force was put to a stringent test on 22 August 1842, when the Chartists attempted to get up simultaneous demonstrations at Kennington Common, Clerkenwell Green and Paddington. The first was an utter failure, as the promoters of the meeting did not put in an appearance, and the

[1] Metropolitan Police Records, New Scotland Yard, Police Order Book, 1848–50: Entries for 15 June and 1 August 1848.

police had no difficulty in clearing the Common of the immense crowd which had gathered there. When it came to freeing the numerous avenues leading to the Common, however, the trouble started. Something must have been missing in the arrangements for directing the crowd, for *The Times* reports that people who were driven down one side of an avenue moved back upon the other, so that a passage was scarcely cleared when it was again filled up.[1] Here the police were dealing not with an angry mob, but with a crowd of would-be spectators, foiled of an evening's entertainment, but at Paddington and Clerkenwell Green they encountered stiffer resistance. Over 10,000 people gathered in the vicinity of the Great Western Railway terminus. The police, concentrated there from three divisions, repeatedly charged the mob, scattering it in all directions and preventing it from uniting by placing constables in double file across the various roads, but about two hours elapsed before the assemblage began to thin.[2]

Similar difficulties were encountered by the police on 6 and 7 March 1848, when disorderly meetings were held in the newly-completed Trafalgar Square. The meeting on the 6th, originally called to protest against the income tax, was illegal from the start, by virtue of the fact that it was held within a mile of Westminster Hall during the sitting of Parliament.[3] The police gave notice of its illegality to the promoters, but, rather unaccountably, took no steps to prevent about 15,000 people from gathering in the Square at the time appointed. After a few speeches had been made, sections of the audience began to indulge in a little rough horse-play against individual constables scattered about the Square, thrusting their hats down over their eyes and pushing the officers about in all directions. It was at this point that the Commissioners made their second mistake, sending a mere 20 or 30 men of the A Division to restore order. These were soon pushed right out of the Square (by a mob now growing angrier and tearing down the hoardings round the unfinished Nelson column, to arm itself with stakes of wood and mud and stones from within the enclosure)

---

[1] *The Times*, 23 August 1842, p. 6.   [2] *Ibid.*
[3] 57 George III, c. 19, s. 23.

to the area round King Charles I's statue at Charing Cross. Individual policemen broke away from their colleagues and made sallies into the crowd for the purpose of arresting or knocking down ringleaders. These tactics seem to have been very highly rated by the exponents of the new police ideal, for they were lauded by Edwin Chadwick in his County Constabulary Report in 1839,[1] and by Superintendent George Martin, an experienced officer of the Metropolitan Force, giving evidence before a parliamentary committee in the eighteen-fifties,[2] but it must be stated that they proved quite ineffective on this occasion. The mob gave way before the rushes of the constables, but closed in again as soon as they had returned to the ranks, and seemed quite unmoved by the sight of two or three of its members being carried away to hospital. No progress was made, in fact, until strong reinforcements of police were sent up. These eventually gained command of the situation by forcing their way into the centre of the Square, taking possession of the enclosure round the column, and eventually pushing the crowd outwards in two directions, until they had cleared a space for the effective disposal of their force, and were able to take the more troublesome of their opponents captive. The disturbances lasted for about two hours, and even after that the concourse did not disperse. Disorder was renewed in the evening and on the following day, and it was not until late on 7 March that the police were able to keep the crowds moving in the vicinity of Charing Cross.[3]

Whatever else these examples show, they do not suggest that the Metropolitan Police were in the habit of employing too much force against the London mobs. Indeed the 20–30 men of the A Division who first attempted to restore order in Trafalgar Square, deferred using their batons for as long as possible.[4] Nevertheless, from time to time during the Chartist period, allegations were made against the police that they behaved with unnecessary brutal-

---

[1] See below, pp. 101–2.

[2] *S.C. on Police:* Second Report, Mins. of Evidence, p. 92; 1852–3 (715) XXXVI.

[3] The foregoing account of the Trafalgar Square riots is taken from *The Times*, 7 March 1848, p. 8, and 8 March 1848, p. 6.

[4] *Ibid.*, 7 March 1848, p. 8.

ity. The most widespread and persistent of these charges related to the happenings at the conclusion of a Chartist meeting on Bishop Bonners Fields on 4 June 1848. A memorial signed by 262 inhabitants of the adjacent parts of Bethnal Green afterwards accused the police of having made an "indiscriminate, wanton, inhuman and brutal attack . . . upon men, women and children",[1] and complaints of a similar character were made by other persons, who denied that they had any connection with the Chartists.[2] There seems little doubt that truncheons were used very freely in dispersing the crowd assembled on the Fields, but not un- necessarily. The police were obliged to clear the ground in order to put an end to the stoning, by a section of the mob, of the win- dows of the church in which they were concealed, and in carrying out this duty the constables encountered a stubborn resistance. Some of the demonstrators carried knives; others hurled stones. A sergeant and seven constables were wounded in the affray, and one police officer only escaped being stabbed in the abdomen by taking the blow on his hand.[3] We may safely acquit the police of using unnecessary violence on the meeting ground, but we cannot ignore the charge that they afterwards pursued the constituents of the crowd into the surrounding by-streets, breaking into houses and dragging the occupants into the streets.[4] Individual constables, exasperated by months of emergencies and alarms, may, on this occasion, have allowed their anger to outrun their discretion, but the behaviour of the Metropolitan Police Force towards disorderly crowds was usually both good-humoured and restrained.

The feature of the new police which most impressed contem- poraries, however, was not its humanity but its preventive character. When Edwin Chadwick was demonstrating, in the report of the County Constabulary Commission, the advantages

[1] Memorial to Sir George Grey of the Inhabitants of Bethnal Green in the Immediate Vicinity of Bonners Fields. H.O. 45/2410.

[2] Groom, Higgins and others to H.O. dated 4 July 1848. H.O. 45/2410.

[3] Report of Inspector Horn, Hans., 3 Ser., XCIX, 506–7; The Times, 5 June 1848, p. 8.

[4] Memorial to Sir George Grey of the Inhabitants of Bethnal Green in the Immediate Vicinity of Bonners Fields. H.O. 45/2410.

of using a police force to maintain public order, he dwelt mainly on the theme that, whereas the employment of the military was attended by lethal consequences, and, therefore, deferrred until property had actually been destroyed, policemen could often prevent a riot by going singly into a crowd to seize the ringleaders. The soldier, with two hands on the musket, was bound to kill; the constable, with baton in one hand and the other free, could take his opponent prisoner.[1] The experiences of the Trafalgar Square riots on 6 March 1848 give grounds, as we have seen,[2] for scepticism as to the value of the particular tactics which Chadwick recommended, but the general point surely stands, viz., that much could be done to forestall mob violence by interposing force at an early stage in an outbreak or even by ensuring that potential rioters knew that they were being watched and could be made to answer for their actions.

For carrying out these purposes a professional police, such as the Metropolitan Force, was peculiarly well adapted. In the first place it was flexible, and capable of being used in dispersion. One of the most serious problems to confront the forces of law and order occurred when a mob split up into small detachments which moved swiftly from district to district, committing acts of violence here and there, and disappearing before troops or policemen could reach the spot. Such an emergency arose in the capital about 9 o'clock in the evening on the first day of the Trafalgar Square riots (6 March 1848). Whilst a large portion of the police force was busy keeping order in the Square, a party of about 200 people, headed by a youth in epaulettes, broke away from the crowd, and proceeded through Pall Mall, St. James's and Westminster, smashing street lamps and windows and entering breadshops, as it went. These rioters quickly shook off the constables who were sent in pursuit of them, by deploying their force in St. James's Park, and not until they had reached Strutton Ground, south of the present Victoria Street, did they encounter any more policemen.[3] On the following day, however,

---

[1] Royal Commission on the Establishment of a Constabulary Force in the Counties of England and Wales, Report, pp. 83–4; 1839 [169] XIX.
[2] See above, p. 100. [3] *The Times*, 7 March 1848, p. 8.

the Commissioners took steps to prevent a recurrence of this kind of disorder by dividing their men into parties of thirty, stationed at various points in the Charing Cross area, from which the constables could quickly descend on any place where a mob was becoming troublesome, and disperse it before it proceeded to serious outrage.[1]

A second asset which the police brought to the task of preventing disorder was the knowledge of the people which they acquired in the pursuit of their routine duties. The importance of this local knowledge was demonstrated during the Birmingham riots of July 1839, when the London policemen who had been sent to Birmingham had to act without it and encountered a furious resistance. The police superintendent stated, many years afterwards, that "a great many of the men who threw brickbats at my men would not have done so if they had known they would be liable to be recognized".[2]

But the real secret of preventive action was to be found in choosing precisely the right moment to intervene, and in this the Metropolitan Police had attained considerable skill, as was shown in the measures which they took to forestall a riot at a Chartist meeting in Clerkenwell Green on 31 May 1848. A crowd gathered on the Green, and in the absence of the conveners of the meeting, who had abandoned it in the face of immense police precautions, "a singular looking being with long hair, a profusion of beard and that 'air distraught' which is generally supposed to mark a child of the Muses" shinned up a lamp-post, and harangued the mob. When he had finished speaking, sections of the crowd began to make those desperate rushes, first in one direction and then in another, which generally precede a riot. At this critical moment a strong body of the police entered the Green from the east, and forming a line across the open space, swept the people at once and without opposition into the narrow streets and alleys opening from Clerkenwell Green on the west. Strong parties of police were then placed at all the entrances to the

---

[1] *Ibid.*, 8 March 1848, p. 6; 9 March 1848, p. 5.
[2] *S.C. on Police*, Second Report, Mins. of Evidence, p. 93; 1852-3 (715) XXXVI.

H

Green, and sections were sent to clear the several streets in the vicinity.[1]

The Metropolitan Police were only able to time their intervention so exactly because they kept a careful watch on the proceedings of large assemblages of the people. Their usual procedure was to plant a few plain-clothes observers on the meeting-ground to bring word of any disorder, holding their main force in concealment nearby so as to avoid giving provocation to the crowd. On the occasion of the Chartist meeting on Bonners Fields on 4 June 1848, the police were hidden in a nearby church, where they remained until, as we have seen, a section of the mob assailed the building with stones at the conclusion of the meeting.[2]

The techniques described in the two foregoing paragraphs enabled the police to prevent disorder without resorting unduly to suppression of the right of public meeting. The attitude of the Commissioners towards the Chartist agitation in the metropolis was, on the whole, tolerant. It is true that in 1839 their discretion was fettered by instructions from the Whig government not to apprehend for political offences "without previous communication to the Secretary of State",[3] but there is evidence to suggest that they had no wish to pursue a repressive policy even if they had been free to do so. During that year, complaint was made to the Home Secretary that the Commissioners were failing in their duty to put down the frequent meetings of the working class which were held on Clerkenwell Green to the alarm and annoyance of the property-owning residents of the district. The Commissioners defended themselves by stating that no breach of the peace had occurred, and that, therefore, there seemed no necessity to interfere.[4]

In August 1842 the Commissioners again showed marked reluctance to suppress public meetings. No interference was made

---

[1] *The Times*, 1 June 1848, p. 8.

[2] Metropolitan Police Records, 'Chartists' Box: Bundle marked 'Chartist Proceedings, 1848'. See also above, p. 101.

[3] H.O. to Rowan dated 18 May 1839. H.O. 65/13.

[4] C. Reith, *British Police and the Democratic Ideal*, 239.

with those held on Stepney Green on the 16th[1] and on Clerkenwell Green on the 17th, and not until it had been made clear by what occurred on the night of the 18th that such meetings were being used as rallying points for unauthorized processions through the streets of London at a late hour, were steps taken, by the direction of the Home Secretary, to put down processions and meetings alike.[2] In 1848, though meetings in Trafalgar Square were vetoed in compliance with the Seditious Meetings and Assemblies Act of 1817 (which forbade assemblages of more than fifty persons within a mile of Westminster Hall during the sitting of Parliament), the police permitted the Chartists to meet on Clerkenwell Green, Bonners Fields and other open spaces in the working-class districts of eastern and central London, until the Home Secretary gave directions, after several such meetings had ended in disorder, to prevent a demonstration on Bonners Fields on 12 June.

The success of the new police in maintaining public order in the capital, without having to be rescued by the troops, contributed to the employment of Metropolitan policemen in the provinces, either as officers of the new provincial forces, or as members of temporary detachments loaned to the magistrates to make up the deficiencies of the local constabulary. Between June 1830 and January 1838 2,246 London policemen were sent to places outside London to preserve the peace and apprehend offenders.[3] This was an average of approximately 300 a year, and in the years of Anti-Poor Law disturbance, 1837 and 1838, the numbers rose to 444 and 764 respectively. Not all of these were sent to put down riots. Many went to perform the more humdrum operation of keeping order at race meetings, but we have evidence that in 1837 some 38 policemen were absent from London for the purpose of suppressing Anti-Poor Law riots in Yorkshire, Essex and the West Country.[4] During the Chartist disturbances of 1839 detachments of Metropolitan policemen were sent to Loughborough,

[1] *The Times*, 17 August 1842, p. 6.
[2] *Ibid.*, 19 August 1842, p. 6. *The Letters of Queen Victoria, 1837–61*, I, 427.
[3] Return by Metropolitan Police Commissioners. H.O. 61/20.
[4] Return dated 14 November 1838. H.O. 61/21.

Mansfield, Monmouth, Bury, Bedlington and Cockermouth. One hundred constables were despatched to Birmingham alone in July.[1] There must have been at least 77 London policemen in South Wales in the autumn of 1843, when the Rebecca Riots were drawing to their close.[2]

The practice of detaching Metropolitan policemen to the disturbed areas of the provinces was attended by certain serious drawbacks. The local authorities were encouraged in their resolution to do nothing for their own defence, and to rely on outside help. Experience was to prove that the despatch of a body of Metropolitan constables to Cardiganshire in 1843 would be followed by the deferment of the question of raising a county force at the ensuing Quarter Sessions.[3]

Furthermore, there was strong opposition to such detachments from the Police Commissioners and from the radicals of the London vestries. The former resented the depletion of their force, which was small enough for the duties which it was required to perform in London, and the government's refusal to allow them to increase numbers drove them to resist applications from the provinces for the loan of constables in 1837 and again at the end of 1838.[4] In June 1844 Colonel Rowan advised the Home Secretary not to comply with a request of the Durham magistrates that 30 Metropolitan Police constables should be sent into the County Palatine to check violence and intimidation during the strike of the miners against the yearly bond. He pointed out that the Commissioners still had 26 of their best men in Wales, to say nothing of 100 absent on other duties, and that in the following week the Sessions would commence, "when the attendance of

[1] Metropolitan Police Records, 'Chartists' Box: Bundle marked 'Birmingham Riots'.

[2] Inspector Martin and two constables proceeded to St. Clears at the end of 1842. Two constables were sent to Carmarthen late in June '43 and two more a month later. Two parties of ten were granted to Colonel Trevor in September and fifty more policemen in October. These figures are drawn from correspondence in H.O. 41/17 and 18, and H.O. 45/454. There may have been other London policemen in Wales, to whom no reference is made in the Home Office Papers.

[3] H.O. to Powell dated 13 November 1843. H.O. 41/18.

[4] Charles Reith, British Police and the Democratic Ideal, 210 et seq.

upwards of 100 men will be required on the ordinary business of prosecutions etc., besides numerous other calls for the attendance of bodies of Police".[1]

The London vestries were quick to pounce on anything which might be construed as a mis-application of the force which their members were rated to support. Shortly after the Birmingham Riots of July 1839, in which the London policemen had been so deeply involved, the vestry of the parish of St. Leonard, Shoreditch, passed the following resolution: "It was resolved that this Vestry does remonstrate against the use of the Metropolitan Police Force in the country, leaving the Metropolitan parishes less protected than heretofore, and interfering with the police of the provincial towns, and the old constitutional plan of quelling riots by magistrates reading the Riot Act, using the local civil force, and if not sufficient, to call to their aid the military."[2]

A further disadvantage was that Metropolitan policemen on service in the provinces were much less successful in controlling crowds than they were when at home in London. Their numbers were often totally inadequate to enable them to cope with the situations which confronted them. Their contact with the provincials was too casual to permit them to form a correct estimate of the amount of force required to disperse a mob; so also was their knowledge of the territory in which they had to operate. Worse still, they had to act under the direction of magistrates whose judgment was often inferior to their own. The first batch of Metropolitans sent to Birmingham in July 1839 was ordered by the magistrates to arrest the speaker at a Chartist meeting in the Bull Ring attended by about 1,000 people, though one of the magistrates subsequently admitted that the crowd was so closely intermingled that it was not possible to take the man. The result was a violent attack on the police, who suffered the unaccustomed humiliation of having to be rescued by a force of cavalry.[3]

[1] Rowan to H.O. dated 6 June 1844. H.O. 45/644.
[2] Resolution dated 1 October 1839. H.O. 61/24.
[3] Evidence of Dr. Booth at the Warwick Assize. *The Northern Star*, 10 August 1839, p. 3.

Moreover, the very presence of the police in the provinces had a pronounced tendency to incite the people to riot. When ten of the A Division of the Metropolitan Force were sent to Bury early in June 1839, their lodgings were surrounded by a mob, and three of their number were accosted by the populace as they patrolled the streets of the town.[1] Two years earlier, in 1837, Alfred Power, Assistant Poor Law Commissioner, persuaded the Bradford magistrates to send them away from Bradford, on the grounds that the employment of them extended the unpopularity of the New Poor Law and its agents.[2] All the hostility to a professional police (arising from the belief that it was unconstitutional) which the Metropolitan Force had battled against in London in the first three or four years of its existence, welled up afresh against its officers serving in the provinces, and deprived them of that approval of the community which is so essential for the proper functioning of a constabulary. It must also be remembered that the constables had little chance to allay this hatred when their only appearance was occasioned by a popular agitation which had to be repressed. Moreover, the provincial magistrates, conscious of the unpopularity of the force which they had summoned to their aid, did not scruple to cast the blame upon it if things went wrong. Thus the civic fathers of Birmingham sought to focus the investigation which they conducted into the Bull Ring Riots on the brutality of the Metropolitan Police.[3]

It was also noticed that discipline tended to deteriorate when the Metropolitan constables were removed from the immediate oversight of the Commissioners. This was especially true when the London force operated side by side with the local police. In Carmarthenshire, for example, the Metropolitan policemen stationed at Llanelly refused to obey the orders of a sergeant of the rural police, which was being introduced gradually, to replace the Metropolitans, in the posts which had been established in various parts of the county to curb the Rebeccaites. The Home

---

[1] *The Northern Star*, 8 June 1839, p. 5.
[2] *Return of Metropolitan Police Sent to Bradford*; 1837–8 (118) XXXVIII.
[3] *The Northern Star*, 14, 21 and 28 September 1839.

Secretary declined to uphold the authority of the Chief Constable of the county over the Londoners.[1]

Because of the disadvantages attending it (and also because of the general improvement in the local police services), the practice of detaching Metropolitan policemen to the provinces was declining before the period ended. Detachments were withheld from Scotland in August 1842,[2] and from Durham during the great colliers' strike of 1844. On the latter occasion, the Home Secretary, Graham, stated quite frankly to the Lord Lieutenant his objections to the employment of the Metropolitan Police in such a service: "It has the effect of impairing its discipline, and sometimes excites a strong public feeling against the Police."[3] In 1848 requests for London constables from Halifax and Bradford were rejected on the grounds that the situation in London was sufficient to absorb the attention of the whole force.[4]

Numerical expansion of the Metropolitan Police and other improvements to the Force were held back, throughout the period, by the rigid economy imposed by the Home Office in matters of police expenditure. Home Secretaries, Whig and Tory alike, were afraid of the clamour which would arise from the vestries of the London parishes (dominated as they were by radicals imbued with a strong hostility to a centralized police force) if an attempt was made to demand from the London rate-payers, for police purposes, more than was exacted under the existing sixpenny rate. This sixpenny rate was already supplemented by the government from the Consolidated Fund, but a bid to increase the subsidy would have been unwelcome both to the Treasury[5] and to members of the House of Commons, whose

---

[1] Scott to H.O. dated 18 November 1843 and minute. H.O. 45/454.

[2] Graham to Peel dated 28 August 1842. *Peel Papers.* Brit. Mus. Add. MSS. 40,447.

[3] Draft of reply to Londonderry to H.O. dated 10 June 1844. H.O. 45/644.

[4] H.O. to Pollard and Waterhouse dated 8 April 1848; H.O. to Tempest dated 29 May 1848. H.O. 41/19.

[5] In transmitting the Police Estimates to the Treasury in 1842 Sir James Graham thought it necessary to explain that a smaller sum from the Consolidated Fund than was actually demanded would not be sufficient to meet the expenditure of the Metropolitan Force in that year. Phillipps to Trevelyan dated 24 February 1842. H.O. 65/14.

sanction would have to be sought before the increase was made.[1] Rather than resort to either expedient, Home Secretaries pared down police expenditure, with the result that there was continuous friction between the Home Office and the Police Commissioners. Faced as they were, in the years 1837–41, by repeated budgetary deficits, the Whigs declined to allow a superannuation fund for Metropolitan Police constables as it meant drawing further on Treasury support,[2] turned down applications for the extension of the Police District[3] and, by directing detachments of policemen to the provinces whilst refusing to consider an increase of strength, provoked a crisis in their relations with the Commissioners at the close of 1838, just when the Chartist agitation was gathering strength.[4]

The following year the purse strings were loosed sufficiently to permit the inclusion of the outlying parishes of the metropolis in the Police District, the making of a few meagre concessions in respect of pay and service and the immediate addition of 100 men to the A Division to meet the inconvenience arising from the detachment of constables to the provinces.[5] Sir James Graham sanctioned further increases in the Force in October 1843[6] and November 1845,[7] on account of the rising demand for the services of the police resulting from the rapid growth of London's streets. He was careful to state on the former occasion, however, that his consent rested upon the assurance that "the cost of this additional number of men will be more than covered by the increased produce of the existing rates, without any further charge on the ratepayers".[8]

[1] Sir George Grey told the representatives of the Middlesex parishes in 1848 that Parliament would not allow him to draw further on the Consolidated Fund for police purposes. "The counties pay 6d., and the Consolidated Fund 2d.; but there are many gentlemen in the House of Commons who object even to that." *The Northern Star*, 8 July 1848, p. 5.

[2] Phillipps to Commissioners dated 11 March 1837. H.O. 65/12.

[3] H.O. to Tottenham Ratepayers dated 8 January 1838. H.O. 65/12.

[4] For a comprehensive account of these developments see Reith, *op. cit.*, 210 et seq.

[5] This increase in numbers was sanctioned in a letter from the Home Office to the Commissioners dated 20 May 1839. H.O. 65/13.

[6] Sutton to Commissioners dated 4 October 1843. H.O. 65/14.

[7] Phillipps to Commissioners dated 6 November 1845. H.O. 65/15.

[8] As above, n. 6.

Graham, in fact, though he held office under the man who brought the Metropolitan Police Force into existence, was no less parsimonious than the Whigs in his attitude towards the police establishment. In 1844 he rejected the Commissioners' application for an increase in the remuneration of Detective Inspector Pearce which would bring his income to the level of that of a Superintendent in the uniformed branch, regardless of the fact that Pearce had worked out the whole plan of a Detective Force, and was indispensable to that branch of the service.[1]

The struggle for economy continued when Sir George Grey assumed the office of Secretary of State, the target now being wasteful expenditure in the office of the Receiver of the Metropolitan Police. In a long stinging letter, written on 5 December 1846, the Under-Secretary, Phillipps, commanded John Wray, the Receiver, to set his house in order, and even suggested that he might release his Chief Clerk for other duties by bringing the cash from the Bank of England in person.

In July 1848, however, the Whigs were compelled by the stir which the Chartists and the Irish Confederates created in the capital to sanction the addition of 627 men to the strength of the Force.[1] To finance this augmentation, they took advantage of the pure coincidence that the Middlesex magistrates had just raised the assessment of the property in their county to the rates. There was opposition from the Middlesex vestrymen who resented having to shoulder a burden which should have fallen equally on all the counties of the Metropolitan Police District, and a deputation waited upon Grey and Mayne at the House of Commons. But the government held firm, and *The Northern Star* was able to rejoice at the discomfiture of the men who had taken part against the Chartists as special constables. "The shopocracy will support 'the system'," wrote the editor, "and our earnest prayer is that the system may grind them to the dust."[2]

By the time that the era of Chartism had dawned, the Metropolitan Force was no longer an isolated experiment in police

[1] H.O. to Commissioners dated 27 July 1848. H.O. 65/16.
[2] *The Northern Star*, 8 July 1848, p. 4.

reform. The Municipal Corporations Act of 1835 had required the reformed municipalities each to establish a Watch Committee, which would appoint a sufficient number of constables paid regularly at the expense of the ratepayers. Unlike their metropolitan counterpart, the borough forces were to be controlled locally by the Watch Committee, in which was vested the power to appoint and dismiss the constables and to frame regulations for their guidance, the prerogative of the Home Secretary being limited to the receipt of a quarterly report of numbers and equipment and an occasional copy of the rules made by the Watch Committee. In short the reformers of 1835 had intended to establish in the boroughs a force as efficient as the Metropolitan Police, but locally controlled. The Scottish towns had been dealt with separately under a general police Act of 1833, which enabled, but did not compel, the larger burghs to elect Commissioners, who were to appoint police officers and make rules for watching. It was not until the close of our period that the privilege was extended to the smaller towns by Acts of 1847 and 1850.

But an extensive social reform is not effected overnight by the mere passage of a bill through Parliament. The administrative process by which it is implemented commonly stretches over a number of years, and resistance is encountered at every turn from those who have a vested interest in frustrating the measure. So it was with the reform of the borough police. Many of the reformed corporations were in no hurry to comply with the requirements of the Act of 1835 regarding the setting up of a police force. It appears from a table cited by Mrs. J. M. Hart in an article entitled 'The Reform of the Borough Police, 1835–56', that at least 53 boroughs (29 per cent of the whole) possessed no police force in the year 1839. Three years later, when the Plug-Plot disturbances convulsed the manufacturing districts, there were at least 36 (20 per cent), and in 1848 at least 22 corporate towns (12 per cent) remained in this position.[1]

---

[1] These figures refer to boroughs listed in Schedules A and B of the Municipal Corporations Act, of which there were 178. The table cited by Mrs. Hart shows the number of these municipalities setting up police forces each year from 1835 to 1853, and the number continuing without police in 1853.

In such boroughs the maintenance of public order was probably entrusted to parish constables, as in Saffron Walden until a few years before 1853,[1] or to bodies of paving commissioners like those of Romsey (down to 1851), who appointed four watchmen "not for their efficiency, but for their being willing to watch for 1s. 6d. a night".[2]

Moreover, even where a police force had been set up, the definition of "a sufficient number" of constables accepted by a Watch Committee anxious to keep down the rates, often differed markedly from what the legislator intended. The Chief Constable of Hampshire, Captain W. C. Harris, told a parliamentary committee in the early fifties that a force of one constable to every 1,000 inhabitants would be required in the boroughs, except in the case of such large towns as Liverpool and Manchester, where it might be necessary to have more than one constable to every 1,000.[3] His estimate was a modest one and it seems reasonable to assume that the exception would apply to most of the rising centres of industry where crime and disorder were serious problems. The Metropolitan Force had one constable to every 443 inhabitants in 1840.[4]

It is instructive to examine the police of the provincial boroughs in the light of these standards. The following table, based mainly on calculations from a parliamentary return drawn up in 1854, classifies those English and Welsh boroughs which are known to have possessed a police force, according to the ratio of constables to inhabitants.[5] The percentages shown in brackets are calculated

I have computed figures for 1839, 1842 and 1848 by adding to the number of boroughs without police in 1853 the number establishing police forces between each of those years respectively and 1853. It is only possible to calculate a minimum, as the table quoted in Mrs. Hart's article classifies 17 boroughs as 'unknown'. See J. M. Hart, 'The Reform of the Borough Police, 1835–1856', *English Historical Review*, LXX (1955).

[1] *S.C. on Police:* Second Report, Mins. of Evidence, p. 35; 1852–3 (715) XXXVI.

[2] *Ibid.*, First Report, Mins. of Evidence, p. 33; 1852–3 (603) XXXVI.

[3] *Ibid.*, p. 11.

[4] J. M. Hart, *The British Police*, 34.

[5] Appendix I gives the detailed figures for individual boroughs on which this table is based.

upon the total number of municipal boroughs existing at the time—i.e. 182 in 1839 and 1842; 191 in 1848.

Year	No. of boroughs with ratios higher than 1 : 600	No. of boroughs with ratios between 1 : 600 and 1 : 900	No. of boroughs with ratios between 1 : 900 and 1 : 1100	No. of boroughs with ratios lower than 1 : 1100	Total
1839	10 ($5\frac{1}{2}$%)	20 (11%)	17 ($9\frac{1}{4}$%)	56 ($30\frac{3}{4}$%)	103 ($56\frac{1}{2}$%)
1842	8 ($4\frac{1}{2}$%)	20 (11%)	17 ($9\frac{1}{4}$%)	69 (38%)	114 ($62\frac{3}{4}$%)
1848	8 ($4\frac{1}{4}$%)	16 ($8\frac{1}{4}$%)	22 ($11\frac{1}{2}$%)	87 ($45\frac{1}{2}$%)	133 ($69\frac{1}{2}$%)

The impression to be gained from a study of the above table is one of insufficient numerical strength. Throughout the period, few boroughs possessed forces with ratios comparable with that of the Metropolitan Police, and even by the less rigorous standards laid down by the Chief Constable of Hampshire, the number of boroughs qualifying as adequate was considerably less than that of the inadequate. Owing to the deplorable inaccuracy of parliamentary returns of police statistics for the period in question, the figures and percentages shown in the table cannot be taken as infallible, but the error probably tells in favour of the boroughs, as corporations submitting returns would be tempted to exaggerate rather than to underestimate the size of their forces. Moreover, if some boroughs which ought to have been included in the calculation are left out, by virtue of the fact that they failed to submit the required information, these would probably be the less efficient boroughs and, therefore, the ones least likely to possess an adequate police. It seems likely then that the true situation was either as represented in the table or slightly worse.

The second important inference which may be drawn from the table is that there was no significant improvement in the borough police forces as the Chartist period progressed. It is true, as we have seen, that the percentage of boroughs possessing no police force fell during the period. But there was no increase in the percentage of well-policed boroughs. Towns which received their charters of incorporation in the middle and later forties established forces which were well below the 1 : 1,000 ratio.

Ashton-under-Lyne had one constable to every 1,660 inhabitants in 1848, and in the same year Honiton had 1 : 1,783, Salford 1 : 1,411, Warrington 1 : 3,620, and Bradford 1 : 1,343. Older boroughs which did not appear in the parliamentary return until the middle forties (either because they did not set up a police establishment until that time, or because they submitted no record of their earlier force) were equally guilty of failing to maintain an adequate force. If the 1854 parliamentary return is to be believed the police ratio in 1848 was 1 : 1,349 in Exeter, 1 : 1,244 in Pontefract, 1 : 2,451 in Preston and 1 : 2,703 in Tiverton.

But the percentage of boroughs occupying the two highest categories of the table did not merely fail to rise: it fell slightly in consequence of the fact that the enlargement of existing forces had not kept pace with the rapid rise in the population. In some cases the Watch Committees, anxious to promote economy and out of sympathy with modern police ideals, had actually reduced their forces in the years intervening between the first and the last outbreaks of Chartist violence.

The record of the borough police forces in dealing with the problem of disorder was largely what might have been expected from a study of their respective sizes. In the handful of large towns—Liverpool, Bristol, Newcastle upon Tyne, Hull, Manchester and Birmingham—falling within the first two categories of the table, the civil force succeeded, if not always in dispensing with military aid, at least in keeping such assistance to a minimum. When the attempt was made, in August 1839, to implement the Sacred Month in Manchester by a series of turnout raids on the factories, it was the borough police force under the control of the Watch Committee which repeatedly charged the mob with no small success, and arrested the ringleaders. Military assistance was only necessary when a party of police unwisely allowed itself to be surrounded in a mill.[1] In Liverpool, in 1848, although a large military concentration was effected as a result of the spread of disaffection among the Irish population, the duties of patrolling

[1] Mayor of Manchester to H.O. dated 12 August 1839. H.O. 40/43. See also below, pp. 119–20.

and of obtaining information remained in the hands of the large, well-disciplined police force, 822 strong, and the troops were kept in the background.[1]

The vast majority of the English industrial towns, however, fell considerably short of the 1 : 1,000 ratio in their police establishments. How ill served they were in the event of disturbances, how dependent upon military aid, is only too evident from a study of the Home Office Records. At Congleton, where the magistrates boasted that the inhabitants were "kept in perfect order and peace by one constable", uproarious scenes occurred during the General Election of 1841[2] and during the Plug-Plot disturbances twelve months later. The response of the Watch Committee to the latter emergency was to add two more constables to the force for six months, with a strong intimation that after the expiration of that period the appointments would not be renewed.[3] Bolton with over 60,000 inhabitants (1851 Census) had a police force of 24 constables in 1848.[4] When, in the course of that year, the attempt was made to blow up a weaving factory in the town, the magistrates were driven to issue a confidential letter to millowners advising them to make private provision for the watching of their premises "especially since the lamentably small number of regular police belonging to the borough is altogether insufficient for a complete day and night watch".[5] At Bradford, in May 1848, the police force, 69 strong, went its rounds in one quarter of the town by special permission of the Chartists.[6]

The Halifax borough force was in process of formation in

[1] Mayor o Liverpool to H.O. dated 28 June and 5 August 1848. H.O. 45/2410A. The number of police is taken from *The Return of the Several Cities and Boroughs of Great Britain, their Population, Number of Police, etc.*; 1854 (345) LIII.

[2] Report of proceedings submitted to H.O. by Mayor and three magistrates. H.O. 45/44.

[3] Hall, Read, Vaudrey and Hogg to H.O. dated 12 September 1842. H.O. 45/242.

[4] *Return of the Several Cities and Boroughs of Great Britain, Etc.;* 1854 (345) LIII.

[5] Enclosed in Winder to H.O. dated 28 July 1848. H.O. 45/2410A.

[6] Mayor and magistrates of Bradford to H.O. dated 22 May 1848. H.O. 45/2410AC. The figure for the strength of the force is taken from the *Return of the Several Cities and Boroughs of Great Britain, Etc.;* 1854 (345) LIII.

1848. Despite the fact that drilling was believed to be practised in private houses, and that one of the magistrates claimed that such buildings could not be surrounded and searched with less than 50 constables,[1] the Watch Committee prepared a force of 25 men. Home Office protests were unavailing. "Taking into account the limited extent of the borough and the usual good government of the town, hitherto with a much smaller number and a much less efficient body of men", the Committee maintained that 25 policemen were "amply sufficient for all ordinary purposes".[2] It is sufficient to add, by way of comment, that some ten days later the Home Office was apprised of the impracticability of removing the military force from Halifax "for a very long time, if ever".[3] One could go on enumerating industrial boroughs—Stockport, Leicester, Wigan, Preston and many others —where, thanks to the parsimony of the Watch Committee, the police force was starved of men, and consequently helpless to resist any serious outbreak of disorder.

Deficiency in numbers was not, however, the only flaw in the borough police system. The division of authority between magistrates and Watch Committee sometimes made for considerable confusion, especially when contradictory instructions were issued by the two authorities. "I have known instances occur", stated John Dunne, an experienced police officer, before a parliamentary committee in the early fifties, "in which the magistrates have suspended a policeman, and recommended his dismissal, and when before the Watch Committee, the Watch Committee reinstated him." [4]

The very mode of appointment, by a committee of the town council, had its dangers. If, as was not unusual, there were publicans on the Watch Committee, the police were impeded in their action against licensing offences and disorderly houses. At Norwich the Committee instructed the police not to summon

[1] Pollard to H.O. dated 22 August 1848. H.O. 45/2410AC.
[2] Town Clerk of Halifax to H.O. dated 25 August 1848. H.O. 45/2410AC.
[3] Pollard to H.O. dated 4 September 1848. H.O. 45/2410AC.
[4] S.C. on Police: First Report, Mins. of Evidence, p. 119; 1852-3 (603) XXXVI.

any publican or beer-house keeper without seeking the prior approval of that body.[1] Furthermore the elective character of the Watch Committee tended to weaken its independence, and to drive the police into political partisanship. At Liverpool, according to the testimony of a Chief Superintendent of Police, attempts were made to penalize policemen on the representations of the electorate to the Watch Committee.[2] At Bath prospective town councillors sought the support of police officers in the municipal elections by promising to promote them when power had been attained.[3] Several months before the Manchester Police Force reverted to the control of the Watch Committee in 1842, it was ominously reported by the Chief of Police that "many of the constables have an idea that the Police Force is shortly to fall into the power of the local authorities, and consequently are inclined to mix themselves with the borough politics of the day".[4]

It was also a charge against the borough police forces that they lacked uniformity in organization, discipline and method. Such objectionable features of the old police system as part-time employment[5] and the remuneration of constables by fees[6] lingered on in certain of the boroughs, whilst in Norwich the night police checked themselves in by a very inefficient clock-system in use in London before 1829.[7]

Finally, the small size of many of the boroughs imposed limits upon the efficient operation of the force. True, the borough constables were also constables for the surrounding county, but there was not always that smooth co-operation between county and borough police which made for good order. Moreover, it was not easy to prevent the police from acquiring undesirable local connections when the restricted area of the borough would

[1] S.C. on Police: First Report, Mins. of Evidence, p. 120–1.
[2] Ibid., 90–1.
[3] Ibid., 128–9.
[4] Shaw to H.O. dated 10 March 1842. H.O. 45/249C.
[5] In Bath and Liverpool the police were allowed to follow other occupations. S.C. on Police: First Report, Mins. of Evidence, p. 68; Second Report, Mins. of Evidence, p. 54.
[6] S.C. on Police: First Report, Mins. of Evidence, pp. 115–16.
[7] Ibid.

not allow constables to be moved about. Of course, these defects could be remedied if the borough authorities consented to merge their police with that of the county, under the Rural Police Act of 1840. In practice they were seldom willing to resign their powers of patronage.

In two outstanding cases, during the period, provisions had to be made for the policing of corporate towns otherwise than by the arrangements which were laid down in the Municipal Corporations Act. The first was that of the City of London, which had been excluded both from the Metropolitan Police reform of 1829 and from the remodelling of the municipal corporations six years later, on account of the peculiar difficulties of its situation. It was left to the Lord Mayor, Aldermen and Common Council to bring their own police up to date, by replacing the wardmote constables and superior nightly watch, which had previously answered for the peace of the City, with a strong, professional force subject to a single control. This they did by a series of reforms in the eighteen-thirties, culminating in the City of London Police Act of 1839, which established a force of 500 men commanded by a Commissioner, who was appointed by the Common Council, but endowed with a wider discretion than the Chief Constable of a provincial borough. The Home Secretary's powers of supervision were also greater than in the reformed municipalities.

The second case was that of the three newly incorporated boroughs of Manchester, Birmingham and Bolton. As we have seen, these towns were raised to municipal status in the year 1838 by the grant of charters of incorporation, but the charters were opposed by manorial authorities, county justices and improvement commissioners, unwilling to surrender their powers to the new corporations. The fact that, in these circumstances, any attempt to levy a watch rate would most certainly meet with considerable resistance, rendered the situation peculiarly dangerous to public order. In Manchester, despite the difficulty, the council managed to raise a strong force of 343 men,[1] which proved its

---

[1] 295 constables and 48 officers of higher rank. Redford and Russell, *op. cit.*, II, 42.

I

worth against the Chartists on 12 August 1839,[1] but the Police Commissioners and the manorial authorities refused to dissolve their forces, and offered every obstruction to the activities of the borough police. The Chartist disturbances aggravated the chaos by causing the Police Commissioners, who had hitherto restricted themselves to the provision of night watchmen, to establish a day police in May 1839.[2] Furthermore, the borough councillors, who had advanced the sum of £20,000 to finance the borough police, and had subsequently failed in their endeavours to levy a rate, soon found themselves confronted with the prospect of disbanding their force.[3] In Birmingham and Bolton the effect of uncertainty about the charters was even more devastating. The corporations of those boroughs failed to form a civil force which was in any way adequate to meet the demands made upon it. Birmingham faced the excitement of 1839 with a police force of thirty very inefficient men including constables, street keepers and watchmen.[4] Bolton raised a force of ten by subscription from members of the council.[5]

The fever of agitation which descended upon Birmingham after the Chartist Convention had transferred its sittings thither amply demonstrated the incapacity of the local civil force. Since it was clearly impossible to allow the burden of maintaining order to fall permanently upon the detachment of Metropolitan Police which was brought in to fill the gap, the government was driven to propose a reform of the police of Birmingham. The original plan, laid before Parliament on 23 July 1839, provided for a loan of £10,000 from the Consolidated Fund to enable the corporation to establish its own police force. The metamorphosis of this simple scheme into a project for the creation of a government-controlled police in Birmingham, was due to the intervention of Sir Robert Peel, who urged in debate the appointment

---

[1] See above, p. 115.

[2] Redford and Russell, *op. cit.*, II, 44.

[3] Hans., 3 Ser., L, 147.

[4] Charles Tindal's letter of 7 May 1839 enclosed in Governor of Bank of England to H.O. dated 8 May 1839. H.O. 40/50.

[5] Darbishire to H.O. dated 19 May 1839. H.O. 40/37; Darbishire to H.O. dated 29 July 1839. H.O. 40/44.

of a Commissioner of Police under the direct supervision of the
Home Office.[1] Thus for the second time in ten years Peel emerged
as the sponsor of a centralized police. Soon measures based on
Peel's suggestion were introduced into Parliament not only for
Birmingham, but for Bolton and Manchester also.

The Mayor of Bolton had applied for the inclusion of his
borough in the reform, though he would have preferred to
borrow money from the government for the establishment of a
locally-controlled force.[2] The Manchester Act, however, was
opposed by the Borough Council, the Ratepayers Meeting and
the Police Commissioners,[3] whilst the Town Clerk of Birmingham wrote angrily to the Home Secretary:

I beg to acquaint Your Lordship that a meeting of the Council of
this Borough will take place on Tuesday next, when the Birmingham
Police Bill will form one of the subjects for their consideration. What
their opinion may be it would not become me to anticipate, but having
already put myself in communication with many of the members, I
find amongst them one strong feeling of indignation at the measure as
insulting and despotic, insulting to themselves personally as members of
the Town Council, and despotic as tending to that system of centralization which every good Englishman must utterly abhor and abjure.[4]

In due course the opposition was overborne, and the bills
became law before the end of August 1839. Sir Charles Shaw, an
ex-soldier who had seen service in the Low Countries towards
the end of the Napoleonic War, and in Portugal during the
campaigns against Dom Miguel, was appointed to the command
at Manchester, with 319 constables and 64 officers selected mainly
from the Borough Police Force. "A very liberal proportion" of
the Police Commissioners' watchmen, however, was also incorporated in the new police.[5] The Birmingham Commissioner was

[1] Hans., 3 Ser., XLIX, 691 et seq.
[2] His original application was for a grant similar in principle though not in
amount to that originally proposed for Birmingham. Darbishire to H.O. dated
29 July 1839. H.O. 40/44. When this was declined he petitioned for the inclusion of Bolton in the plans for the establishment of a centralized police.
Darbishire to H.O. dated 4 August 1839. H.O. 40/44.
[3] See Redford and Russell, op. cit., II, 44-5.
[4] Redfern to H.O. dated 2 August 1839. H.O. 40/50.
[5] Redford and Russell, op. cit., II, 46.

Captain Francis Burgess, who had served under Wellington in Flanders and France in 1815,[1] and had also practised as a barrister.[2] He set to work with a force of 307 men.[3] In Bolton the post of Commissioner was first conferred on Lieutenant-Colonel Angelo, a gentleman whose military pride was wounded by the paucity of his command, for he resigned his office on 8 October 1839, writing to the mayor that "it would be a complete robbery upon the inhabitants of Bolton to receive from them the sum of £500 per annum for the fulfilment of an office no more important than the business of a common corporal in the regular service viz. the management of 20 men".[4] The Bolton Force was then committed to the charge of the Manchester Commissioner, Sir Charles Shaw, who was to train Boyd, his second-in-command, for eventual leadership in the smaller town.[5]

Necessity rather than design had thus brought into being in three of the great industrial centres of the provinces police establishments fashioned on the Metropolitan model and intended to last for just under three years. In Bolton the experiment was not a success. Owing to the smallness of the funds at his disposal Sir Charles Shaw was compelled to limit the size of the force to forty men,[6] with the result that it never became effective as a means of maintaining order. Boyd, the Head of the Police, told Colonel Wemyss in November 1841 that he could do nothing even on the most trifling occasions if it were not for the confidence inspired by the troops.[7] The Manchester and Birmingham establishments, however, were in many respects, model forces, grappling not unsuccessfully with disorder by methods which were based on the police principles already worked out by the Commissioners at Scotland Yard.

Though less than adequate numerically in the estimation of its commander, Sir Charles Shaw's force at Manchester achieved a

[1] Burgess to H.O. dated 18 November 1839. H.O. 65/10.
[2] Burgess to H.O. dated 12 March 1840. H.O. 65/10.
[3] *Return of the Several Cities and Boroughs of Great Britain*, 1854 (345) LIII.
[4] *The Times*, 14 October 1839, p. 5.
[5] *The Manchester Guardian*, 26 October 1839, p. 2.
[6] *The Times*, 6 November 1839, p. 5.
[7] Wemyss to H.O. dated 14 October (? November) 1841. H.O. 45/43.

high standard of efficiency in dispersing mobs. So great was its prestige that its approach during an election riot in Salford in July 1841 was sufficient to cause a mob of Irish rioters to flee in all directions.[1] It failed to preserve the peace without recourse to military aid during the riots of August 1842, but on that occasion the disaffected in Manchester were strengthened, at first, by 5,000 invaders from the poorly-policed manufacturing districts to the east of the town, a mob which Shaw would have prevented from entering Manchester, but his advice was not adopted by the stipendiary magistrate.[2]

True to the preventive principle of police the forces of Manchester and Birmingham sought rather to forestall disorder than to suppress it. Great emphasis was laid upon the necessity of obtaining accurate information concerning Chartist proceedings. As early as 4 February 1840 Shaw was able to boast to the Home Office that the movements of the Chartists in Manchester were completely under police surveillance, and that the whereabouts of Feargus O'Connor and Dr. Taylor, who had just arrived in Manchester, were exactly known to him. It was also claimed that the activities of the government police were driving the Manchester Chartists to take refuge in Salford.[3] Meanwhile the agents of Captain Burgess were sounding the depths of Birmingham Chartism. The preventive principle was also seen at work in Birmingham in 1842 when, the borough authorities having forbidden the holding of public meetings, Burgess's constables took prior possession of the ground on which each meeting was to be held,[4] instead of waiting to disperse it when it had assembled in defiance of the law.

Modern police principles recognize that the power of the police depends upon public approval of their existence, actions and behaviour and upon their ability to win respect. As may well be imagined from the bitterness of the struggle to pass the police bills through Parliament, the statutory forces were far from

---

[1] Wemyss to H.O. dated 2 July 1841. H.O. 45/43.
[2] Shaw to H.O. dated 26 August 1842. H.O. 45/249C.
[3] Shaw to H.O. dated 4 February 1840 (Private). H.O. 40/54.
[4] Burgess to H.O. dated 21 August 1842. H.O. 45/261.

possessing that approval and respect at the beginning of their careers. This was particularly so in Birmingham, where both the Chartists and the members of the Corporation were in arms against the police. Immediately after his arrival, however, Captain Burgess set about the task of breaking down the opposition to his force by raising it above the spirit of faction, and by representing it to the public as an impartial guardian of the law. His first approach was to P. H. Muntz, the ex-Chartist, who had become Mayor of Birmingham in 1839. To him he addressed a courteous and conciliatory letter, expressing the hope that the differences of opinion concerning the Police Act might be forgotten now that it was the law of the land, assuring him of willingness to co-operate with the council, and appealing for common action against "the lawless depredators on property and the disturbers of peace and good order".[1] This tactful move had the very best effect on Burgess's relations with the mayor, who even offered to undertake Burgess's duties whilst the Commissioner visited London.[2]

A good deal of opposition was still encountered from a party among the ratepayers and councillors led by Joseph Sturge, the Quaker, who wanted to bring the force under local control, and from the Chartists, who desired "to have no Police whatsoever until the working classes had a voice in the making of the laws of the land".[3] These two factions joined in a monster demonstration at the Town Hall on 25 November 1839. But Francis Burgess did not despair of winning further support. In July 1840 an incident occurred which increased the prestige of the police with the working class. On the 23rd a Chartist deputation waited upon the Commissioner to solicit his aid in keeping order at the reception which the Chartists were giving to Collins and Lovett on their release from gaol. By acceding to their request for a small body of police to keep watch during their open-air dinner,

[1] Burgess to Muntz dated 11 November 1839. H.O. 40/50.
[2] Burgess to H.O. dated 13 November 1839. H.O. 40/50.
[3] They carried a resolution to this effect at the joint meeting with the Sturgeites on 25 November 1839. Schofield to H.O. dated 25 November 1839. H.O. 40/50.

and by assuring them of his intention to protect them against all disorderly persons, even, if necessary, against the emissaries who, they believed, were to be employed by the authorities to excite confusion and riot, Burgess strove to convey the impression that the one object of his force was to preserve the peace—not to beat down the political opponents of the government.[1] It would be unjust to allow Burgess to take all the credit for the popularity which the police gained from this affair since he would have prevented the Chartist procession if the Home Secretary had not advised against such a course,[2] but he must be credited with tact in his treatment of the Chartists once the decision to permit the demonstration had been made. Meanwhile the ratepaying class was being won over to the support of the police by the activity of the latter in the detection of crimes against property.[3] "I am hourly gaining friends and losing enemies," wrote Burgess on 24 February 1840, "and this with a strict performance of duty." [4]

In Manchester, too, Sir Charles Shaw was struggling to increase the popularity of his force by maintaining its independence, incurring thereby, he was convinced, the hostility of the Anti-Corn Law Leaguers who wanted the police to take sides. During the disturbances which broke out in June 1841 between the Chartists and the Irish, he was able to save the meeting-houses of the former from destruction by the latter, who had gained the upper hand. Unfortunately he had somewhat rashly promised the Chartists protection to their meeting in the Carpenters Hall, but subsequently found it necessary to prevent the meeting in order to allay the wrath of the Irish.[5] This brought charges of partiality from a Chartist correspondent, who also alleged that he had been threatened with violence by the Irish, and asserted that in consequence he would in future go out armed to meet any Irishman

[1] Burgess to H.O. dated 23 July and 27 July 1840. H.O. 40/56.
[2] Burgess to H.O. dated 5 July 1840 and Minute. H.O. 40/56.
[3] When the borough sessions commenced on 26 December 1839, there were more than four times the number of people for trial than at previous sessions. Burgess to H.O. dated 26 December 1839. H.O. 65/10.
[4] Burgess to H.O. dated 24 February 1840. H.O. 65/10.
[5] Shaw to H.O. dated 5 June 1841. H.O. 45/46.

or policeman who interfered with him.[1] To this Shaw drafted a carefully worded reply:

> To the first part of your letter I beg to assure you that if you lodge with me any information on which I can act, I shall at once take steps that any person ever threatening you, as you state, shall be brought before the magistrates to be punished as the law directs. You will be glad to learn that the information you have received as to the Police Force under me either encouraging or supporting breaches of the peace is totally false and unfounded, as I not only issue orders, but take care to have them executed that people of all nations, of all political and religious sects and of all ranks and gradations of society be treated with justice, and no distinction be made. . . . As you state your intention is not to stir out unarmed, I beg to call to your recollection the 'Cutting and Maiming Act', therefore, (in your own words) if you interfere with an Irishman or Policeman, or indeed with anyone, you must take the consequences.[2]

Unpopularity was not the only handicap which the government police forces had to fight. Their activities were also hampered by financial stringency. Sir Charles Shaw admitted in 1840 that his police was insufficient to protect property in some districts of the town. For this he blamed his inability under the powers of the Manchester Police Act to raise a sum of money equal to the establishment of a more competent force.[3] The Birmingham Commissioner was unable to offer stipends high enough to prevent his best officers from being drained away to the newly formed Worcestershire County Police, where they would receive salaries almost twice as high.[4] The fault lay partly with the Birmingham Police Act of 1839, which did not guarantee a sufficient financial backing, and partly with the difficulty of levying a rate in a parish like Aston, only a portion of which was situated within the Birmingham police district. Burgess, himself, was treated by the Whig Home Office with a parsimony and niggardliness reminiscent of that which was meted out to the Metropolitan Police. His application for an increase of salary was resisted;[5]

---

[1] Richardson to Shaw dated 7 June 1841. H.O. 45/46.
[2] Shaw to Richardson dated 8 June 1841. H.O. 45/46.
[3] Redford and Russell, op. cit., II, 48.
[4] Burgess to H.O. dated 19 December 1839. H.O. 40/50.
[5] Burgess to H.O. dated 6 February and 18 July 1841. H.O. 65/10.

he was refused permission to employ a policeman as a groom; his stable allowance was fixed at £50, whereas the Metropolitan Commissioners had £63.[1] Eventually he was driven to dispense with the services of an assistant despite a severe attack of rheumatic fever in February 1842, which deprived him temporarily of the use of his limbs.[2]

Before the end of 1842 the government police forces in Manchester, Birmingham and Bolton had run their allotted span. Dictated originally by an emergency, the Manchester and Birmingham forces at least had demonstrated the value of modern police principles in coping with the problem of disorder. But the centralization of police power implicit in these arrangements was odious to men of all parties, and sometimes even prejudicial to good order, in that disputes might, and indeed did, arise between the magistrates of the borough and the Commissioner, whose responsibility was to the Home Office rather than to them.[3] The future of the borough police was to be identified with Watch Committee control. Into such hands fell the management of the police of Manchester, Birmingham and Bolton in 1842.

During the period under review the modern police system spread from the metropolis and the provincial boroughs to the counties. A not very successful beginning of rural police reform had been made under the Cheshire Police Act of 1829 (which divided that county into nine police districts and appointed a salaried high constable and between six and eight salaried petty constables to each), but it was not until ten years later that a general police Act, applicable by adoption to all the counties of England and Wales, found its way into the statute book.

Interest in the reform of the arrangements for policing the

---

[1] Burgess to H.O. dated 5 November 1841. H.O. 65/10.

[2] Burgess to H.O. dated 19 February 1842 (Private and Confidential). H.O. 45/261.

[3] Sir Charles Shaw was brought to a recognition of the danger by his own differences with the stipendiary magistrate on the propriety of allowing the turn-outs of August 1842 to enter Manchester. A few days later he wrote to the Home Office asking that there might be one head in Manchester. Shaw to H.O. dated 12 August 1842. H.O. 45/249C.

English counties was rising in the later eighteen-thirties. In 1836 Edwin Chadwick, the Secretary to the Poor Law Commissioners, who regarded police reform not only as desirable in itself, but as the means of enforcing the New Poor Law, prevailed upon the government to issue a Royal Commission to investigate the question, and this commission presented its report in March 1839.[1] There was also a growing concern among the county magistrates that "the great increase of population and the extension of the trade and commerce of the country" had rendered the existing constabulary useless. Shortly before the report of the Royal Commission was published, the Shropshire bench passed a resolution to this effect, and recommended that "a body of constables appointed by the magistrates, paid out of the county rate and disposable at any point of the shire where their services might be required", should be established.[2]

In the opening months of 1839 the Whig government was cautiously feeling its way towards reform. On 2 February the Home Secretary circulated a copy of the resolution of the Shropshire magistrates to the chairmen of Quarter Sessions of all counties except Lancaster and Salop, requesting them to bring it before their respective benches. Thirty-five replies were received, of which fifteen gave a more or less unqualified acceptance of the Shropshire resolution and three more accepted the principle of the need of a new force whilst refusing to consider details.[3]

It is now clear, however, that the Rural Police Act of 1839 was precipitated by the Chartist disturbances of that year and, in particular, by the desire to relieve the military of a pressure which was in the highest degree inconvenient and injurious.[4]

---

[1] S. E. Finer, *The Life and Times of Sir Edwin Chadwick*, 126–7. Chadwick served in the Commission, and, it would appear from Professor Finer's account, compiled the report.

[2] *Copy of a Circular Letter addressed by Lord John Russell to the Chairmen of the Quarter Sessions; and copy of any resolutions of Justices of the Peace at General Quarter Sessions relative to the establishment of a constabulary force.* 1839 (259) XLVII.

[3] *Ibid.*

[4] The point that it was Chartist unrest, and not the alleged exodus of criminals from the reformed municipalities, that led to the establishment of the rural police in 1839 has been cogently and conclusively argued by Mrs. J. M.

The generals commanding the Northern District had in fact taken a leading part in campaigning for the reform of the provincial police forces. In December 1838 Sir Richard Jackson suggested the establishment of a constabulary force on the basis of the Poor Law Unions,[1] and in the following July his successor Napier renewed the pressure upon the Home Office.[2]

In their report the Constabulary Commissioners had contemplated a large measure of central control for the county police. They wished to vest in the Commissioners of the Metropolitan Police the power to fix the size of the force which was to be employed in each county, to make the appointments, and to frame regulations regarding the general management of the police. All this, of course, flew in the face of mid-nineteenth-century prejudice against centralization, and the measure which Lord John Russell saw fit to introduce into the House of Commons on 24 July 1839 excluded the more objectionable recommendations of the Royal Commission. It was a compromise between the extremes of centralization and local control. The magistrates in Quarter Sessions were allowed to fix the strength of the force, and to appoint and dismiss the Chief Constable. Once appointed, however, the latter, unlike his borough counterpart, was to have absolute rights of appointment over his subordinates. The Home Secretary was to frame the rules and regulations as to the government, pay, clothing, accoutrements and necessaries of the constables, a task which in practice he delegated to Scotland Yard.[3] The cost of the new force was laid upon the county ratepayers.

Separate legislation similar in character was introduced for

Hart in an article previously referred to. See above, p. 112. It is also supported by a letter written by Lord John Russell to the Queen on 9 July 1839, stating that "Lord John Russell still hopes that the session may be closed early in August". Correspondence of Queen Victoria with Lord John Russell, 1838–9. Royal Archives. Russell would hardly have been so optimistic had the government intended to introduce so contentious a measure as a rural police bill. It seems more probable that the Whigs were driven to bring forward the measure in haste by the Chartist disturbances in Birmingham and elsewhere later in the month.

[1] Jackson to H.O. dated 12 December 1838. H.O. 40/39.
[2] Napier, *op. cit.*, II, 57.
[3] Phillipps to Mayne dated 31 August 1839. H.O. 65/13.

Scotland in 1839. In that country a fund known as "Rogue Money", levied first by the freeholders, and later by a body of local landowners in each county known as the Commissioners of Supply, had been available since 1724 to defray the cost of apprehending and prosecuting criminals. In 1839, after the Lieutenant of Fife had made representations to the Home Office concerning the uneasiness in his county arising from combinations among the colliers, and from the religious strife of the Established Church and the voluntaries,[1] the government procured an Act of Parliament[2] extending the purpose of the "Rogue Money" assessment to the establishment of a Constabulary Force, much as the Lieutenant had suggested in his letter.

The legislation affecting both Kingdoms was, of course, permissive in character, and the response of the county authorities was uneven. Out of 52 English and Welsh counties 15 had adopted the Rural Police Act for the entire county by the end of 1840, and a further 5 had done so for a portion of the county.[3] Of these 20 counties or parts of counties 10 lay in the industrial North and Midlands, and one was a Welsh county which experienced its share of disorder during the Chartist period. But many of the densely populated manufacturing districts, notably the West Riding of Yorkshire, the Potteries of North Staffordshire and the Lanarkshire coalfield preferred to remain outside the new police arrangements, as indeed did the mass of rural England, Scotland and Wales. The reluctance to adopt the legislation of 1839 sprang from several causes.

One of them was lack of confidence. Writing to the Home Office in October 1842, Lord Wharncliffe epitomized the attitude of many magistrates when he claimed that the authorities of the West Riding would do nothing to establish a permanent police "inasmuch as for common times and purposes they conceive the present force sufficient, and that upon occasions of outbreak or riot . . . no addition to the Police Force which can be contem-

---

[1] Ferguson to H.O. dated 1 August 1839. H.O. 40/52.

[2] 2 and 3 Vict., c. 65.

[3] See *Returns of Police Established in Each County or Division of a County in England and Wales under the Acts 3 Vict. c. 93 and 3 & 4 Vict. c. 88*; 1842 (345) XXXII. This return gives the date of establishment for each force.

plated would be sufficient for their protection".[1] In rural Cardiganshire it was raised as a further objection that the establishment of a rural police in a county placed upon the inhabitants "the stigma of being classed with those who had broken the laws".[2]

In almost every case, however, the outstanding obstruction to police reform was a financial one, for the decision rested with the magistrates who, as the principal landowners of the county, had a vested interest in keeping down the rates. Moreover the organization of the new police on a county basis meant that the rural districts of a county, remote from industrial unrest but heavily rated on account of the large amount of landed estate situated within them, would be footing the bill for the maintenance of public order in the relatively distant manufacturing towns and villages, where property of high rateable value was more scarce. Thus the objections entertained by the agriculturalists of the eastern portions of the West Riding to a rate which was designed to provide a police force for Bradford, Dewsbury, Halifax and the area around Sheffield wrecked the proposals for police reform in the Riding in 1840.[3] Similar considerations were found retarding the establishment of county police forces in Lanarkshire in 1842[4] and in Cardiganshire in 1843.[5] In the amending act of 1840[6] an attempt was made to meet this difficulty by permitting the division of counties into separately rated police districts. Staffordshire for example was thus enabled to levy a police rate of 5d. in the pound in the Potteries, 3d. in the mining area, and 1d. in the rural district.[7] Even this arrangement, however, did not completely solve the problem, for sometimes,

[1] Wharncliffe to H.O. dated 3 October 1842. H.O. 45/264.

[2] Memorial enclosed in Williams to H.O. dated 30 January 1844. H.O. 45/642.

[3] S.C. on Police: Second Report, Mins. of Evidence, pp. 26–7; 1852–3 (715) XXXVI.

[4] The majority of the Commissioners of Supply resided outside the mining districts of the county. Alison to Graham dated 9 August 1842. H.O. 45/266.

[6] Williams to H.O. dated 30 January 1844 and enclosure. H.O. 45/642.

[5] 3 and 4 Vict., c. 80.

[7] S.C. on Police: Second Report, Mins. of Evidence, p. 8; 1852–3 (715) XXXVI.

as in the case of County Durham,[1] the geographical intermingling of the rural, mining and manufacturing areas defied division into police districts, and always there was the item of general expenditure, which had to be borne by all parts of the county without reference to the police demands of each.

It was hardly to be claimed that the counties had taken the fullest advantage of the powers offered to them in the legislation of 1839–40, and the Home Office frequently found it necessary to intervene to procure a more widesprred adoption. In September 1842 Sir James Graham took up she cause of police reform in the West Riding of Yorkshire and the Staffordshire Potteries, two areas which had been reduced by the recent Plug-Plot disturbances, first to chaos, and then to a dependence on military aid resented by every conscientious army commander. His efforts, which were unavailing in Yorkshire,[2] resulted in the establishment of a rural police force in the Potteries district of Staffordshire before the close of the year.[3] He achieved this success by threatening to remove the troops from Newcastle under Lyme if the magistrates did not improve their police.[4] With the same object in view, Graham held back for as long as he could from sending assistance in the form of Metropolitan policemen and troops into Wales at the time of the Rebecca Riots,[5] and, at a later stage in the disturbances, threatened to withdraw such aid, when the magistrates of Cardiganshire, having received it, coolly deferred the establishment of a county police.[6] The policy

[1] Memorandum enclosed in Arbuthnot to H.O. dated 13 June 1844. H.O. 45/650.
[2] The Lord Lieutenant replied that there was not the slightest probability of a rural police force being established in the Riding. Wharncliffe to H.O. dated 3 October 1842. H.O. 45/264.
[3] *S.C. on Police:* Second Report, Mins. of Evidence, p. 11; 1852–3 (715) XXXVI.
[4] Minutes on Wood to H.O. dated 3 September 1842, and Wise to H.O. dated 16 September 1842. See also Wise to H.O. dated 23 September 1842. H.O. 45/260.
[5] See Home Office minute written on Lloyd Davies to H.O. dated 21 April 1843. H.O. 45/454 I.
[6] Memorial of sixteen Cardiganshire magistrates dated 30 January 1844. H.O. 45/642; H.O. to Powell dated 21 November 1843. H.O. 41/18.

was so far successful that rural police forces were actually set up in Carmarthenshire[1] and Cardiganshire[2] during the riots.

Even where county forces had been established the new arrangements often left much to be desired. A marked deficiency in numbers was one of the outstanding difficulties under which the early rural police forces laboured. A contemporary estimate put the optimum police ratio for the rural districts at one constable to every 1,200 of the population,[3] and it will be seen from the table overleaf how far the achievements of this early age of police reform fell short of its ideals, which in themselves were not exacting when judged by modern standards, or even by those of the force operating in the metropolitan district at that time.[4]

In Scotland the situation was worse than in England, where the police forces outside London have, on an average, always been, and still are, 75 to 100 per cent larger than in Scotland.

The basic reason for the smallness of the size of many of the rural police forces was of course the opposition of the magistrates to unnecessary expense. It is worth noting, however, that the division of the county into separately rated police districts under the Act of 1840 worked against the maintenance of any adequate police establishment. For then the magistrates considered each district in isolation from the rest, and settled the number of constables to be maintained in it by reference only to the narrowest and most parochial estimate of its needs. When the Lancashire Constabulary was re-organized upon this basis in 1842, using the petty sessional divisions as police districts, the total strength of

[1] Dynevor to H.O. dated 28 June 1843. H.O. 45/454 I.

[2] Williams to H.O. dated 30 January 1844 and enclosed Memorial. H.O. 45/642.

[3] Asked to state what number of men would be required in England and Wales if the Rural Police Act were made compulsory, Captain W. C. Harris quoted the figure of one constable to every 1,200 people for the areas lying outside the boroughs. Interrogated further on this point Harris, who was the Chief Constable of Hampshire, agreed that the figure was a maximum (i.e. that there should not be fewer than 1,200 people per constable), but it is difficult to believe that he wished for many more than 1,200 to every constable as he had originally suggested that ratio as the one which would be required. *S.C. on Police:* First Report, Mins. of Evidence, p. 11; 1852–3 (603) XXXVI.

[4] See above, p. 113. In 1949 the police ratio for the provinces was one constable for every 803 persons. J. M. Hart, *The British Police*, 34, Table.

THE POLICE OF THE ENGLISH COUNTIES, 1841[1]

County or part of county	Number of police	Police Population ratio	County or part of county	Number of police	Police Population ratio
Bedford	47	1/2101	Salop	50	1/3474
Cambridge (Isle			Southampton	106	1/2249
of Ely)	38	1/1397	Stafford (Offlow		
Cumberland			South		
(Derwent			Hundred)	21	1/3727
Div.)	4	1/7325	Suffolk (East Div.)	64	1/2687
Durham	81	1/2700	Sussex (East Div.)	26	1/4885
Essex	136	1/2305	Warwick		
Gloucester	250	1/1219	(Knightlow		
Hertford	71	1/2038	Hundred)	45	1/1308
Lancaster	502	1/1978	Wiltshire	201	1/1115
Leicester	25	1/6597	Worcester	65	1/3050
Norfolk	143	1/2142	Denbigh	28	1/3174
Northampton	50	1/3312	Glamorgan	39	1/3414
Nottingham	42	1/4379	Montgomery	15	1/4045

the force was reduced from 500 to 350, on the very eve of the Plug-Plot disturbances.[2]

[1] The numbers of policemen quoted in this table, which refers to the year 1841, are drawn from three parliamentary returns—*Abstract return of the number of rural police in each county of England and Wales . . . since the passing of the 2 & 3 Vict. c. 93 and 3 & 4 Vict. c. 80;* 1854 (211) LIII; *Return of counties or divisions of counties which have adopted the County Constabulary Acts;* 1841 (121) XX; *Returns of police establishment in each county or division of a county . . . under the acts 3 Vict. c. 93 and 3 & 4 Vict. c. 88:* 1842 (345) XXXII. These returns do not entirely agree, and there are good reasons for believing that the first-named of them has been carelessly compiled. Nevertheless in 8 out of the 23 cases cited in the table there is absolute agreement as to the number of police between the first and the second of these returns. In a further five the margin of disagreement is not wider than 5 per cent. In one other case, where the third return has been drawn on to supply a deficiency of information in the second, the former agrees absolutely with the first return. Where disagreements exist between the first and the second return, the latter has been preferred, on the grounds that it was compiled in 1841, and would thus be more likely to be accurate than a retrospective return drawn up 12 years later. It cannot be too firmly stated, however, that much caution is required before accepting any parliamentary police statistics for this period. The ratios in the above table are calculated on the basis of population-figures exclusive of the corporate towns.

[2] *S.C. on Police:* Second Report, Mins. of Evidence, pp. 82–3; 1852–3 (715) XXXVI.

Nor was the best disposition always made of the existing strength. In some counties the police were distributed by districts on the Irish model, with stations spread over the county, and a certain number of policemen under a superintendent at each, but in others they were placed singly or in twos and threes, in separate parishes. When the police were first placed in the rural districts of Staffordshire in 1843 some of the magistrates insisted on the second mode of distribution,[1] which prevailed also in Wiltshire right down to 1852.[2]

Severe problems of recruitment confronted the architects of the new rural police forces. Even the selection of a Chief Constable was not accomplished without difficulty. The officers of the Metropolitan Force supplied the most obvious field of recruitment, but when the Home Secretary applied to Colonel Rowan on behalf of the Gloucestershire magistrates, he was told that there was "not a description of man in the Metropolitan Force" suitable to be appointed Chief Constable of Gloucestershire.[3] A little later Lord Normanby was giving as his opinion to magistrates in quest of Chief Constables that "he ought not to lay upon the Metropolitan Police Commissioners the responsibility (as they consider it) of recommending persons to that situation".[4] When the Worcestershire county justices, acting on their own initiative, chose a Metropolitan Police Inspector as their Chief Constable, the Commissioners did their best to forestall his appointment by casting doubt on his fitness for the job.[5] The underlying reason for their unco-operative attitude was probably the fear of losing valuable personnel. Its result was that the Home Secretary had to turn to the Inspector General of the Irish Police for names.[6]

It was also difficult to attract the right kind of man to the lower grades of the police establishment. As in the Metropolitan

---

[1] *Ibid.*, 12.

[2] *Ibid.*: First Report, Mins. of Evidence, p. 146.

[3] Fox Maule to Charles Bathurst dated 25 October 1839. H.O. 65/4.

[4] Phillipps to Pakington dated 7 November 1839. H.O. 65/4.

[5] Phillipps to Pakington dated 4 December 1839. H.O. 65/4.

[6] Phillipps to Clerk of Peace for Gloucestershire dated 14 November 1839. H.O. 65/4

K

Force salaries were low,[1] and only the intervention of the Home Secretary prevented the employment in Lancashire of constables unable to read or write,[2] whilst the admission into the Essex force of a man dismissed from the Metropolitan Police for highly improper conduct led to the formulation of a Secretary of State's regulation against the employment in one police force of persons discharged from another.[3] On the other hand, the government sometimes had to intervene to combat senseless discrimination in the choice of police officers, as when a Mr. Tyner was refused admission to the Essex force on the ground of his having served in the Spanish Legion, a British volunteer force, liberal in character, which had fought for the constitutionalist cause in Spain.[4]

The county police forces were also in difficulty in respect of facilities for detaining prisoners. In 1841 the Norfolk Police were reported to be in the habit of chaining prisoners to mangers in stables and to bed-posts, for want of adequate lock-ups.[5] Where lock-ups did exist, they were not infrequently grimy little hovels in which the prisoners became so contaminated with filth and vermin that, when they were removed to the County Gaol, the warders thereof were compelled to subject them to a rigorous inspection, and cleansing. Much of the indignity complained of by the Chartist leaders, Lovett and Collins, during their detention in Warwick Gaol stemmed from this source.[6] In 1847, however, Sir George Grey embarked upon a campaign for providing adequate lock-ups, allowing the magistrates to borrow money for their erection on the security of future instalments of the police rate.[7]

[1] In Essex there were two classes of constables, paid at 21s. and 19s. per week respectively, whilst inspectors received 25s. Maule to Essex Clerk of Peace dated 2 November 1840. H.O. 65/4: In Gloucestershire constables started at 16s. Maule to Gloucester Clerk of Peace dated 7 November 1840. H.O. 65/4.

[2] Phillipps to Woodford dated 17 March 1840. H.O. 65/4.

[3] Maule to Chairman of Essex Quarter Sessions dated 3 October 1840. H.O. 65/4.

[4] Phillipps to McHardy dated 26 March 1840. H.O. 65/4.

[5] Phillipps to Oakes dated 10 December 1841. H.O. 65/4.

[6] Report of Visiting Magistrates of Warwick Gaol. H.O. 52/43.

[7] Phillipps to Peers dated 5 March 1847. H.O. 65/4.

Inferior in strength and efficiency to the Metropolitan model, the county constabularies had yet to endure a hostility as venomous as ever confronted the London Police in the early years of their existence. Their subordination to a body so thoroughly un-representative as the Court of Quarter Sessions rendered them odious to radicals and Chartists alike. Hence the formation of a rural police in Lancashire threatened initially to provoke disorder rather than to repress it. A Todmorden magistrate wrote to the Home Office in May 1840: "The County Police will shortly be established here, and the very circumstances of their introduction being odious to the greater portion of our inhabitants, renders it more than probable some serious disturbance will be attempted."[1] A "serious disturbance" did occur at Colne in August 1840, the new police being "so dumbfounded by the strength and sudden-ness of the attack that their own real power was never put fairly to the test".[2] The riot was strictly non-political and stemmed only from hostility to the police.[3]

This extreme unpopularity, together with the aforesaid defects of size and organization and the general inexperience of the force, greatly marred the performance of the rural police in the battle against disorder. The Lancashire Constabulary was woefully unequal to the task. In the riot at Colne, of which mention has just been made, the "tolerably strong" force of county policemen assembled in the town was completely routed by a body of dis-ciplined rioters (some of whom were armed with firearms, others with uprooted garden palings), and troops had to be summoned from Burnley barracks.[4] Less than twelve months later, on 30 June 1841, sixty-five constables from the Ashton and Manchester Divisions were foiled in an attempt to disarm an electioneering mob at Ashton-under-Lyne, and driven to take refuge in the police station. The mob tore up paving stones and hurled them at the police.[5] Later in the day the magistrates decided to appease

---

[1] Crossley to H.O. dated 19 May 1840. H.O. 40/54.
[2] Bolton to H.O. dated 10 August 1840. H.O. 40/54.
[3] Napier, *op. cit.*, II, 138.
[4] Bolton to H.O. dated 10 August 1840. H.O. 40/54.
[5] Captain Woodford's Report of the Ashton Riots dated 5 July 1841. H.O. 45/46.

the angry populace by sending the police out of the town.[1] In November 1841 Colonel Wemyss affirmed that the county constables in the Bolton district, "cannot be collected in any force without considerable delay, and when collected they can do little, and are thought nothing of by riotous assemblages unless troops are at hand to protect them".[2]

The Lancashire County Constabulary was further weakened by the reduction of 1842,[3] and when the Plug-Plot Riots began, about a week later, the force was completely swept aside. Captain Woodford, the Chief Constable, concentrated his men at vital points, but did not thereby succeed in raising a sufficient force to check the progress of the mobs; the concentration only weakened the defences of neighbouring localities. All the constables of the Warrington Division, assembled at Leigh, failed to turn a mob of many thousands out of the town,[4] whilst nearby Hindley was abandoned to the mercy of another mob, because the police who normally served it were doing duty elsewhere.[5] The county was reduced to a dependence on military aid which could hardly have been exceeded had there been no rural police. Two years later, during the Colliers' Strike of 1844, the police were only able to grant protection to a party of blacklegs imported into the mines of St. Helens by placing them all together in one pit.[6] In 1848, the county force remained so defective that a large mob was allowed to assemble on 31 May and march, armed with bludgeons, across country from Oldham to Manchester, turning out the factories as it went; no effective resistance was offered to it until the boundaries of Manchester were reached.[7]

In Shropshire the rural police was so small that the outbreak of disturbances among the colliers in August 1842 necessitated the concentration of more than 80 per cent of the force (50 constables

---

[1] Wemyss to H.O. dated 30 June 1841. H.O. 45/43.
[2] Wemyss to H.O. dated 14 October (? November) 1841. H.O. 45/43.
[3] See above, pp. 133–4.
[4] Lacy to H.O. dated 15 August 1842. H.O. 45/249.
[5] Gaskell to H.O. dated 17 August 1842. H.O. 45/249.
[6] Arbuthnot to H.O. dated 1 March 1844. H.O. 45/650.
[7] Mellor, Lees, Rowland, etc. to H.O. dated 31 May 1848. H.O. 45/2410A; Arbuthnot to H.O. dated 31 May 1848. H.O. 45/2410AB.

out of 58) in the Wellington district, and other parts of the
county were left to be molested by bands of beggars.[1] The area
round Coventry was likewise denuded of protection, in the same
month, because much of the constabulary of the Knightlow
Hundred of Warwickshire was needed in the Bedworth collieries
to prevent disturbances among the miners.[2]

Nevertheless it would be wrong to regard the county police
forces as wholly useless and inefficient. Examples may be cited to
show that they were learning the art of dealing with disorderly
crowds and that, when mustered in reasonable strength or
supported by special constables, they sometimes succeeded in
dispersing a mob without recourse to military assistance. Even
the precariously placed Lancashire Constabulary managed to
clear the streets of Blackburn on 29 April 1842 after a disturbance
had broken out and the Riot Act had been read. They did so
speedily, without the help of troops and without inflicting material
injury on anyone.[3] Furthermore, it was in Glamorganshire,
alone among the counties of South Wales in having adopted the
Rural Police Acts before the beginning of the Rebecca Riots,
that some of the earliest and most effective resistance was offered
to the rioters.[4]

Moreover, the directors of the new police forces of the counties
also realized that the proof of the efficiency of a constabulary force
was the absence of riot not the energy shown by the police in
dispersing crowds. They resisted the inclination of magistrates to
provoke disorder by launching attacks upon peaceable assemblies.
At Ashton-under-Lyne, during the election ferment of 1841, of
which mention has been made, the county police officers at first
remonstrated against the order issued by the magistrates to disarm the mob, as there was at that time no actual riot, and secured
the deferment of the operation for about an hour. When at
length an attempt had been made to execute the command, and

[1] Eyton to H.O. dated 19 August 1842. H.O. 45/258.

[2] Aylesford to H.O. dated 22 and 26 August 1842. H.O. 45/261A.

[3] Woodford to H.O. dated 30 April 1842. H.O. 45/249.

[4] For details of the exploits of Captain Napier, Chief Constable of Glamorganshire, in putting down Rebecca, see D. Williams, *The Rebecca Riots*,
221–3, 249–51.

the police had been beaten, one of the superintendents said to the magistrate who had originated the order: "Now sir you are satisfied we are no cowards, and you see the melancholy consequences of bringing on a riot without any provocation on the part of the mob."[1]

Slowly but surely, too, the implacable hostility of the masses towards the police died away. As early as May 1842 the nailmakers of Northfield, who had been compelled by intimidation to leave their employment, returned to work under the protection of the Worcestershire County Police, promising to co-operate with the police if interfered with by strangers.[2] Such incidents were both illustrative of and contributory to the decline of a conception of the police as an instrument of class domination. And they prepared the way for a smoother functioning of the force.

To sum up, police reform in the age of the Chartists was but a partly completed process. Many important areas, boroughs no less than counties, still lay outside its reach, and even where reform had been attempted, parsimony and prejudice marred its success. And yet, reorganization had proceeded far enough to demonstrate the immense superiority of the new police forces over what had gone before. Extremists in the Chartist camp might protest that the introduction of the former "was the first step to a despotism, and its general adoption synonymous with one". They might also lavish praises on "the old English law that the Sheriff should call out the force of the county" which "consisted of every male person in it".[3] In practice, however, the alternative to police was anarchy followed by bloody repression. The new professional police forces were based upon the principle that prevention was better than cure, and that when remedial measures had become inevitable the less painful they were the better.

[1] Captain Woodford's Report dated 5 July 1841 and enclosures. H.O. 45/46.

[2] Taylor to H.O. dated 1 May 1842. H.O. 45/261A. For a similar incident in Staffordshire in 1843, see Hatton to H.O. dated 11 May 1843. H.O. 45/431.

[3] These sentiments were expressed by Whittle when the Chartist Convention debated the question of the need for a Rural Police. *The Northern Star,* 23 March 1839, p. 4.

CHAPTER V

THE MILITARY FORCE

SAVE perhaps in London and one or two of the largest towns, the police forces of England remained, throughout the Chartist period, inadequate to answer unassisted for the peace of the districts which they were appointed to watch. Moreover, even where the civil force was capable of dispersing riotous assemblages with little or no reinforcement, the authorities nevertheless insisted upon marshalling an array of military power, either to quell their own fears, or to lend moral support to the police in the execution of their duty. And so, according to a pattern which had become an established feature of English life, the outbreak of disturbances quickly led to a heavy demand for troops. There were three main sources from which this demand might procure satisfaction.

The first was the territorial force of the county, which meant in practice the Yeomanry. The Militia, that other great local military resource, which had been used to suppress disturbances in Stuart days,[1] had been allowed to lapse after the Napoleonic Wars. Only the permanent staff, the strength of which in 1839 amounted to 1,144,[2] remained available for use in aid of the civil power, its services being confined for the most part to the guarding of public buildings.[3] The Yeomanry corps, though of more recent origin, in that they were called into existence in 1794

---

[1] Max Beloff, *Public Order and Popular Disturbances, 1660–1714*, 148 et seq.
[2] *Abstract of Return for Each Year 1835/6 to 1851/2 Inclusive, of the Number of All Ranks of the Regular Army, Militia Staff etc.*; 1852 (260) XXX.
[3] The Second West Yorkshire Militia Staff guarded York Castle during the riots of August 1842, thus releasing the regular troops for service in the disturbed districts. Hague to H.O. dated 7 September 1842. H.O. 45/264.

to counter Carnot's invasion project, survived the post-war disarmament, and were available to preserve order during the Chartist period.

Unlike the Militia, the Yeomanry was a purely voluntary force, served by tenant farmers and small landowners, and officered by the landed gentry and aristocracy. In other respects, however, it possessed all the merits of a regular cavalry force. It was armed and well trained. The members of the several corps assembled for six days' permanent duty each year, and for inspection by a Field Officer of the Regular Army before they dispersed. Under the terms of an act of 1804 the Yeomanry was subject to military discipline for such periods as it was acting against rioters. Moreover, it possessed a high degree of mobility, being available for service anywhere within the county to which it belonged, and even, if the occasion demanded it, in neighbouring counties.[1]

Notwithstanding its military character, the Yeomanry was normally under the direction of the civil authority. It was the Home Secretary who decided annually what the strength of the force in the coming year should be, communicating his decision to the War Office:[2] no departure from the usual routine of assembling the corps each year, for permanent duty and inspection, was permissible without his authority.[3] In times of trouble the Yeomanry force of the county might be called out by the Lord Lieutenant or by the magistrates: it was not, however, at the disposal of the military commander of the area,[4] except for short periods of general unrest, when the Home Secretary saw fit to confer upon the commanding officers of the military districts subject to disturbance the power to call out the Yeomanry. Napier received such authority in respect of the county forces of the vast Northern district early in May 1839.[5] And in the

[1] Both the Shropshire and the Montgomeryshire corps were employed in restoring order in Central Wales in April 1839. Oskar Teichman, 'The Yeomanry as an aid to Civil Power (1795–1867)', *Journal of the Society for Army Historical Research*, Vol. XIX (1940).

[2] See correspondence between the Home Secretary and the War Office. H.O. 51/165–6.

[3] Grey to Maule dated 30 January 1849. H.O. 51/166.

[4] H.O. to Arbuthnot dated 4 March 1848. H.O. 41/19.

[5] H.O. to Napier dated 2 May 1839. H.O. 41/13.

anxious days of August 1842, when the disturbed areas of England were combined into a single command, the Yeomanry of a block of counties, stretching from the Scottish border southwards to Worcestershire, was placed at the disposal of General Arbuthnot, whose headquarters were at Manchester.[1] Early in October 1843 the government once more placed the Yeomanry corps of those English counties which were normally subject to disturbance under the control of the military authorities.[2] The measure was a purely precautionary one, as there was no real threat to public order in England at the time. It was probably dictated by the need to amass regular troops for service in Ireland, where the government had determined to suppress O'Connell's Clontarf meeting. When excitement returned to England in 1848, the Yeomanry forces of individual counties were again ordered from time to time to obey the requisitions of the military commanders,[3] but there was no general instruction to that effect.

Numerically the Yeomanry cavalry force available in Great Britain during the Chartist period was a good deal smaller than that which existed in the turbulent years following the conclusion of the Napoleonic Wars. Its strength had been allowed to fall from 17,818 in 1817[4] to something in the vicinity of 14,000 in 1838.[5] In fact, the last great reduction, which was of the order of 25 per cent,[6] had been effected in the early months of 1838, on the very eve of the Chartist troubles. It seems likely that the financial embarrassments of the Whigs in the late thirties furnished the immediate motive for this curtailment of the force, for a number of corps containing approximately 680 men were

---

[1] H.O. to Arbuthnot dated 24 August 1842. H.O. 41/17.

[2] H.O. to Wellington dated 7 October 1843. H.O. 41/18.

[3] In April 1848, for example, the Duke of Rutland was ordered to place the Leicestershire Yeomanry at the disposal of Sir Thomas Arbuthnot. H.O. to Arbuthnot dated 9 April 1848. H.O. 41/19. Towards the end of July the Lancashire and Cheshire forces were made subject to General Arbuthnot and General Warre. Arbuthnot to H.O. dated 2 August 1848. H.O. 45/2410AB.

[4] *Journal of the House of Commons*, Vol. 72, 1817, Appendix, p. 604.

[5] In a House of Commons debate Lord John Russell gave the figure 13,594 men for 1838. Hans., 3 Ser., XLII, 651. To these may be added about 680 allowed to serve gratuitously. See above.

[6] Troops containing a total of 4,717 men exclusive of officers were disbanded. Phillipps to Sulivan dated 23 January 1838. H.O. 51/165.

allowed to retain their existence on condition that their members agreed to serve gratuitously.[1] At the same time, it must be admitted that the uncompromising Toryism of many of the Yeomanry corps did not commend them to a Whig government and its liberal supporters. This latest reduction did little to weaken the forces of order which confronted Chartism in the ensuing years, for most of the corps singled out for dissolution emanated from the agricultural districts of the south of England. One of them, however, came from Wigton in Cumberland, a town which was to experience the problem of disorder quite acutely in August 1842.[2] But apart from its effect upon the strength of the Yeomanry force, the reduction of 1838 left in the minds of the members of that body and more particularly in those of its officers, a legacy of disaffection towards the government. Lord Sondes, the major commandant of the Norfolk corps, which escaped the axe, wrote to his officers and men in a somewhat intemperate strain, advising them to resign before the government decided to dispense with their services also. "I am willing to prove my loyal attachment to the Throne by serving her Majesty," he wrote; "but I will not, as an independent man, subject myself to the capricious and uncertain conduct of the present Administration." His letter was quoted by Joseph Hume in the House of Commons in the course of an exceedingly acrimonious debate on the reductions in April 1838.[3] The Whigs and the Yeomanry were thus at loggerheads when internal disorder was about to call for their close co-operation. It is not surprising that General Napier found the commanders of the local forces apathetic and unco-operative in the spring of 1839.[4]

The geographical distribution of the Yeomanry of Great Britain was far from even. The strength of the force lay in the Midlands

---

[1] The Gilston, Lymington, Andover, Taplow, Ilminster, West Essex, Taunton, Long Milford and Suffolk Borderer corps. See correspondence between the Home Office and the War Office and Horse Guards, 12 March–3 July 1838. H.O. 51/165. The strength of these units is also listed in H.O. 51/165, pp. 41–3.

[2] For list of corps disbanded see Phillipps to Sulivan dated 23 January 1838. H.O. 51/165.

[3] Hansard, 3 Ser., XLII, 637.   [4] Napier, op. cit., II, 30.

and in the Western counties, from the mouth of the Mersey down
to the borders of Devon and Cornwall. In the East, in the South-
east with the exception of Kent, in the North with the exceptions
of Yorkshire and Northumberland, and in Wales, the Yeomanry
Cavalry was less abundant. From this it follows that the manufacturing districts of the Midlands had at their disposal, for the
suppression of the disturbances with which they were so frequently
confronted, a sizeable body of volunteer cavalrymen. The three
adjoining counties, Staffordshire, Warwickshire and Worcestershire, which included within their boundaries the Potteries and
the Black Country, had between them 25 troops of Yeomanry,
a force which totalled 1,886 men.[1] The East Midland shires,
Derbyshire, Leicestershire and Nottinghamshire, teeming with
half-starved and desperate framework knitters, were also relatively
well off, having at their command 1,450 men assembled in 20
different troops.[2] It is not without significance that Major Teichman, dealing with the Chartist period in an article which stresses
the contribution of the Yeomanry to the preservation of public
order,[3] draws heavily upon the experience of these Midland
counties. In Lancashire, with its three troops totalling 171 men,[4]
to control a population larger than that of Staffordshire, Warwickshire and Worcestershire combined, it could hardly be
claimed that the Yeomanry was the foundation of the county's
defences. With the best will in the world the Lancashire corps
could meet but a small proportion of the demands of the civil
power for military aid in times of serious disturbances. The great
mining county of Durham did not boast a single troop in 1839,
and with the single exception of Pembrokeshire, the counties of
South Wales, scene of the Newport Rising and the Rebecca
Riots, experienced the same deficiency.[5] It would, therefore, be
an exaggeration to claim, as is sometimes done, that the Yeomanry
stood, during this period, between England and anarchy.

[1] *Return of the Number of Troops etc. of Effective Yeomanry . . . dated 4 June
1839*. 1839 (364) XXXI.
   [2] *Ibid.*   [3] Teichman, *op. cit.*
[4] *Return of the Number of Troops etc. of Effective Yeomanry . . . dated 4 June
1839.*
   [5] *Ibid.*

It was no part of government policy to encourage a too frequent or protracted use of the Yeomanry in the suppression of civil discord. Lord John Russell admitted, in the debate on the reduction of the Yeomanry in 1838, that "for his own part he would rather that any force should be employed in case of local disturbance than the local corps of Yeomanry".[1] He frankly admitted having called upon regular troops and Metropolitan policemen in preference to Yeomanry corps in cases of disorder provoked by the introduction of the New Poor Law. The following year he restrained General Napier from placing the whole of the Yeomanry of the disturbed districts on permanent duty against the Chartists.[2]

No doubt the Whigs had their own peculiar reasons for not wishing to be rescued from the Chartists by a force which they had openly contemned in Parliament some twelve months earlier. But the policy of restricting the use of the Yeomanry was continued by their Tory successors. "I much prefer the assistance of regular troops to calling on a Yeomanry force",[3] wrote Sir James Graham to the Vice-Lieutenant of Staffordshire on the outbreak of the Colliers' Strike in the Potteries in July 1842. Twelve months later the military commander in South Wales, who had made extensive use of the Pembrokeshire Yeomanry against the gate-breakers, received from the Home Office a letter stating: "Sir James Graham thinks you must not look upon the Yeomanry as a permanent Force." [4]

There were, in fact, three outstanding disadvantages inherent in the employment of a Yeomanry force to put down popular disturbances. The first was financial in character. Resort to the Yeomanry involved the government in additional expenditure, for whereas the regular troops were entitled to payment whether in use against rioters or safe within barracks, the Yeomanry became liable to remuneration only when embodied. The second disadvantage accrued to the members of the corps. Several of the

[1] Hans., 3 Ser., XLII, 651.
[2] Napier to H.O. dated 11 May 1839. H.O. 40/53.
[3] Graham to Dartmouth dated 13 July 1842. H.O. 41/16.
[4] H.O. to Love dated 7 July 1843. H.O. 41/17.

most severe disturbances of the period occurred at a time of the year when the farmers who composed the Yeomanry troops needed to devote all their attention to the gathering of their crops. The Birmingham excitement of July and August 1839, the Sacred Month Riots, the strikes of 1842, could not have taken place at a less convenient season for the agriculturalist, a fact which did not escape mention in official correspondence.[1] Consideration for the agricultural interest certainly accounted for much of Sir James Graham's reluctance to overwork the Yeomanry. "I am to inform you", wrote his Under-Secretary to Colonel Love in September 1843, "that in any arrangement respecting the keeping on duty of the Yeomanry Cavalry, due regard must be had to the time of the year and the inconvenience and loss which may be occasioned to them by their being detained from the getting in their crops." [2] By long descent a landowner, living among landowners and tenant farmers, Graham was able to enter fully into the problems of those whose lot it was to cultivate the soil. He served, moreover, in an administration which could not afford to alienate the agricultural interest.

Last but not least, among the difficulties arising from the employment of the Yeomanry, was the fact that their presence exasperated the populace, and tended to bring on a riot, where otherwise none might have occurred. In explaining to the House of Commons his objections to the use of the Yeomanry, Russell in 1838 alleged that a corps of that force would "create more animosity than the regular army would do in putting down local riots".[3] This, he attributed to the local connections of the county forces, which gave them the character of parties to the dispute. It was also due, however, to a belief, inherited from Peterloo, that the Yeomanry was peculiarly prone to savage repression. Even so responsible an officer as General Napier accused the yeomen of being "over-zealous for cutting and slashing".[4]

---

[1] Thorn to H.O. dated 16 August 1839. H.O. 40/53; Swanwick to H.O. dated 14 August 1839. H.O. 40/41; Lyttelton to H.O. dated 13 August 1842. H.O. 45/263.

[2] H.O. to Love dated 8 September 1843. H.O. 41/18.

[3] Hans., 3 Ser., XLII, 650.

[4] Napier, *op. cit.*, II, 73.

Nothing in their conduct during the Chartist period gave the slightest support to this opinion, and against it may be cited the example of a Yeomanry commander in the West Riding who, in April 1848, showed the utmost reluctance to bring his force into collision with the people, unless it was absolutely necessary.[1] But the impression remained, so that the very presence of the Yeomanry at a scene of disorder tended to add to the intensity of the conflict. At Stoke on Trent in 1837,[2] at Birmingham in 1839,[3] at Chard in 1842[4] and at Exeter in 1846[5] the county forces were subjected to ferocious assaults by mobs, assaults which betokened an animosity not usually shown to regular troops.

Despite the intention of governments to use regular troops rather than yeomen, and to restrict the latter to the task of filling the gap until a detachment of regulars arrived on the scene, the county forces were frequently called upon to assist the civil power, and to assist it for lengthy periods. Shortly after taking up his command in the spring of 1839 General Sir Charles Napier formulated a scheme which would have involved the Yeomanry in immense commitments. He planned to place them on permanent duty in the more seriously disturbed districts, in order that he might use them for local defence, thus freeing the regular troops for concentration at focal points.[6] Faced with the hostility of the Yeomanry commanders, still smarting under the insult inflicted upon them by the Whigs in the previous year,[7] and having no more than the grudging assent of the Home Secretary,[8] Napier abandoned his project. But the summer months of 1839 saw the Yeomanry forces well in the field against the Chartists. In the excited days which followed the incendiarism in the Bull Ring on 15 July 1839, the districts around Birmingham were patrolled day and night by troops of yeomen,[9] the last of which

---

[1] Pollard to H.O. undated. H.O. 45/2410AC.
[2] Teichman, *op. cit.*, 138.   [3] *Ibid.*, 140.
[4] Loveridge to H.O. dated 26 August 1842. H.O. 45/259.
[5] Teichman, *op. cit.*, 141–2.   [6] Napier, *op. cit.*, II, 20.
[7] One of them told Napier that his men would resign if kept out on duty. *Ibid.*, 30.
[8] Napier to H.O. dated 11 May 1839 and Minute. H.O. 40/53.
[9] Teichman, *op. cit.*, 140.

was not dismissed until 24 August.[1] In the summer of 1842 the Staffordshire Yeomanry averaged 22 days' duty per troop; whilst the Himley troop of that regiment did 50 days' continuous duty.[2]

Serious efforts were made from time to time to minimize the hardship inflicted upon the yeomen by these long spells of duty. Troops were relieved by other troops after a certain time had elapsed. In Worcestershire, in the month of August 1842, the Lord Lieutenant proposed to relieve the Dudley troop, which had been on duty for nearly a fortnight, by forming two new troops selected from members of the regiment who could spare the time for protracted duty.[3] Despite these arrangements, however, considerable inconvenience was experienced by the farmers enlisted in the Yeomanry corps. Nor was it limited to troops called out on active service. When disturbances broke out on a large scale in the summer of 1842, the Lords Lieutenant of the counties affected were requested by the Home Office to hold their Yeomanry corps in readiness. What this meant in terms of hardship to members of the corps is best illustrated by the following extract from a letter written by the officer commanding the Sherwood Rangers, describing the manner in which he complied with the Home Office order which had been transmitted to him three weeks before he wrote: "I at once issued a regimental order, which brought some members of the corps from the North of Scotland, and which has since kept every man at home in readiness to act if called upon. Nor will an individual consider himself at liberty to absent himself until he has received an intimation from me that his services are not likely to be required." [4] Farmers were thereby prevented from attending distant markets, and trade was hampered in numerous ways.

The usefulness of the Yeomanry force as an instrument of public order was so clearly demonstrated during the disturbances of 1842 that the policy of reducing its strength was reversed. The Whigs, those arch-enemies of the Yeomanry, were now out of office,

---

[1] Thorn to H.O. dated 24 August 1839. H.O. 40/53.
[2] Teichman, *op. cit.*, 141.
[3] Lyttleton to H.O. dated 12 and 13 August 1842. H.O. 45/263.
[4] White to Arbuthnot dated 7 September 1842. H.O. 45/268.

their place having been taken by the more friendly Tories. "The conduct of the Yeomanry Cavalry in every district has been admirable and we must consider an extension of this force," wrote Peel to Wellington on 24 August 1842.[1] By 27 December it had been decided that the increase should not exceed 950 men exclusive of officers.[2] It took the form of a restoration to the permanent establishment of six troops which had been serving gratuitously since 1838, and of an expansion of the strength of the Yeomanry force in Cumberland and Westmorland, Stafford-shire, Derbyshire, Lancashire, Oxfordshire, Midlothian and the West Riding.[3] Further additions were made to the Yeomanry in the centres of disturbance—Lancashire and Glasgow in particular —before the close of the period, but these were offset by the dis-appearance of troops in the Eastern and South-eastern districts of England.[4] The total strength of the Yeomanry forces of Great Britain shows a slight decrease in 1850 as compared with 1839.[5]

A second auxiliary military force, locally recruited, came into being about halfway through the period—the Enrolled Pensioners. As we have seen, the transformation of the Chelsea out-pensioners from a civil into a military arm began during the Plug-Plot Riots with the emergency measures effected by Colonel Angelo at Manchester and by Captain F. Unett at Birmingham.[6] At that time, however, the Home Secretary also requested the Secretary-at-War to mature a more permanent plan[7] which received legis-lative sanction in August 1843. At first approach, the idea that pensioners could constitute an efficient military force seems absurd, for few, except the permanently disabled, would draw

[1] *Peel Papers*, Brit. Mus. Add. MSS. 40, 459.
[2] Graham to Hardinge dated 27 December 1842. H.O. 51/166.
[3] Graham to Hardinge dated 1 February 1843. H.O. 51/166.
[4] See correspondence in H.O. 51/166.
[5] 13,676 men in 1850. See list enclosed in Cornewall Lewis to Fitzroy Somerset dated 9 March 1850. H.O. 51/166.
[6] See above, pp. 89–90.
[7] Graham to Wellington dated 22 August 1842 (Private). The Graham Papers, Bundle 52B.

their pensions below the age of forty.[1] But if, man for man, pensioners in their forties and fifties were hardly the equals of stalwart young rioters, they could, if properly armed and organized, be made superior. The Enrolled Pensioners Act of 1843 conferred these advantages on the best of the old soldiers, who were to be compulsorily enrolled in local uniformed corps, armed with muskets and bayonets and acting under military discipline when called together to assist the civil power. There was provision for assembling each year for eight days' training and inspection, and members of the corps were to be liable to fines and forfeiture of pension if they lost or damaged their arms or equipment.[2] Pensioners who were physically unfit for service were exempted, as were those over fifty-five years of age, though volunteers were taken down to the age of fifty-eight.[3]

The authorities had difficulty in finding sufficient pensioners to enrol in some areas, particularly the more remote rural districts, such as the parts of South Wales visited by the Rebecca Riots,[4] but in the larger towns sizeable corps were formed. By the beginning of 1844 Manchester had 400 Enrolled Pensioners, Liverpool had 300 and Birmingham 240, whilst smaller towns like Stockport and Bolton had 70 or 80.[5]

One important problem which impeded the formation of corps was that of providing safe custody for their arms when the men were not mustered for inspection or assembled in aid of the civil power. Where barracks existed they were used for the purpose, but elsewhere a serious difficulty occurred. In Bristol, Derby and five other large towns, the magistrates had stored the arms in jails and court houses, protected by the strength of the building and a small guard of warders or police. At Bath and Gloucester

[1] Hardinge's reform of the pensions system in 1829 had restricted pensions, except in cases of permanent disability, to soldiers who had served for at least 21 years. John Fortescue, *A History of the British Army*, XI, 437.
[2] 6 and 7 Vict., c. 95.
[3] War Office Circular to Staff Officers signed by L. Sulivan and dated 7 September 1843. War Office Papers 4/847.
[4] Sulivan to H.O. dated 7 October 1843. H.O. 45/454 II.
[5] W.O. to Byham, Secretary of Ordnance, dated 18 December 1843 and 2 January 1844. W.O. 4/847.

L

60 or 70 stand of arms were kept in private houses with only a sergeant or two resident in the building.[1] In 1848, however, the Secretary-at-War was busying himself to ensure safer keeping for weapons issued to the pensioners. The failure of the magistrates to comply with his requirements frustrated the projects for the enrolment of the pensioners at Lincoln, Oxford, Reading and Shrewsbury,[2] whilst at Dudley the problem was only solved by maintaining a military detachment in the town to protect the arms, which were deposited in a small lock-up house.[3] Such an expedient defeated the object of enrolment, which was to effect an economy of regular military force.

Despite difficulties the new force gained in strength. An amending Act of 1846 rendered the Greenwich (naval) out-pensioners liable to enrolment also,[4] and by 1847–8 the number of veterans, Chelsea and Greenwich, mustered in Great Britain amounted to 8,720.[5] They performed a useful service on the return of agitation in 1848. They shared with the military the duty of guarding the bridges over the Thames and of garrisoning the Bank, the Mint and the Tower on 10 April, a total of 1,290 pensioners being employed to preserve the peace of the metropolis on this occasion.[6] In Leicester their backing enabled the police to disperse unruly mobs during the Labour Test Order Riots;[7] it is recorded that when the pensioners moved forward with levelled bayonets the mob broke and fled.[8] They co-operated with regular troops in Manchester on 31 May 1848, the day of the combined demonstration of Chartists and Irish Repealers, and their conduct was commended by the Home Office in a letter to the Horse Guards.[9]

Power to call out the Enrolled Pensioners was vested in the

---

[1] Sulivan to H.O. dated 15 April 1848. H.O. 45/2410.   [2] Ibid.

[3] Arbuthnot to H.O. dated 20 and 27 April 1848. H.O. 45/2410AB.

[4] 9 Vict., c. 9.

[5] Return Showing the Expense . . . attending the Enrolling, Clothing and Drilling of the Pensioners' Force, etc. etc., 1849 (533) XXXII.

[6] Metropolitan Police Records, 'Chartists' Box: Bundle marked 'Special Reports and Documents Relative to Chartist Meetings'.

[7] Stone to H.O. dated 16 and 19 May 1848. H.O. 45/2410R.

[8] A. T. Patterson, Radical Leicester: A History of Leicester, 1780–1850, p. 360.

[9] H.O. to Fitzroy Somerset dated 2 June 1848. H.O. 41/19.

Home Secretary, who might delegate his rights to the local authorities by issuing warrants under an Act of 1847. In practice such warrants were granted only to Lords Lieutenant and the mayors of corporate towns. The Home Secretary refused to issue them to stipendiary magistrates[1] and chairmen of petty sessions.[2] In times of emergency, however, the Enrolled Pensioners, like the Yeomanry, might be placed at the disposal of the military commanders. Thus, before the Chartist demonstrations of 10 April 1848, the Earl of Harewood and the mayors of Manchester and Leeds, as holders of warrants to call out the pensioners, were warned by the Home Secretary to be ready to answer the requisitions of General Arbuthnot.[3]

It was the Regular Army, however, which furnished most of the military aid required by the civil authorities.

For the performance of this duty, and for sundry other purposes of a routine character, a combined force of rather less than 30,000 regular infantry and cavalry was maintained in the United Kingdom exclusive of Ireland.[4] With the exception of about 12,000 men stationed at Windsor and in the capital, this force was divided up into military districts, each with a district commander, whose rank varied with the size and importance of his command.

The largest of these districts and the one containing most of the disturbed areas of England was the Northern, which extended from the Scottish border through the North-eastern coalfield and the textile belt of Lancashire and Yorkshire into Leicestershire and Nottinghamshire. Over the troops in this vast and densely populated area presided a succession of able generals, all veterans of the Peninsular campaigns. The first of these was Lieutenant-General Sir Richard Downes Jackson, K.C.B., who was possessed of a

[1] Rose to H.O. dated 13 March 1848 and Minute. H.O. 45/2410Y.

[2] H.O. to Maude dated 2 August 1848. H.O. 41/19.

[3] H.O. to Harewood dated 6 April 1848; H.O. to Mayor of Manchester dated 6 April 1848; H.O. to Mayor of Leeds dated 6 April 1848. H.O. 41/19.

[4] Sir William Molesworth, speaking on the Army Estimates in the House of Commons in 1848, calculated an average of 29,500 r. and f. for the preceding ten years. Hans., 3 Ser., XCVII, 1173-4. The figure for January 1840 was 29,345, and for December of the same year 28,497. Returns of the Distribution of the Army in Great Britain. H.O. 50/16.

balanced judgment and much common sense, and was respected by men of diverse positions and outlooks.[1] It fell to his lot to command the Northern District during the Anti-Poor Law agitation and the opening phase of Chartism. When, at the end of March 1839, he left the District to take up the post of Commander-in-Chief of the British forces in North America, he was succeeded by Major-General Sir Charles James Napier, undoubtedly the greatest of the officers concerned in the maintenance of public order throughout the Chartist period. Napier stood apart from the dominant tradition in the British Army in the early nineteenth century. In a force which accepted almost without question the stern views of the Duke of Wellington in matters of discipline, he upheld the more humane principles of Sir John Moore (with whom he had served at Corunna), and strove to establish his authority over his men on a basis of confidence and affection rather than fear.[2] Moreover, although the army was in his day largely controlled by Tories, Napier, who was the cousin of Charles James Fox, tended to the ultra-radical in politics, agreeing with the Chartists not only in their 'Six Points', but also in their dislike of the New Poor Law.[3] He had no sympathy, however, with direct action as a method of procuring reforms,[4] and threw himself energetically into the task of frustrating the devices of physical-force Chartism in 1839. Nevertheless he abhorred the prospect of shedding civilian blood, and this led him to devote a great deal of his attention to preventing the outbreak which he knew he would have to suppress if it actually occurred.

[1] Early in March 1839 the Tory Lord Lieutenant of Nottinghamshire wrote to the Home Secretary asking that Jackson should not be replaced by Napier as commander of the District. The Lord Lieutenant described Jackson as "sensible and provident". Newcastle to Russell dated 11 March 1839. H.O. 40/47. But Napier, who was a radical, also thought Jackson "a very good and very clever man". Napier, *op. cit.*, II, 10.

[2] Napier, *op. cit.*, II, 54–5.

[3] *Ibid.*, 63.

[4] "Good government", he wrote in his journal, "consists in having good laws well obeyed. England has abundance of bad laws, but is every man to arm against every law he thinks bad? No! Bad laws must be reformed by the concentrated reason of the nation gradually acting on the legislature, not by the pikes of individuals acting on the bodies of the executive." Napier, *op. cit.*, II, 63.

Napier relinquished the Northern command in September 1841 to join the Indian staff. His successor, Major-General Sir William Gomm, may be dismissed with a mention, as he left the command in June 1842 to become Governor of Mauritius, after holding it for no more than three relatively undisturbed months.[1] Gomm was succeeded by Major-General Sir William Warre, who like Napier had been with Moore at Corunna.[2] Warre remained in the Northern District until the end of the period, but fell into disfavour with the Duke of Wellington and the Tory government for not showing enough vigour in putting down the Plug-Plot disturbances.[3] From 17 August 1842 his command was made subordinate to that of a general commanding the whole of the disturbed districts, and his authority was greatly diminished.

Adjacent to the Northern lay the Midland District, also subject to much disorder as it comprised the industrial counties of Stafford, Worcester and Warwick. It was commanded from Birmingham, first by Colonel Thorn and later by Colonel Arbuthnot. A separate command in Monmouthshire and the adjacent counties of South Wales was instituted immediately after the Newport Rising and given to Colonel Considine, and a similar procedure was followed in West Wales at the time of the Rebecca Riots, when Colonel James Frederick Love, a veteran of Waterloo and the Peninsular campaign, was sent to take charge. Scotland was a single military district known as North Britain, and the remaining area commands were the South-western, the Western and those of Jersey and Guernsey.

[1] D.N.B., XXII, 101–3. Gomm to H.O. dated 22 March 1842. H.O. 45/268. Annual Register, 1842, List of Gazette Promotions—13 June 1842.

[2] D.N.B., LIX, 407–8.

[3] When harassed by requests for military aid which he could not meet by reason of the inadequacy of his force, he ventured to advise the magistrates who applied to him for such assistance to "temporize with the people where they feel themselves quite unequal to enforce the law". Warre to H.O. dated 11 August 1842. H.O. 45/268. For this he was mildly rebuked by the Home Secretary, Sir James Graham. Graham to Warre 12 August 1842. Graham Papers, Bundle 52A. Two days later he failed to carry out Graham's instructions to procure the arrest of some trade union delegates in Manchester. This was not his fault, but the Duke of Wellington, then Commander-in-Chief, expressed to Graham his want of confidence in Warre. Graham to Wellington, 19 August 1842; Wellington to Graham 19 August 1842. Ibid.

In the middle of the Plug-Plot disturbances the government reorganized the administration of the two English districts which suffered most from disorder—the Northern and the Midland. Whilst he held the command of the Northern District, Napier had suffered much from overwork, and when during the tumults of 1842 Warre complained of the inadequacy of his staff the Home Secretary requested that an additional officer should be despatched into the District.[1] At a meeting between Graham and the Duke of Wellington (recently appointed Commander-in-Chief) two days later this proposal was metamorphosed into a completely new arrangement. Lieutenant-General Sir Thomas Arbuthnot, brother of Charles Arbuthnot, the Duke's friend and political ally, was sent to Manchester to take charge of the whole disturbed District, the Midlands as well as the North.[2] Colonel Thorn's command at Birmingham was made subordinate to his; Major-General Brotherton was given a command in Yorkshire similar to Thorn's; and General Warre was continued at Chester under the more immediate surveillance of Arbuthnot.[3] This revision, though intended to promote unity of control over a wide area, was also almost certainly a reproof for the discredited Warre.

Theoretically, when acting to maintain internal order, the Army was a mere instrument in the hands of the civil power. By numerous conventions the control of the latter over the former was secured. The real authority for altering the stations of troops on home service was the Home Office, not the Horse Guards: it was at the Home Secretary's behest that the Commander-in-Chief issued the necessary instructions to move a company of infantry or a troop of horse from one town to another, and though the Home Office usually consulted the General in charge of the District before ordering such a movement, it was not bound to do so.

At a somewhat lower level, it was the magistrates who were

[1] H.O. to Fitzroy Somerset dated 15 August 1842. H.O. 41/16.
[2] Graham to Queen Victoria dated 17 and 18 August 1842. Graham Papers, 52A.
[3] H.O. to Arbuthnot dated 13 October 1842. H.O. 41/17.

expected to direct the operations of the military force against rioters. They had the power to requisition troops when rioting had broken out or when it was imminent, and were under an obligation to accompany those troops to the scene of the disturbance, and if necessary to read the Riot Act and instruct the officer to order his men to fire. The military were to be found extremely reluctant to act without specific instructions from a justice of the peace. At Rochdale during the Plug-Plot disturbances the troops failed to stop the progress of a mob because, when the magistrate who was accompanying them rode on ahead into the middle of the mob, the officer in command wheeled back his men, and allowed the crowd to pass quietly on.[1] This was not an isolated instance,[2] for though Lord Chief Justice Tindal had given a clear ruling after the Bristol Riots of 1831, that "where the danger is pressing and immediate . . . and from the circumstances of the case no opportunity is offered of obtaining a requisition from the proper authorities, the military subjects of the king, like his civil subjects, not only may, but are bound to do their utmost to prevent the perpetration of outrage etc.",[3] the soldiers were slow to appreciate their responsibilities in this matter.

In practice, however, the subordination of the military to the civil power was qualified by the important rôle assigned to the officer in charge of the military district in the maintenance of public order. Because of the defects of the magistracy, and because of the scope he had to exercise a unified control over an area wider than the town or village or even the county, the district commander tended to assume important executive functions and to plan the general strategy of resistance to popular uprisings real or anticipated. Sir Richard Jackson conducted, through his subordinate officers, an investigation into the number of Yeomanry and Volunteer forces in each county of his district, the size of the civil force in every large town, the state of prosperity (or depression) of the leading industries and the operation of the

---

[1] Captain Forrest to Fitzroy Somerset dated 26 August 1842. H.O. 45/249.

[2] See Balcarres to H.O. dated 13 August 1839. H.O. 40/37, for the occurrence at Hindley on 13 August 1839.

[3] H.O. to Balcarres dated 14 August 1839. H.O. 41/14.

New Poor Law, in order to be able to "move troops in aid of the civil power, upon the shortest notice, without the necessity of previous reference to the Civil and Military Departments in London".[1] His successor, Napier, laid plans for defeating a Chartist insurrection that never came off, conferred with the magistrates to arrange concerted action, and tendered advice to the government and to the Horse Guards on political questions affecting the condition of his district. During the disturbances of August 1842 Sir William Warre and Sir Thomas Arbuthnot, rather than any civil magistrates, were used by the Home Secretary to carry into effect his most vital and confidential plans for combating the outbreak. It was also by no means unusual to find a high-ranking Army officer mediating in trade disputes in the area of his command. Sir Thomas Arbuthnot was urged to do so by the Home Office in August 1842.[2]

Just as the military commander was obliged to assume functions more properly belonging to the civil executive, so the force at his command was compelled to take over, to a very large extent, the work of the only partially reformed constabulary. But if the Army was the mainstay of public order it can hardly be said to have provided a satisfactory solution of the problem. It is true that regular troops with their advantages of discipline and weapon-power could usually be trusted to triumph over a mob in a straightforward fight, provided that the soldiers were used resolutely and not placed at an exceptional disadvantage by being split up into minute parties. A company of foot-soldiers could disperse an angry concourse many times its size by opening fire on it: and although mounted troops could be more easily out-manœuvred if the rioters assailed them with missiles from the upper storeys of houses or from natural eminences, in circumstances which made it possible a cavalry charge was a fearful thing, and few had the courage to withstand it. Nevertheless the

[1] Jackson to Fitzroy Somerset dated 28 October 1838. H.O. 50/16. This investigation came to light because the Mayor of Leeds, on being presented with a questionnaire seeking information on the above points, sent it to the Home Office with the comment that he thought it odd to receive such instructions from the military. Tottie to Russell dated 11 October 1838. H.O. 50/16.

[2] Graham to General Arbuthnot dated 25 August 1842. H.O. 79/4.

opinion expressed by Lord Melbourne, early in 1831, that a military force could produce "but a partial and uncertain tranquillity"[1] was substantially borne out by the experiences of the Chartist period.

The trouble lay partly in shortage of numbers. The British Army had passed under a cloud in the years after Waterloo. "Peace, retrenchment and reform" had been the slogan, and drastic cuts had been made in the armed forces. The last of these, which was ordered in the Army Estimates for 1834, provided for a reduction by about 8,000 men, which was to be effected gradually over a period of three years.[2] When it had been completed, Britain became involved in a number of overseas entanglements which made it necessary to maintain a substantial army abroad. Rebellion in Canada and warfare in China and Afghanistan made heavy demands on military resources in the years 1837–1842, when acute social discontent prevailed at home. The result was that the strength of the armed force in the Northern District fell considerably below what it had been in former times, as the following figures testify:

	Artillery	Cavalry	Infantry	Total
1820	282	1761	5481	7524
1826	235	1587	6315	8137
1829	197	1479	4759	6392 (? 6435)
1832	287	738	4716	5741
1837	288	1147	3003	4438
1839 (Jan.)	292	1416	3596	5304 [3]

As the year 1838 drew to its close, and demands for troops began to pour into Manchester from magistrates of the towns of Lancashire and the West Riding alarmed by torchlight meetings and the arming of sections of the working class, General Jackson and his Assistant Adjutant General, Colonel Wemyss, found their disposable force quite inadequate. After sending a troop of

[1] *Lord Melbourne's Papers*, ed. L. C. Sanders, 122–4.
[2] Hans., 3 Ser., XLVI, 1128.
[3] Enclosed in Jackson to H.O. dated 27 February 1839, H.O. 40/53. The figure for January 1839 includes six troops of the 2nd Dragoon Guards and the 96th Regiment of Infantry—altogether about 900 men—recently switched from Ireland. The size of the force in the Northern District down to the end of 1838 was probably not greater than in 1837.

Dragoon Guards to Todmorden, Jackson was left with a single troop of cavalry at Burnley barracks: at Manchester he had only four troops.[1] Despite the addition of 11,000 men to the Army in 1839 and 1840[2] the military situation was again critical when the Plug-Plot disturbances began. The garrison at Manchester, which consisted of 150 cavalrymen, 480 rifles and some artillery,[3] was found "barely sufficient to preserve the peace of the town",[4] and utterly incapable of supplying aid to the neighbouring towns.[5]

In the following year the Tories reduced the establishment by nearly 6,000 men,[6] and as the government was called upon to supply troops, at one and the same time, for the suppression of the Rebecca Riots in South Wales and for the maintenance of order in Ireland (which was stirred by O'Connell's revived Repeal agitation), the pressure on the military force in the British Isles in 1843 was considerable. The Estimates for 1847 and 1848, framed under the supposed threat of French invasion, raised the strength of the Army by about 14,000 men.[7] Nevertheless, when disorder returned in 1848, the military authorities found difficulty in meeting the demands which were made upon them, as they were also required to despatch troops to Ireland to counter the subversive activities of the Confederates and their supporters.[8]

Two main factors tended, however, to alleviate the shortage of troops in England in the age of the Chartists. The first was the tranquillity of Ireland during the early years of the period. It has been seen that from 1843 onwards Ireland competed with Great Britain for troops at times of acute social unrest. In the late eighteen-thirties, however, the sister isle enjoyed an unusual tranquillity as a result of the *rapprochement* between O'Connell

---

[1] Jackson to H.O. dated 13 December 1838. H.O. 40/38.

[2] Hans., 3 Ser., LII, 1088.

[3] Warre to H.O. dated 10 August 1842. H.O. 45/268.

[4] *Ibid.*, 11 August 1842.   [5] *Ibid.*

[6] Fortescue, *op. cit.*, XIII, 4.   [7] *Ibid.*, 9, 15.

[8] In the middle of his preparations to preserve order in Manchester on 10 April 1848 General Arbuthnot found himself obliged to send a whole regiment from Manchester to Ireland. When Smith O'Brien's insurrection broke out in July, three regiments were suddenly withdrawn from the Northern command, and these could only be replaced by bringing troops from distant places. Arbuthnot to H.O. dated 7 April and 2 August 1848. H.O. 45/2410AB.

and the Whigs and the enlightened administration of Thomas
Drummond as Irish Under-Secretary. The government was able,
therefore, to draw troops extensively from Ireland when Chartist
unrest first came to a head. Between December 1838 and August
1839 no fewer than three infantry regiments and three of cavalry[1]
were brought across the Irish Sea into the Northern District. This
was done entirely without detriment to the Irish command, for
the Lord Lieutenant informed Lord John Russell on 2 May 1839
that four or five regiments might safely be withdrawn from his
lieutenancy, in addition to the two which had just been com-
mandeered.[2] Geographically the ports of the east coast of Ireland
were well placed for sending reinforcements by sea into the
Northern District. Even in the 1820s the voyage could be made
in fourteen hours by steam packet.[3]

The second influence was the coming of the railways. The
construction of the British railway network raised markedly the
efficiency of the military force which was maintained on home
service, by making the troops stationed in the southern part of
England more readily available for the restoration of order in the
manufacturing districts of the north. The Quartermaster General
put the point clearly before a parliamentary committee in 1844:

> Then I should say [he testified] that this mode of railway conveyance
> has enabled the army (comparable to the demands made upon it, a very
> small one), to do the work of a very large one; you send a battalion of
> 1,000 men from London to Manchester in nine hours; that same
> battalion marching would take 17 days; and they arrive at the end of
> nine hours just as fresh, or nearly so, as when they started. . . . Without
> that conveyance, you could not have done one tenth part of the work
> that it was required of the troops to do, and necessarily to do, in the
> year 1842.[4]

---

[1] The 96th Regiment of Infantry and the 2nd Dragoon Guards in December
1838 and January 1839; the 10th Regiment, the 79th Regiment of Highlanders
and the 1st Royal Dragoons early in May 1839; the 8th Hussars early in
August 1839.

[2] *Dispatch written by the Lord Lieutenant of Ireland to the Secretary of State,
2nd May 1839, stating what Regiments could be spared from Ireland*, 1844 (30)
XXXIII.

[3] A. Redford, *Labour Migration in England, 1800–1850*, 81.

[4] *Select Committee on Railways, 1844*, 5th Report, Mins. of Evidence, pp.
144–5; 1844 (318) XI.

The transport of troops by rail was not only speedier than on foot. It was also cheaper, on account of the saving of time, for every day the soldier marched he cost the public 1s. 1d. more than he would have done in barracks. The bulk of this additional expenditure was paid to publicans on the line of march. The Quartermaster General estimated that the cost of moving troops from London to Birmingham by rail would be 10s. 7d. per man, by the old and tried method of marching, 10s. 10d., a saving of 3d. per head.[1] An Act "for the better regulation of railways and for the conveyance of troops" which received the royal assent six days before the Plug-Plot disturbances commenced and was probably influenced by the disturbed condition of the country at the time,[2] allowed the Secretary of State to contract with the railway companies for the transport of troops. The rates agreed upon were actually less than the normal third-class passenger fares. A further Act, passed in 1844, fixed the maximum charge at 2d. per mile for officers and 1d. per mile for other ranks.

The habit of moving troops by rail was growing in the thirties and forties of the nineteenth century. It was in the hope of being able to utilize this mode of transport that a large military depot was established at Weedon in Northamptonshire early in the Chartist period, for Weedon was situated on the London and Birmingham Railway.[3] Sir Richard Jackson had planned to make extensive use of railroads for moving troops to the scene of riot, when he commanded the Northern District in the early months of 1839, and his successor, Napier, had used the Liverpool and Manchester line to transport reinforcements from Ireland from the former to the latter town.[4] It was in 1842, however, that railways were first employed to convey large numbers of troops from the garrisons of the south to deal with an emergency in the industrial north and midlands. On 13 August the 3rd Battalion the Grenadier Guards, which was stationed in St. George's Barracks, Charing Cross, was despatched to Manchester by rail.

[1] *Select Committee on Railways, 1844,* 5th Report, Mins. of Evidence, p. 144.
[2] The clause affecting conveyance of troops, which was quite irrelevant to the main purposes of the Bill, was added at the last moment. H. G. Lewin, *Early British Railways,* 134.
[3] *Ibid.*
[4] Napier, *op. cit.,* II, 39.

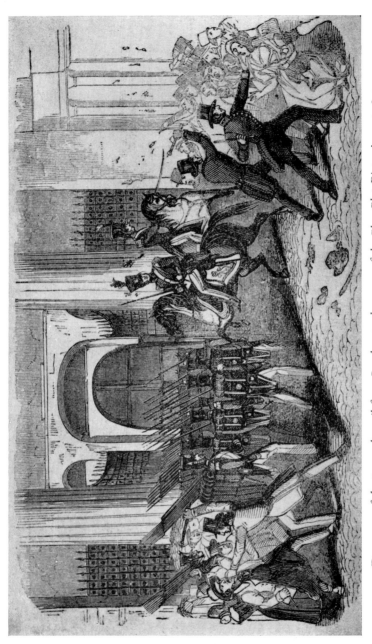

Departure of the troops by rail from London to the scene of the Plug-Plot Riots, August 1842

With it proceeded a troop of Royal Horse Artillery with two guns, and the entire force was in Manchester by 5 o'clock on the following morning. In the ensuing twenty-four hours a further troop of the Artillery from Woolwich and 600 men of the 34th Regiment of Foot from Portsmouth passed along the London and Birmingham Railway to the scene of tumult.[1]

By drawing on the resources of the Irish command, and by using the railroads to convey troops from distant parts of Great Britain, the governments of the period were able to build up heavy military concentrations in the disturbed areas, and to do so with reasonable rapidity once the necessity had been made clear. By the end of 1839, a force consisting of 10,527 men had been concentrated in the Army districts subject to Chartist disorder. Of these, 7,686 were in the Northern District, 969 under the Midland command, and 1,872 in South Wales.[2] In August 1842, once the initial shortage had been recognized, a regular force of 10,000 men was speedily drawn together for the restoration of order.[3] Eighty-two officers and 1,167 men were serving in South Wales in the early months of 1844, when the Rebecca Riots were drawing to their close.[4] In London alone, in 1848, 7,123 officers and men were assembled in preparation for the expected Chartist demonstration of 10 April. Nine hundred and fifty-eight were drawn from Windsor, 532 from Chichester, 781 from Dover and 678 from Chatham.[5] The remainder was supplied from garrisons within, or in the immediate vicinity of the capital. A second large concentration, consisting of 5,303 men of all ranks, was effected in the metropolis on 12 June 1848, the day of the prohibited Chartist meeting at Bonners Fields.[6]

The worst shortages were, therefore, local shortages capable of

[1] *The Manchester Guardian*, 17 August 1842, pp. 1–2.

[2] The figures are for January 1840. See Returns of the Distribution of the Army in Great Britain. H.O. 50/16.

[3] Figure quoted by Sir Henry Hardinge when presenting the Army Estimates in February 1843. Hans., 3 Ser., LXVI, 1363.

[4] Extract from United Services Gazette reproduced in *The Welshman*, 16 February 1844, p. 3.

[5] Memoranda by the Duke of Wellington with Statement showing the Distribution of the Troops in 1848. War Office Papers 30/81.

[6] *Ibid.*

being met, after some delay, by switching troops from one part of the British Isles to another. But a more general shortage arose when large numbers of troops were required simultaneously in more than one region. Thus when, a week after the departure of the Grenadier Guards from London to restore order in Manchester in August 1842, the disorders began to spread to the capital, the Duke of Wellington, who was Commander-in-Chief, found it necessary to press for the return of the Guards to London, on the grounds that they would be needed there.[1] The continuance of unrest in the Manchester area made it impossible, however, to comply with his wishes until a regiment had been brought up from Plymouth to relieve the Guards from duty at Manchester, and owing to the lack of railroad communications in the south-western sector of England it was a matter of a day or two before the relief movement could be carried out.[2] It is evident that a large concentration of troops could only be built up in one area by denuding another of protective force. Had the Chartists succeeded in producing a truly general rising affecting several widely separated regions at once, it would probably not have been possible to supply troops to put it down—at least not for a considerable time.

It was not merely a want of sufficient numbers that hindered the troops in the performance of the duty of maintaining public order; shortage of good barrack accommodation was a further impediment. An extensive campaign of barrack building had been waged during the French Revolutionary and Napoleonic era, partly because the anti-Jacobin alarm of the 1790s had turned attention to the need to provide safe accommodation for the troops stationed in the manufacturing districts of England. And by the end of the French Wars there were 159 barracks capable of housing 16,854 cavalry and 138,410 infantry. Of these, however, only a dozen or so were situated in or near the industrial areas of the North and Midlands.[3] Moreover the post-war retrenchment in military expenditure left its mark on barrack accommodation.

---

[1] Wellington to Graham dated 20 August 1842. Graham Papers, Bundle 52B.
[2] Graham to Wellington dated 21 August 1842. *Ibid.*
[3] John Adolphus, *The Political State of the British Empire*, II, 293–7.

The wooden temporary barracks which had multiplied during the war period were abandoned, and many more permanent structures were allowed to fall into decay.[1] Hence, when the Chartist disturbances called for the stationing of a large military force in the industrial areas, a serious want of barracks was felt. The majority of the smaller towns and manufacturing villages had no barracks at all, and the temporary barracks in the larger towns of Lancashire were of such a character as to prejudice the health and security of the soldiers lodged in them. Those at Bolton, Blackburn and Rochdale, which had been hired for a temporary purpose about twelve years before the commencement of the Chartist disturbances, and had been continuously occupied ever since, gave grave disquiet to Jackson and Napier. At Bolton 48 soldiers were accommodated in a room 72 feet long, 36 feet broad and 12 feet high. When Captain Boldero of the Ordnance visited the building in 1842 he could not see the men for smoke.[2] These temporary barracks were not only unhealthy; they were also insecure. Napier, who visited them in June 1839, noted in his journal that "the Chartists may place marksmen at windows commanding egress from the barracks, and setting fire to the last, shoot the soldiers as they attempt to form".[3]

The shortage of barrack accommodation placed difficulties in the way of stationing a large military force in the manufacturing districts and of diffusing it throughout those districts for the protection of the scattered towns and villages threatened with riot.

Principally concerned to have troops on hand in their several localities the magistrates were well content to solve the problem of accommodation by billeting the soldiers upon the innkeepers in the manner prescribed in the Mutiny Act, but the military authorities objected to this method of housing their force. They argued quite justifiably that it exposed the soldiers to the risk of being overpowered. In order to distribute the burden fairly

[1] Copy of Major-General Burgoyne's Memorandum to the Ordnance, 1848. H.O. 45/2410AB.
[2] Hans., 3 Ser., LXVII, 324.
[3] Napier, *op. cit.*, II, 47.

among the innkeepers, who were apt to complain if asked to take more men than their neighbours, the magistrates usually billeted the troops with the maximum dispersion. A squadron of the 3rd Dragoon Guards, which proceeded to Huddersfield in December 1838, was scattered dangerously in billets, despite the request of the commanding officer that his men should be billeted as compactly as possible.[1] At Halifax 42 troopers were placed in 21 distinct billets situated at a distance from one another, the men being also separated from their horses.[2] A resolute band of insurrectionists could have wiped out a whole troop thus accommodated by attacking its members singly as they slept.[3]

A further objection to private billeting, in the minds of the Army chiefs, was that it rendered the soldiers more liable to be corrupted or suborned than they would otherwise have been. Troopers billeted upon innkeepers were more susceptible than those in barracks to the influence of disaffected persons who would chat to them in the public houses, treat them to free beer and present them with copies of the "publications of a strong republican nature and containing the most plausible arguments against the constitution" which habitually circulated in such places.[4] We learn, for example, from a letter written by a magistrate of Abergavenny two days after the Newport Rising, that immediately before the outbreak several of the troopers stationed in his locality had been found by the sergeants drinking with strange men who were treating them.[5] Moreover, it was far more difficult to detect cases of disaffection in the ranks when the men were in billets, and the taint might thus spread without any effective measures being taken to counteract it.

In every respect private billeting was accounted bad for discipline. The Military Secretary at the Horse Guards wrote

[1] O.C. Squadron 3rd Dragoon Guards to Wemyss dated 24 December 1838. H.O. 40/39.

[2] Napier, *op. cit.*, II, 16.

[3] In April 1839 General Napier received information that a plan to cut off the soldiers in their billets had actually been discussed in the public houses of Halifax. *Ibid.*

[4] Napier to H.O. dated 13 February 1841. H.O. 45/41.

[5] Powell to H.O. dated 6 November 1839. H.O. 40/45.

to the Home Office in July 1839 complaining that, in the three companies quartered in billets in the Chartist strongholds of Newtown and Llanidloes, "crime has considerably increased ... as compared with the companies stationed at Montgomery, where a temporary Barrack has been afforded, and that no less than 15 desertions have taken place from Newtown and Llanidloes".[1]

As an alternative to this obnoxious policy of quartering the soldiers upon innkeepers, the generals who commanded the Northern District in 1838 and 1839 strove to keep their men together in masses at places where barrack accommodation was available. When Chartist excitement intensified in the winter of 1838-9, Sir Richard Jackson advised against bringing troops into the District from Ireland on the grounds that he had not adequate barracks to contain more men. He suggested that arrangements should be made instead to send reinforcements speedily from Dublin when they were required.[2] He aimed to keep large reserves at centres which lay outside the disturbed portions of his District, e.g. at Chester, Hull and Weedon barracks in Northamptonshire, and to make extensive use of the railways, in the event of emergency, to bring an adequate force to bear on points where its services were needed.[3] As the magistrates were hostile, and the Home Office (which had supreme authority to determine the location of troops on home service and could over-rule the commanders of the districts) pursued a rather vacillating policy, Jackson was no more than partially successful in preventing the dispersion of his force. His subordinate, Colonel Wemyss, managed to talk round the civil authorities at Leigh and Ashton-under-Lyne in December 1838 when they and other magistrates of Lancashire were clamorous for a system of small military detachments based on a precedent of several years earlier,[4] but the head of the Northern District was unable to avoid sending troops to be stationed in billets in Huddersfield, Todmorden and

---

[1] Fitzroy Somerset to S. M. Phillipps dated 12 July 1839. H.O. 50/16.
[2] Jackson to H.O. dated 27 February 1839. H.O. 40/53.
[3] Jackson to H.O. dated 6 January, 25 February and 9 March 1839. H.O. 40/53.
[4] Jackson to H.O. dated 19 and 21 December 1838. H.O. 40/39. Wemyss to H.O. dated 14 December 1838. H.O. 40/38.

M

Halifax.[1] When he handed over his command to Napier at the end of March 1839, his force consisted of some 26 detachments.[2]

Sir Charles Napier was a more uncompromising opponent of detachments than most of the other leading military figures of his time. His experiences in Ireland during the rebellions of 1798 and 1803 had bred in him a persistent fear that isolated troops of cavalry dispersed in billets might fall victims to a sudden and unexpected attack, and in his zeal to protect the men under his command from such a disaster he thrust aside the arguments which reconciled so many of his brother officers to the practice of stationing troops in towns where adequate barracks did not exist.[3] His policy was to have as few detachments as possible, and to make it a condition of the grant of troops that suitable barracks should be provided, free of charge to the government, by the inhabitants of the districts receiving the protection. He insisted that such barracks should be perfectly comfortable for the private soldiers, with officers' quarters adjacent to those of the men, and that they should be situated in the suburbs of towns where they

---

[1] The choice of Halifax as a station was due to the intervention of the Home Office. Jackson to H.O. dated 23 December 1838. H.O. 40/39.

[2] Napier, *op. cit.*, II, 7.

[3] Wemyss was willing to admit the necessity for having troops on hand in the towns threatened with disturbance for the purpose of encouraging the well-disposed. Napier, *op. cit.*, II, 13. Jackson, while deprecating the condition of the barracks at Bolton, Blackburn and Rochdale, affirmed his belief that "it is positively absurd to suppose that the above towns, possessing an immense population (increasing, impoverished and most excitable) can be left without troops at any time, or under any circumstances". Extract of a Letter from Lieutenant General Sir Richard Jackson, K.C.B., to the Quarter Master General of the Forces dated 14 February 1839. H.O. 50/16. Lord Hill, the Commander-in-Chief, agreed with Napier that "all troops required for the assistance of the Civil Power against insurgents should be kept as much apart as possible from the insurgents", but he also held that it should be the "first and special care" of the general commanding the Northern District to "employ the force under his command to aid and assist the magistrates in preserving the public peace, however difficult the circumstances attending such duty may be". Fitzroy Somerset to S. M. Phillipps dated 5 August 1839, giving Lord Hill's comments on a letter written by Napier to the Home Office relative to the state of accommodation for troops in the Northern District. H.O. 50/16. To Napier, however, the safety of the troops was the overriding consideration. Napier, *op. cit.*, II, 13.

would not be hemmed in by other buildings.[1] "A strong detachment lodged in the skirts of a town", he wrote to the Home Office in July 1839, "commands that town, whereas if it be posted in the midst of the town it is likely to be commanded by that town."[2]

Within a month of his assumption of the command of the Northern District he had won over the Home Secretary to support him in refusing to station troops in localities which would not provide suitable lodgement.[3] Faced with the alternatives of supplying barracks and failing to obtain troops, the wealthier inhabitants of several manufacturing towns came together in their localities and subscribed to guarantee funds for defraying the expense of hiring buildings and converting them into barracks.[4]

[1] Fenwick, Shepperdson and Fawcett to Russell dated 21 July 1839. H.O. 40/42.

[2] F. Somerset to Phillipps dated 5 August 1839, giving extracts from Napier's letter to the Home Office dated 24 July 1839. H.O. 50/16.

[3] At first the Home Secretary was inclined to side with the magistrates against Napier, but the latter's strong representations against private billeting soon gained the backing of government. From the end of April onwards Lord John Russell was to be found rejecting the frantic pleas of the magistrates for detachments, and ordering those who already possessed troops to house them more compactly. See Napier, op. cit., II, 21. Also H.O. to Harewood dated 3 May 1839. H.O. 41/13, and minute written on Napier to H.O. dated 25 April 1839. H.O. 40/53. But Home Office support of Napier was not absolutely consistent. Towards the end of July 1839, the excitement prevailing on the North-eastern coalfield caused Lord John Russell to order detachments to key points, without insisting on the provision of barracks which conformed to Napier's standards. Napier protested, and the Home Secretary conveyed his letter to the Commander-in-Chief, who wrote back in rather equivocal terms. See F. Somerset to Phillipps' dated 5 August 1839. H.O. 50/16. Extracts from this letter are cited above, p. 168, n. 3. The Home Office response was to draft a letter to Napier, laying upon him the responsibility of deciding whether or not detachments should be granted, but exhorting him to "make such arrangements as shall be best calculated to ensure the safety and comfort of the troops, and at the same time to afford the readiest support to the civil authorities under all circumstances in every part of your District". Phillipps to Napier dated 7 August 1839. H.O. 41/14. When Napier replied to these self-cancelling instructions by asking for advice as to how he should act in a specific instance, the Home Secretary not only declined to give it, but proclaimed his lack of confidence in Napier by offering to send Lord Strafford into his District to assist him. Phillipps to Napier dated 10 August 1839. H.O. 41/14.

[4] Mence to Cooke dated 3 August 1839. H.O. 40/51. Evans to H.O. dated 10 May 1839. H.O. 40/37.

Thus Napier obtained new temporary barracks, conformable to the high standards which he laid down, at Loughborough, Barnsley, Mansfield, Bradford, Bury and Ashton-under-Lyne.[1] These new barracks provided a partial solution of the problem of local defence at a time when the provinces were grossly under-policed. They also eased the overall shortage of barrack accommodation in the Northern District, and helped to make possible the further augmentation of the military force in the District which Jackson had hesitated to recommend on account of the want of proper quarters, and which was effected under Napier in May and August 1839 by drawing troops from Ireland.[2] Not all the reinforcement went, however, into outlying detachments; Napier had been granted permission to hire barracks at the government's expense at Manchester and Nottingham, two strategically important centres,[3] and substantial concentrations of troops were built up there in the spring of 1839.

The arrangement whereby the inhabitants of the disturbed districts provided barrack accommodation at their own expense for the troops who protected them was not destined to endure. Nevertheless, as the Chartist period progressed, steps were taken by the central government to ease the situation by building new permanent barracks. At first the work of improvement was held up by financial difficulties. The Treasury scotched a plan launched in 1833 for building a permanent barrack at Blackburn to replace the temporary ones at Bolton, Blackburn and Rochdale,[4] which had been hired some six years earlier for a temporary purpose, and had

[1] Napier to H.O. dated 2 November 1839. H.O. 40/53.

[2] It is clear, however, that the supply of barracks was still inadequate to the demand for them. After the second instalment of reinforcements had been brought over from Ireland in August 1839, all the cavalry barracks in the north of England were full, and the only alternative disposition for a troop of horse billeted in Carlisle was a similar mode of billeting in Newcastle. Napier to H.O. dated 28 August 1839. H.O. 40/53. See Home Office minute written on this letter.

[3] Napier, *op. cit.*, II, 27. Manchester was expected to be the scene of the main Chartist rising in May 1839. *Ibid.*, 23, 28-9. Troops stationed at Nottingham might be used to check the proposed march on London from the north of England which the Chartists threatened to make about that time. *Ibid.*, 33.

[4] Fitzroy Somerset to H.O. dated 8 April 1839. H.O. 50/16.

afterwards been kept continuously occupied,[1] although they were manifestly unfit for the soldiers to live in, being both unhealthy and unsafe.[2] The budgetary problems of the Whigs in the later eighteen-thirties rendered the government even more indisposed to sanction an outlay of public money on barracks. But the pressure applied by Generals Jackson and Napier and a forceful speech delivered by Colonel Thomas of the 20th Regiment in the House of Commons, when the Ordnance Estimates for 1839 were presented, succeeded in inducing a change of policy, more especially as the need for a contribution from the central government towards the provision of accommodation for the troops was further emphasized shortly afterwards by demonstrations of the unwillingness of the subscribers to the temporary barracks to continue to foot the whole bill for these, once the Chartist crisis of 1839 was over.[3] The Ordnance Estimates for the year 1841 provided for the expenditure of £20,000 on barrack accommodation in the disturbed areas of England;[4] £30,000 was voted for the purpose in 1842, £45,000 in 1843,[5] whilst in 1844 £117,000 was allocated for the construction of a new barrack in Manchester.[6]

There had been much discussion by the heads of departments as to whether the money should be spent on building a large number of small barracks or on a few large ones centrally situated.[7] Thanks to the influence of Sir Charles Napier, it was the latter view which prevailed, and the first of the new barracks were ordered to be built at Bury, which occupied a central position

[1] Extract from Jackson to Quarter Master General dated 14 February 1839. H.O. 50/16.

[2] Napier, op. cit., II, 47.

[3] In January the Committee of Merchants, Manufacturers and Inhabitants of the Town and Parliamentary Borough of Bury, which had raised funds for the barrack, asked for assistance in paying the rent of the buildings. Walker to H.O. dated 23 January 1840. H.O. 40/54. Early in February the magistrates of Hyde and Ashton resolved that the government should be recommended to refund the expenses incurred in fitting up the barrack at Ashton. Brooke and Hall to H.O. dated 6 February 1840. H.O. 40/54.

[4] Hans., 3 Ser., LVII, 37.

[5] Ibid., LXVII, 324.

[6] Ibid., LXXIII, 779.

[7] Napier, op. cit., II, 118.

among the towns of Rochdale, Bolton and Wigan,[1] and Ashton-under-Lyne, which stood in a similar relationship to Oldham, Hyde, Glossop and Stalybridge.[2] Meanwhile, the task of supplying troops in the event of an emergency to such towns as were not favoured with barracks was simplified by the filling in of the railway network and the growth of the habit of moving troops by rail. The magistrates of these localities were advised by the military commanders to hold railway carriages in reserve to bring troops when needed, instead of clamouring for a detachment to be stationed on the spot.[3]

These developments led to the withdrawal, one by one, of the detachments stationed in the temporary barracks. Those at Ashton-under-Lyne, Bury, Todmorden and Haydock Lodge were given up in 1841, before work on the new permanent barracks at Bury and Ashton had even been commenced.[4] Bolton, on the other hand, succeeded in preventing the withdrawal of its military force, both the mayor and Colonel Wemyss thinking it too risky to rely on assistance brought from Manchester by rail, as the track might be destroyed by rioters.[5] But confidence gradually increased, especially after the Plug-Plot disturbances, when the authorities had proved their ability to keep open the lines of railway communication amidst widespread turbulence. In 1845 there was a marked reduction in the number of military detachments. Troops were withdrawn from South Wales, Huddersfield and Preston in February, from Stalybridge in March, from Newtown and Llanidloes in July and from Newcastle-under-Lyne in September.[6] As a policy for the future, General Burgoyne, the Inspector General of Fortifications, suggested in a Memorandum for the Ordnance drawn up in October 1848, that reserve depots for between 3,000 and 5,000 men, situated away from the great towns, should be created to house the additional troops

---

[1] Napier to H.O. dated 2 March 1841. H.O. 45/41; H.O. to Napier dated 31 March 1841. H.O. 41/16.

[2] Wemyss to H.O. dated 14 October (? November) 1841. H.O. 45/43.

[3] Wemyss to H.O. dated 30 June 1841. H.O. 45/43.

[4] Wemyss to H.O. dated 14 October (? November) 1841. H.O. 45/43.

[5] *Ibid.*; Hans., 3 Ser., LXVII, 324.

[6] Letters from H.O. to Fitzroy Somerset. H.O. 41/18.

which he thought would be required to maintain order in England in consequence of the disaffection occasioned by the example of the revolutionary movement in France.[1]

The decision to build centrally situated barracks represented a victory for the policy of keeping the troops together in masses, which was advocated by several of the leading military figures of the age. That policy did not arise entirely (though in large measure it did) from considerations appertaining to the supply of barracks; it was also due to a very natural and well-founded apprehension that if the number of detachments was allowed to grow, the size of each would be reduced to such a level as to place the soldiers at a disadvantage in encounters with the mob, and the reserve at the disposal of the General commanding the District would be whittled away. Napier aimed at detachments of not less than two companies of infantry and a troop of cavalry, thinking that the two arms should always be combined.[2] In practice, however, he did not always realize his objective. He sent single troops of cavalry to several towns during the Chartist unrest of 1839,[3] and his brother officer, Colonel Thorn, who commanded the Midland District, detached his men in even smaller numbers. Withdrawing a company of the 79th Regiment from Lane End in the Potteries in June 1839, he left a party consisting of one sergeant and eleven rank and file to co-operate with the civil power.[4]

The danger was increased when the already small detachments were subdivided for the purpose of operating against the Chartists. Owing to the absence of a professional police force in many places, there was considerable pressure upon the military to perform duties which required that they should act in minute

[1] Copy of Major-General Sir John Burgoyne's Memorandum. H.O. 45/2410AB.

[2] Napier, *op. cit.*, II, 58.

[3] To Mansfield and Loughborough in July. Napier to H.O. dated 15 July 1839. H.O. 40/53. To Barnsley and Bradford in August. Mence to Cooke dated 3 August 1839. H.O. 40/51. Napier to H.O. dated 22 August 1839. H.O. 40/53.

[4] Thorn to H.O. dated 4 June 1839. H.O. 40/53. On 22 July 1839 Thorn detached a subaltern, a sergeant and 20 rank and file of the 1st Bn., Rifle Brigade, to Coventry. Thorn to H.O. dated 22 July 1839. H.O. 40/53.

parties. They were called upon to guard public buildings, to patrol the streets of the large and turbulent towns, to escort prisoners taken in the course of disturbances, and on at least one occasion to execute distress warrants for non-payment of poor rates.[1] For nearly two months after the incendiary riots in the Bull Ring on 15 July 1839 the 4th Dragoon Guards patrolled the streets of Birmingham by night,[2] and a sergeant's guard, consisting of twelve privates, mounted daily at the Public Office.[3] During the disturbances in the West Riding in the summer of 1842, parties of ten were employed to escort Chartist prisoners.

One such party, which was composed of cavalrymen of the 11th Hussars under the command of Lieutenant W. G. Pitt, set out from Halifax on 16 August to convey seventeen prisoners, taken in an affray at Messrs. Ackroyds' mill, to Elland station, whence they were to be transported by rail to Wakefield for safe custody, prior to their examination by the magistrates. For the journey by road to Elland the prisoners were placed in two horse-drawn omnibuses guarded by the soldiers. An attempt was made to rescue them, but this was unsuccessful, and the charges were safely lodged in the train for Wakefield. Now it happened that, just after the two omnibuses arrived at Elland, a third omnibus left the station with a load of ordinary railway passengers who were travelling to Halifax from places like Leeds and Manchester, and had alighted from the train at Elland. This vehicle proceeded towards Halifax along the road which had just been used by the military escort. When it arrived at Salter Hebble, where the road runs alongside a very steep hill, it was met by a mob of several thousand working men anxious to be avenged on the authorities for the arrest of their comrades. Having ascertained that the omnibus contained only railway passengers, and that none of the officials participating in the escort were inside, the mob was about to grant it a safe passage, when the party of soldiers return-

---

[1] In the Cardigan Union during the Rebecca Riots. Love to H.O. dated 21 September 1843. H.O. 45/453.

[2] The order for the cancellation of the patrols was issued on 13 September 1839. H.O. 40/53.

[3] Thorn to H.O. dated 27 August 1839. H.O. 40/53.

The attack on the military at Salter Hebble, August 1842

ing from Elland came up behind it. Immediately the crowd began to hurl enormous stones—some of them weighing as much as 20 lbs—down on to the troops and omnibus. Arrayed on the heights the mob enjoyed a tremendous advantage. Under the impact of the volley of stones the omnibus horses shied, and became entangled with the cavalrymen, three of whom were felled from their steeds and left lying on the ground. A section of the mob rushed down upon the prostrate soldiers, who had been abandoned by their comrades, destroyed their muskets and swords and kicked and beat their bodies in a brutal fashion. From this predicament they were rescued by the return of their companions, who loaded with ball and opened fire on the crowd.[1] At no time during the Chartist period had regular troops come nearer to being overwhelmed by rioters, and although the plight of the former was in large measure due to the unfavourable nature of the terrain, the incident furnished a striking illustration of the danger of employing troops in small parties.

But the military authorities were very conscious of the risk, and succeeded in imposing a check on such practices. During the disturbances which swept over the manufacturing districts in the summer of 1842, the officers commanding the troops in several of the towns visited by rioters and turnout mobs rigidly declined to split up their forces. On 11 August a large body of strikers poured into Stockport from the Hyde district, and proceeded to turn out the mills. The military force was kept drawn up in the market place under the command of the magistrates, and when the proprietors of Messrs. W. & J. Bradshaw's mill (which was not more than five minutes' walk away from the market place) appealed to the mayor for the assistance of six soldiers to beat off the attack on their factory, the request was refused on the grounds that the commanding officer would not divide his men.[2] The consequence was that the mill was broken into by the mob, and

[1] This account of the incident is constructed from two separate accounts appearing in *The Times* and from one received by the magistrates of Leeds. See *The Times*, 19 August 1842, p. 5; Mayor and Magistrates of Leeds to H.O. dated 16 August 1842, and enclosed report. H.O. 45/264.

[2] Statement of evidence by Messrs. Bradshaw's cashier enclosed in Bradshaw to H.O. dated 6 September 1842. H.O. 45/242.

James Bradshaw was roughly handled.[1] Four days later, whilst the town of Hanley lay at the mercy of a mob of incendiaries on the night of 15 August, the troops stood idly by at Newcastle-under-Lyme. The commanding officer, Sir Robert Douglas, stated that he could not divide his force, and that its removal would endanger the peace of Newcastle, where many families and much property had been placed for safety, and whither all the prisoners had been brought.[2] Furthermore, it was the policy of Sir William Warre, who commanded the Northern District, that the troops should remain in barracks until riot was actually apprehended. On these grounds the sergeant's guard which had been placed for the defence of the Court House at Stockport was withdrawn at the height of the Plug-Plot unrest, despite the protestations of the mayor.[3] Likewise at Bolton the officer commanding the troops was ordered to retire the guard at the Police Office unless the utmost emergency existed.[4]

Such restrictions (and the reluctance of the military leaders to station forces in towns which could not supply proper barracks) inevitably complicated the problem of local defence, by leaving certain districts and certain parts of districts unprotected by regular troops. It seems probable, however, that the concentrating policy favoured by Jackson, by Napier and by Warre, was the one best calculated to promote not only the safety of the private soldier, but the stability of the state and of society. For, as Napier never tired of pointing out,[5] had a small military detachment been overthrown by rioters the moral effect would have been incalculable. The disaffected throughout the country would have been encouraged to rise in rebellion, and to throw themselves confidently against the troops, and the latter would have suffered a

---

[1] H. Heginbotham, *Stockport: Ancient and Modern*, I, 101–2.
[2] Rose to H.O. dated 18 November 1842. H.O. 45/260.
[3] Nelstrop to H.O. dated 12 August 1842. H.O. 45/242.
[4] Winder to H.O. dated 18 August 1842. H.O. 45/249.
[5] "If only a corporal's guard was cut off", he wrote to Wemyss, "it would be 'a total defeat of the troops' ere it reached London, Edinburgh and Dublin; and before the contradiction arrived the disaffected in the moral exaltation of supposed victory, would be in arms." Napier, *op. cit.*, II, 14. See also *ibid.*, 16, 24–5 and 59.

lowering of morale which might have led them to desert in large numbers to the side of the populace.

No assessment of the efficiency of the Regular Army in the machinery of public order would be complete without consideration of the loyalty of the force. It is necessary to inquire whether the private soldiers showed any marked sympathy with the popular aspirations of the time, and whether they were likely to be deflected from their duty by such sympathies. The soldiery had much in common with the discontented populace of the towns. They belonged to the same race, spoke the same language, believed in the same religion, endured the same pecuniary hardships, and joined in a common hatred of the police. So great was the animosity between the troops and the new professional police forces that even the officers of the former were prone to insult the police in the execution of their duty, as at Coventry on the night of 15 October 1838.[1] Other clashes between military and police occurred at Ipswich in December 1838,[2] at Hull in July 1839,[3] and at Newcastle in June 1841.[4] The discord arose in part from the disparity in the payment received by the soldiers and the police respectively, but mainly, it would seem, from the resistance which the police were compelled to offer to the drunken frolics of the soldiery. To obviate such unpleasantness, the Metropolitan Force was instructed not to arrest drunken or disorderly soldiers.[5]

Radical demagogues and the Chartist press were not slow to play upon this common feeling between the military and the masses. Richard Oastler was the author of numerous newspaper-articles and pamphlets written with a view to seducing the troops from their loyalty.[6] In February 1838 *The Northern Star* took up the subject of the brutal practice of flogging as a military punishment, in a series of letters and articles accompanied by lurid pictorial illustrations. At Stockport, where the *Northern*

[1] Macdonald to Ewart dated 3 November 1838. H.O. 50/16.
[2] H.O. to Mayor of Ipswich dated 5 December 1838. H.O. 41/13.
[3] Napier to H.O. dated 24 July 1839. H.O. 40/53.
[4] Napier to H.O. dated 12 June 1841. H.O. 45/41.
[5] W. M. Somerville to the Metropolitan Police Commissioners dated 22 September 1846. H.O. 60/15.
[6] Wemyss to H.O. dated 24 February 1839. H.O. 40/43.

Liberator was issued to the soldiers at the inhabitants' expense, a man of the 20th Regiment handed to his Commanding Officer a pamphlet which began:

Soldiers. The following little paragraph is copied from the *Northern Liberator*. Read it, and, after you have done so, ask yourself the following questions: Must I, at the word of command, fire and destroy my fellow creatures, more especially when policemen have aggravated them almost to madness, hired ruffians at 3/6d. per day, who enjoy all the pleasures of life, and I, as a soldier at 13d. per day, exposed to all kinds of weather, harassed almost to death in protecting those very policemen who have been the aggressors? Forbid it humanity! Forbid it Justice! Forbid it God ! ! !

Then followed the moving story of how the widow of a Waterloo veteran, when nearly blind and afflicted with rheumatism, had been deprived of outdoor relief, and compelled to enter a 'bastille'.[1]

Some of the propaganda undoubtedly reached its mark. When Napier went to Nottingham in July 1839 he discovered that one of the riflemen stationed there attended all the Chartist meetings in the town. This soldier was a man of ability, a chosen man.[2] By way of contrast there was the "drunken rascal of the 81st" at Hull who exclaimed, "Damn your eyes we are all Chartists!"[3] In May 1839 Colonel Wemyss received an anonymous letter, purporting to come from a soldier, to the effect that he and his comrades were resolved to make common cause with the people, that they (the soldiers) were the first to suffer from the New Poor Law when discharged, and that they would not fire on their countrymen. It is of course open to argument that this letter may have been a fake, but Napier suspected that it was genuinely written by a soldier of the 20th Regiment.[4]

It is difficult, however, to measure the extent of the disaffection in the British Army as the evidence is somewhat conflicting. On the one hand it is clear that Napier regarded the Chartist threat to the morale of the troops with some concern. In pressing the Home Office to bring additional troops from Ireland towards the end of

---

[1] Napier to H.O. dated 29 July 1839. H.O. 40/53.
[2] Napier, *op. cit.*, II, 49.   [3] *Ibid.*, 62.   [4] *Ibid.*, 35.

July 1839, he urged that regiments containing the greatest number of Irishmen should be selected. "The difference of religion and country", he wrote, "offers additional guards for the soldier's fidelity."[1] He wished to reason as man to man with the Chartist rifleman of Nottingham, and was only prevented from doing so by the intervention of the Home Secretary, who feared that the incident might get into the newspapers.[2] Napier's concern does not prove that Chartist opinions were already widespread among the Queen's troops—merely that he feared that such a situation might develop. In his letters to his brother, Colonel William Napier, however, the General conveyed unmistakably the impression that at least a substantial minority of his force was infected with Chartism. "There are many Chartists among the Rifles", he wrote in July.[3] In January 1840 he stated that the men were "making long strides in liberal opinions".[4]

The first of these assertions is not easily reconciled with a statement made by Napier in a letter to Lord Fitzroy Somerset that the Chartist rifleman at Nottingham was "remarkable for having no comrade and keeping aloof from the other men".[5] Nor is the view that a substantial number of soldiers was Chartist in any disloyal sense of the word compatible with the fact that, when Napier wrote to Lord Fitzroy Somerset on 31 July 1839, to impress upon him and upon the government the danger to the loyalty of the troops arising from small detachments, he was able to cite no more than a few isolated instances of disaffection.[6] On this occasion he could have had no motive for minimizing the amount of unrest in his force—quite the contrary. It seems likely then that the kind of political outlook which was liable to

[1] *Ibid.*, 61.
[2] *Ibid.*, 54. "My whole success, or hopes of it", Napier wrote to his brother, "rested on my being known to hold the man's own opinions, and only differing as to the means taken to give them effect: upon the general himself reasoning with him; on my being an old rifleman." *Ibid.*, 54-5.
[3] *Ibid.*, 54.   [4] *Ibid.*, 114.   [5] *Ibid.*, 49.
[6] *Ibid.*, 62. There is room for argument that a more considerable number of soldiers, like Napier himself, held opinions of an advanced radical nature without sympathizing with physical-force methods. Napier's letter to his brother in January 1840 seems to suggest this. *Ibid.*, 114. But this can hardly affect the argument.

produce a refusal to obey orders was limited to a few exceptional soldiers.

The view that the vast majority of the men was unaffected by the attempts to seduce the troops is supported by the testimony of Alexander Somerville, late of the Scots Greys, who had actually been the spokesman of political unrest in that regiment in the days of the Reform Bill struggle. "Let not the window breakers deceive themselves," he wrote in March 1848, when disorder flavoured with Chartism was extending in the metropolis, "the soldiers are not with them. In 1832, the nation and the House of Commons were almost unanimous, with a well defined purpose before them. There is no great political purpose before the nation now."[1]

There is no evidence that the troops ever faltered in their duty when called upon to put down Chartist and other disturbances. On the contrary, we know that at Bolton in August 1839, at Newport in the November of the same year, and at Preston, Burslem and Halifax during the riots of August 1842, the soldiers obeyed the word of command to fire on the mob without demur. On some occasions, when they had been severely harassed, they lost patience completely with the disturbers of the peace. Thus, according to information received by the magistrates of Leeds, the soldiers in the Halifax district vowed vengeance on the mob for the ill-treatment of their comrades at Salter Hebble in August 1842.[2] Greville tells us that in June 1848 the military stationed in the capital were "so savage that Lord Londonderry told the Duke of Wellington he was sure, if a collision took place, the officers of his regiment would not be able to restrain their men".[3]

In the circumstances in which it was actually required to function during the Chartist period, the British Army proved perfectly reliable. Whether it would have remained loyal if it had been used to uphold a more arbitrary form of government—to break up peaceful meetings, or to compel strikers to resume

---

[1] A. Somerville, The Autobiography of a Working Man, 250.

[2] Mayor and Magistrates of Leeds to H.O. dated 16 August 1842 and enclosed report. H.O. 45/264. For details of the Salter Hebble incident see above, pp. 174–5.

[3] C. C. F. Greville, A Journal of the Reign of Queen Victoria, 1837–52, III, 190.

work at the point of the bayonet—is, however, problematical. There is at least a strong presumption that, in such conditions, the liberal opinions which, according to Napier's correspondence, were fast spreading in the ranks, would have asserted themselves, and that this would have led to a widespread refusal to obey orders.[1] It is equally doubtful whether the loyalty of the troops would have held if they had been scattered about the country as the magistrates wished, a dozen here and a dozen there, and if the Chartists had succeeded in overpowering a number of small detachments. Only when they found themselves hemmed in on every side by barricades, and exhausted by the manœuvres of the Parisian mob did the French troops go over to the side of the people in the July Revolution of 1830, and, if sufficiently harassed and demoralized, English troops might do the same.

But such considerations take us out of the realm of history into that of conjecture. As matters stood the troops at the disposal of the British government were quite ready to do their duty to maintain public order, and those who proclaimed the contrary were guilty of fostering a dangerous delusion.

[1] This supposition is corroborated by the fact that during the Reform Bill agitation soldiers who were perfectly willing to fire on rioters demurred at the prospect of being used to put down agitation. Somerville, *op. cit.*, 245–6.

CHAPTER VI

INTELLIGENCE AND SECRET SERVICE

THE maintenance of a sound system of information is essential to the preservation of good order. Without adequate intelligence no conspiracy can be frustrated, no riot checked in time, no rebel convicted before a court of law. Hence, in depicting the resources arrayed against physical-force Chartism, it is as necessary to describe the methods of obtaining information as to count the number of soldiers available for duty.

Naturally enough, Her Majesty's government relied for much of its information upon the exertions of the civil authorities in the provinces—the Lords Lieutenant and the magistrates of town and county. The Home Office Papers for the period under review are very largely composed of the reports of such dignitaries, though these gentlemen could not always be relied upon to exercise the necessary vigilance in their localities,[1] and were often prone, from fear, self-interest or ignorance, to exaggerate the dangers of disturbance in the districts committed to their charge. Moreover, as the Lord Lieutenant of Leicestershire pointed out in a letter of January 1840 to the Home Office, the county magistrates, even with the best will in the world, were ill-equipped for obtaining information. The justices of the peace acted in insulated parties, each attending the market town of his neighbourhood, and were, therefore, unable to obtain a wider conspectus of the state of the county. The parish constables, who were not paid for the prevention of crime, and trembled under the threat of private vengeance, often failed to communicate vital information to the magistrates, and there was the additional disadvantage that no fund existed in the counties, out of which

---

[1] Napier complained of magistrates who went grouse-shooting in times of crisis. Napier, *op. cit.*, II, 79.

intelligence services might be requited.[1] The Rural Police Act of 1839 had gone far to neutralize these defects, but it was permissive, and was by no means universally adopted.

The stipendiary magistrates, stationed among the turbulent populations of Manchester and the Potteries, stood in a relationship of peculiar intimacy with the Home Office. They were in fact the confidential agents of the Secretary of State in their localities. This arrangement was quite informal and unofficial, being initiated in the case of Daniel Maude, the Manchester stipendiary, by a confidential letter of 7 December 1838, requesting him to communicate local information from time to time confidentially to the Home Secretary, and to allow himself to be used, as his predecessor in office, John Frederick Foster, had been used, to carry out confidential investigations on behalf of the government.[2] Both Maude[3] and Bayley Rose,[4] his counterpart at Stoke-on-Trent, were called upon by the Secretary of State to report on the character and reliability of parties offering private information about the Chartists.

Independently of the civil magistrates, the government also drew upon the military commanders of the disturbed districts for information. In fact the Home Office sometimes preferred to rely upon the military rather than upon the civil arm for the conduct of investigations, as when Colonel Wemyss was entrusted with the task of finding out the identity of the person who gave the signal for the outbreak of the Todmorden riots of November 1838, by ordering the ringing of the factory bell.[5] Throughout the period the Home Secretary was the recipient of frequent and regular reports from the district commanders touching upon every aspect of the public order situation. General Napier elaborated a systematic military-intelligence service designed to dispel the

---

[1] Rutland to H.O. dated 11 January 1840. H.O. 40/55.
[2] H.O. to Maude dated 7 December 1838 (Confidential). H.O. 41/13.
[3] Maude to H.O. dated 28 December 1838. H.O. 40/38.
[4] H.O. to Rose dated 12 July 1842. H.O. 41/16.
[5] H.O. to Wemyss dated 22 November 1838. H.O. 41/13.

N

blindness as to the state of his district which rendered the first weeks of his command so difficult. On 11 April 1839 he despatched a circular letter to the officers in command of the numerous detachments into which his force was divided, conveying to them the following instructions:

> I also wish that you would give me your opinion as to the feelings of the labouring class in your neighbourhood. Do you consider them to be generally speaking favourable or unfavourable to the Chartists (I mean to the system of arming)? Are the middling class alarmed, or are they disposed to believe that there is more talk than reality in the threats of the misled people who make a show of purchasing arms? I am quite aware of the difficulties which attend answering my questions, but you may nevertheless be able to overcome them, and give me confidentially a tolerably correct account of the state of the country about you, especially from talking to the most intelligent of your soldiers, for the privates can and do learn much in their daily inter-course with the labouring people. You may yourself get into conversa-tion with the country folks and thus sift them, and pick up their opinions . . . ; but I do not wish you to consult with any magistrate upon this point. I want to have your own unbiased opinion formed by the observations made by yourself and your soldiers. . . . I will conclude by requesting of you to write to me direct, whenever you hear of any circumstance which you deem important—such as the sale of arms or other appearances of intended violence and insurrection. When relieved, you will give over this letter to the relieving officer, being careful yourself, and cautioning him, to keep its contents secret, for you will perceive that, if this mode of obtaining intelligence became known, its power would at once be lost.[1]

Napier was delighted with the results of his experiment. The reports came in "all well written and with a degree of military sagacity beyond my expectations".[2] Detached from local interests, humane in their attitude to the people, and immune from panic in the face of disorder, the officers in charge of the troops sub-mitted to their superior information which was "less influenced by any party, personal or political bias"[3] than that which the magistrates proffered to the Home Secretary. Moreover, the

[1] Napier to Officers i/c Detachments dated 11 April 1839. H.O. 40/53.
[2] Napier, op. cit., II, 11.
[3] Napier to H.O. dated 13 April 1839. H.O. 40/53.

arrangement was such as to be capable of eliciting information of a confidential character. For the residence of the soldiery among the people, which Napier and other commanders deplored, was in one respect useful to the authorities, viz. that the privates could glean information of Chartist plans, as they sat drinking in the public houses. The pensioners were useful as intermediaries. Enjoying the confidence of the masses to a greater extent than the regular troops, they would "drink and talk with the young soldiers, and, from love or vanity or heat of argument, tell them what is going on".[1] "Thus", said Napier, "I make spies of them despite themselves."[2]

The governments of the Chartist period were not restricted in their quest for information to what they could obtain from magistrates and military commanders. Already they had forged certain bureaucratic links with the provinces, which might be transformed into channels of intelligence when danger threatened. One of the oldest of these links was that between the General Post Office in London and the provincial post offices. Official Instruction No. 19 of the Post Office required the local postmasters "to transmit for the information of the Post Master General an account of all the remarkable occurrences within their districts".[3] In obedience to this command, the postmasters of Bolton, Birmingham and other towns submitted reports on the state of their districts from time to time to Lieutenant Colonel W. L. Maberley, the Secretary of the Post Office, who immediately despatched the information to the Home Secretary. One of the most assiduous correspondents of the General Post Office was William Moore, postmaster of Huddersfield, who reported frequently during the Anti-Poor Law disturbances of 1838 and the Plug-Plot Riots of 1842. In January 1838, Moore, in an excess of zeal, tore down one of Richard Oastler's placards from the walls of the town, and sent it to the Post Office in the company of one of his own reports.[4] Unhappily for him, his action was discovered, and on the

[1] Napier, *op. cit.*, II, 11. [2] *Ibid.*
[3] Gottwaltz to Maberley dated 5 July 1839. H.O. 40/50.
[4] Moore to Maberley dated 16 January 1838. H.O. 40/40.

following day Oastler published a placard in the form of an open letter to the Home Secretary:

> Yesterday it so happened that I caused a placard to be posted upon the walls of Huddersfield which gave great umbrage to Your Lordship's friends, the Whigs. Billy Moore, the Postmaster, who, it is understood, has received Your Lordship's appointment of Government Spy in this neighbourhood, endeavoured to clean his fingers (and everybody knows how nasty they are) by scraping one of them off the wall, and stuffing it all pasty and dirty and wet into the Mail Bag for Your Lordship. . . . Now, my Lord, let us have a word with each other. I have no objection that Your Lordship should employ a Spy to watch my movements; I tell you plainly that I employ one to watch yours. My Spy regularly occupies a stool in your own office at one of your own desks; and from him I regularly receive an account of your proceedings. So long as your London Spy remained here I did not grumble, but I think, my Lord, it is hardly fair to degrade the office of Post Master into that of a Spy.[1]

A foolish official had been caught in his folly, and Oastler was no doubt entitled, as a politician, to make what capital he could of the incident. In fairness to the government it must be admitted, however, that the instructions to postmasters did not in themselves require the establishment of a system of espionage, though they were certainly capable of being interpreted in such a sense by postmasters whose zeal exceeded their discretion.

The information derived from the postmasters' reports supplemented that submitted by the magistrates. It had, however, two advantages over the latter. The first was that the postmasters mixed more freely with the people, and on that account were able more readily to size up the feelings and plans of the disaffected; the second that, having first-hand contact with the mail bag, they could put in reports right down to the point of departure of the mail coach. For this reason their information of disturbances was often more up-to-date than that tendered by the magistrates.

When the Chartist disturbances began, the postmaster was not the only salaried officer in the provincial towns who maintained a regular and constant communication with the central government. Already the social problems of an industrial society had

---

[1] Placard dated Fixby Hall 17 January 1838. H.O. 40/40.

required an enlargement of the sphere of State action, and the setting up of new official posts, the holders of which might be required, in times of disturbance, to furnish information. Lord Althorp's Factory Act of 1833 provided for the appointment of four Inspectors of Factories, who were to carry out the terms of this Act, and, for this purpose, to have access to factories and factory schools. They were to be assisted in their work by Sup intendents. Acting under the control of the Home Office, and in contact through their occupations with the operative class, Factory Inspectors and Superintendents were naturally regarded as a convenient and reliable source of information concerning disaffection. In May 1837 each of the four Inspectors received a letter from the Under Secretary of State, requesting him to report from time to time "respecting the state of trade, the wages of labour, and the state of tranquillity or excitement in the district in which you act". Two years later, in July 1839, Leonard Horner communicated to his fellow Inspectors at their statutory meeting instructions from Fox Maule "to report weekly respecting the Chartist meetings". Owing to the indiscretion of one of the Inspectors, James Stuart, and the malice or carelessness of Beal, his Superintendent at Dundee, the rôle of the Factory Inspectors in the accumulation of information about internal disorder was made known to John Fielden, the Radical member for Oldham, a vigorous opponent of the factory compromise of 1833. The consequence was a motion in the House of Commons for a Select Committee to consider the question of the employment of Inspectors and Superintendents "in other matters than those assigned to them by the authority of Parliament, and to ascertain how far they have been employed by the Government in the capacity of political spies". Fielden's motion was defeated by 113 votes to 11, but not before a good deal of extravagant language had been publicly voiced.[1]

The information which the government derived from its servants in the provinces was supplemented by the voluntary

[1] For a full account of these proceedings see M. W. Thomas, *The Early Factory Legislation*, 108–13.

contributions of private citizens, who were moved to write to the Home Secretary by a desire for favour or reward, by an irrepressible public spirit, or by a strong distrust of the way in which the local magistrates were handling the problems which threatened the public peace. The last of these three motives was uppermost in the mind of E. C. Lloyd Hall, a barrister, living on the scene of the Rebecca Riots, who deplored the violence of the rioters, but remained appreciative of the hardships inflicted upon the farmers by the turnpike tolls.[1] He was one of the most frequent correspondents of the Home Office during the disturbances, furnishing much detailed information of the state of the country, and castigating the magistrates with a merciless pen.

On occasions, when serious outrage had occurred, and remained unpunished owing to the inability of the local justices to procure such intelligence as would justify a prosecution, the government assumed complete control of the quest for information through its own confidential agents despatched to the scene of the trouble. Thus for example in December 1838 the Home Secretary decided to send Sir Frederick Roe, the Chief Magistrate of Bow Street, and Mr. George Maule, the Treasury Solicitor, to Todmorden in Lancashire, to supervise the inquiry, begun by the magistrates, into the authorship of the recent Anti-Poor Law riots.[2] Maule was subsequently engaged in the district round Manchester, collecting evidence for the prosecution of Joseph Rayner Stephens.[3]

Among the tasks involved in bringing political prosecutions was that of obtaining such evidence as would convince a court of law that the Chartist meetings were illegal according to the Common Law definition of illegality,[4] and that the speeches

---

[1] *The Times*, 26 June 1843, p. 6.

[2] H.O. to Todmorden Magistrates dated 2 December 1838. H.O. 41/13.

[3] G. Maule to S. M. Phillipps dated 27 February 1839. H.O. 48/33.

[4] The definition included "all assemblies, not held by lawful authority, attended by great numbers of people, with such circumstances of terror as are calculated to excite alarm and to endanger the public peace". *Copy of a letter from Her Majesty's Principal Secretary of State for the Home Department to Colonel Rolleston, M.P., dated Whitehall, 3 June 1839, on the Subject of Unlawful Meetings*; 1839 (448) XXXVIII.

uttered from Chartist platforms were seditious according to the law of sedition. For it was the policy of the Whig ministry, when confronted, as in the winter of 1838–9, by rowdy meetings which threatened to degenerate into riots, not to interfere with the meetings unless violence actually occurred, but to proceed against the speakers for sedition or attendance at unlawful meetings.[1] Given that the meetings were as dangerous as they were held to be, the policy was a sensible one, far superior to the provocation of riot by active interference. But it necessitated the compilation of a sufficient quantity of accurate information concerning the circumstances of the meeting and the language used by the speakers, to convince a jury of the guilt of the parties accused. Such information was not easy to collect in times of disturbances, notwithstanding the fact that the proceedings of the Chartists were largely conducted without concealment.

The case of Joseph Rayner Stephens is illustrative of the difficulties involved in the prosecution of Chartist speakers. Wanted by the authorities on account of the excitement raised by his public utterances, that perfervid orator, who brought to the task of political agitation all the emotional appeal of the Evangelical Revival, enjoyed for some time an immunity from arrest which was solely due to the impossibility of obtaining evidence against him.[2] Few indeed were prepared to take the risk of testifying against one so popular with the masses. And little wonder! William Manley of Hyde, a constable of the Cheshire Constabulary, was waylaid, brutally beaten and disfigured, because, at a later stage, he became a witness against Stephens.[3] Moreover, even when evidence was procured, it was seldom reliable. Witnesses spoke from their recollection of events which had passed many weeks before; they could hardly have been expected to take notes on the spot. Thus, in December 1838, the Home Office found the depositions brought up for it from Leigh in Lancashire,

---

[1] H.O. to Mayor and Magistrates of Stockport dated 18 December 1838. H.O. 41/13. H.O. to Hyde Magistrates dated 22 November 1838. H.O. 41/13.

[2] Wearmouth, *Some Working-Class Movements of the Nineteenth Century*, 200.

[3] Chorlton and Hibbert to H.O. dated 29 June 1839. H.O. 40/37.

where Stephens had spoken somewhat forcefully in the previous month, "seldom of the least consequence".[1] When eventually the authorities plucked up enough courage to arrest Stephens, they brought forward against him at his examination in the New Bailey, Manchester, two witnesses who spoke only from memory, having made no record of the offending speech to which they testified. The result was an altercation between the accused and the magistrates, who were compelled to extricate themselves ignominiously by remanding the case to another day.[2]

As far as it arose from defects of the memory, the difficulty of obtaining accurate reports could be met by enlisting in the service of the magistrates the public reporters who attended Chartist meetings on behalf of the press. These were capable of using their skill in shorthand to record the speeches and the proceedings with the requisite fidelity, and were able to gain access even to meetings of a semi-private character. No fewer than three reporters attended an assembly of Chartist delegates at Ashton-under-Lyne on 22 April 1839, notwithstanding the fact that a sentinel was stationed at the door to prevent the entrance of those who could not produce proper credentials.[3] It was difficult, however, as the magistrates discovered to their discomfiture, to find reporters willing to co-operate in proceedings against the Chartists. Such persons as were eligible for the job were deterred from coming forward by fears of private vengeance. Daniel Maude, the Manchester stipendiary magistrate, complained to the Home Secretary on 25 April 1839 that the persons who reported for newspapers refused to make any depositions, or to come forward as witnesses in cases arising out of Chartist meetings in that great town.[4] When it became known that the government was seeking information through these channels, press reporters toned down their reports from fear of being compelled to testify to the truth

[1] J. W. Edwards to Russell dated 12 December 1838, Home Office minute. H.O. 52/37.

[2] *The Northern Star*, 5 January 1839, p. 6.

[3] Clerk of Ashton Magistrates to H.O. dated May 1839 and accompanying depositions. H.O. 40/37.

[4] Maude to H.O. dated 25 April 1839. H.O. 40/43.

of them in a court of justice.[1] P. B. Templeton, who boasted that he had attended almost every Chartist meeting in Lancashire and Yorkshire, as a reporter for *The Northern Star,* was sufficiently appreciative of the scarcity value of his products to ask £40 for a report of a single meeting which he had covered.[2] As a remedy the authorities had recourse to the importation of shorthand writers from a distance great enough to liberate them from the pressure of local influences. At a general meeting of the borough magistrates of Manchester towards the end of July 1839, when the reports of recent Chartist meetings were reviewed and adjudged insufficiently decisive or accurate to justify a prosecution, it was resolved that the Head Constable should engage competent reporters from Liverpool, as their local counterparts would not incur the odium of giving their evidence in public.[3] In 1848 appeals were made to the government to send reporters into the disturbed districts. These were refused at first, but later acceded to. The Home Secretary agreed to despatch a reporter from London to take down a speech which was to be delivered by Mantle in Birmingham on 11 June 1848.[4] Several days later, the Ashton magistrates received a general assurance of the government's willingness to afford assistance of this character.[5]

Before long a further problem presented itself to the authorities, as the Chartists reacted to the threat of prosecution by excluding from their assemblies all but those on whom they could implicitly rely. On 24 July 1839 reporters were ejected from two Chartist meetings in Manchester,[6] and in the months which followed, a veil of secrecy fell over the proceedings of the movement throughout the country. The effect was to drive the authorities to devices of a more clandestine and deceitful character, with the result that Chartism became riddled with sinister personalities pretending a

[1] Templeton to H.O. dated 24 April 1839. H.O. 40/43; Hall and Taylor to H.O. dated 16 June 1848. H.O. 45/2410A.

[2] Templeton to H.O. dated 24 April 1839. H.O. 40/43.

[3] Mayor of Manchester to H.O. dated 25 July 1839. H.O. 40/43.

[4] H.O. to Mayor of Birmingham dated 10 June 1848; H.O. to Beales dated 12 June 1848. H.O. 41/19.

[5] H.O. to Hall and Taylor dated 17 June 1848. H.O. 41/19.

[6] Mayor of Manchester to H.O. dated 25 July 1839. H.O. 40/43.

sincere enthusiasm for the cause, but using their position in the movement to obtain information for the government and its servants, the magistrates. It was a wiser course that Samuel Kydd pressed upon his fellow Chartists in July 1848, when he urged them to encourage government reporters to attend their meetings, "as he was convinced that to them he owed his safety during the late sittings of the National Convention in John St., for if they had not been present to report all that had occurred, in all probability he should now be in the walls of a prison". On his advice, permission was formally granted to three reporters to attend a lecture given by him on 12 July in the Milton St. Theatre in London, whilst two plain-clothes policemen were thrown out with much violence.[1]

The task of collecting information was greatly simplified in those localities which were equipped with a professional police force of an up-to-date character. Prevention rather than repression of disorder was one of the cardinal principles of the new police systems, and to implement it the utmost vigilance was required. In the exercise of that faculty the police received far more brickbats than bouquets. Accusations of espionage, foreign in character, and incompatible with the liberties of Englishmen, were frequently levelled against them in their early years of operation. Even in the democratic England of the mid-twentieth century some degree of secrecy is inseparable from police efficiency. As Mrs. J. M. Hart sensibly remarks, the police "could not possibly perform the duties expected of them if they did not on occasion behave secretly, i.e. in plain clothes or incognito, or if they did not use secret methods for detecting crimes and watching suspects".[2] It would be unsafe, however, to conclude that, during the Chartist period, police constables were freely and regularly

---

[1] Metropolitan Police Records, 'Chartists' Box: Bundle marked 'Confidential Information by Persons of Chartist Proceedings and Disaffected Persons, 1848–53'. N.B.—£986 6s. 3d. was paid to Messrs. Gurney and Sons, official shorthand writers, for attendance and transcript of speeches at the Chartist Convention of 1848 and other meetings. C. E. Trevelyan to G. C. Lewis dated 2 January 1849. H.O. 45/2619.

[2] J. M. Hart, *The British Police*, 185–6.

used as spies. In the absence of centralized control there was, in fact, no uniformity of practice for the country as a whole.

In the Metropolitan Force the constable's freedom to practise deception in his quest for information was severely limited by official instructions. There was no absolute ban on the wearing of plain clothes at political meetings, a practice which might be dictated purely by prudential motives, since the presence of constables at such assemblages, if known, might provoke an outbreak of violence, but only the strongest cases of necessity were held to justify the assumption of disguise,[1] and even then there must be no elaborate play-acting to deceive the public. From December 1845 onwards, superintendents of divisions were not allowed to appoint any of their men to exclusive plain-clothes duties.[2] Twelve months later plain-clothes officers were instructed to disclose their identity to anyone who interfered with them in the execution of their duties.[3] How frank and open was the behaviour of Metropolitan Policemen who were sent to watch Chartist meetings in civilian clothes is evident from the conduct of the two officers who attended a Chartist committee meeting on 4 April 1840, but preferred to retire rather than furnish the secretary with fictitious names and addresses. Subsequently they turned up in uniform, and requested formal permission to be present.[4] Some officers of the force may have exceeded their instructions. In January 1840 a policeman named Michael Conway was said to have contributed money to the London Democratic Association, and to have incited others to acts of incendiarism, but the case against him rests on unsubstantiated Chartist allegation.[5] There can be little doubt, however, that the Commissioners, fearful of a repetition of the Popay scandal,[6] discouraged the members of their force from using too much ingenuity in the investigation of political conspiracies. Thus, for example, on

---

[1] Metropolitan Police Records, Police Order Book, 1845–6; entry dated 10 December 1845.

[2] *Ibid.*   [3] *Ibid.*; entry dated 26 December 1846.

[4] Reith, *British Police and the Democratic Ideal*, 248–9.

[5] *The Northern Star*, 25 January 1840, p. 1.

[6] Popay, a sergeant of the Metropolitan Police, was publicly accused of acting as an *agent provocateur* in 1833.

10 August 1839 Richard Mayne issued the following instruction: "Superintendents to gain the necessary information of the political meetings as far as can be possibly ascertained, but not to allow P.C.s (as ordered on former occasions) to go into private meetings." [1]

In the provinces policemen were at greater liberty to practise deception. Some allowed themselves to be drilled that they might lay accurate information against their fellow transgressors.[2] P.C. John Pashley told the sentry posted on the door of a Chartist meeting in Birmingham that "he was a shoemaker from Northampton, and that he came there through motives of benevolence, wishing to contribute his mite towards the family of the unfortunate Frost". This subterfuge he freely confessed in an official police report.[3] Sergeant Michael Daly, also of the Birmingham force, walked about arm in arm with the Chartist leaders of that town.[4] Superintendent Redin of the Liverpool borough police joined the Irish Repeal Club in June 1848, when membership implied participation in subscription for arms and in the study of the art of street warfare.[5]

It was not easy, however, to employ a regular constable to conduct political investigations by methods as secret as these. The experience of Barnett, a member of Captain Burgess's Birmingham force, in so far as it may be ascertained correctly from his own reports, illustrates the difficulties involved. Renewed strength had been infused into Birmingham Chartism by the release of Lovett and Collins from Warwick Gaol on 24 July 1840. The resumption of open-air meetings and demonstrations in the borough caused the Police Commissioner to probe the new movement by sending P.C. Barnett of the first division to attend a Chartist dinner and raffle at the Cross Guns, a public house, on 29 July. Although Barnett attended in plain clothes, he was,

[1] Metropolitan Police Records, Police Order Book; entry dated 10 August 1839.
[2] *The Northern Star*, 11 May 1839, p. 7.
[3] Report of P.C. 276, John Pashley. H.O. 40/56.
[4] *The Northern Star*, 3 September 1842, p. 6.
[5] Report of Head Constable of Liverpool dated 30 June 1848. H.O. 45/2410A.

at first, treated with suspicion, the conversation falling to a whisper as he entered, but, by giving the impression that he had formerly been a member of the Chartist Association, he wormed his way into the confidence of the members, and was introduced to other meetings.[1] On 7 August he played a seditious game of marbles with the Chartist delegates at Bland's Beer Shop in Lancaster Street, and claimed that, when he left, he was "looked upon as entirely one of themselves".[2] On 10 August he was accorded the privilege of a seat on the platform at an open-air meeting at Holloway Head.[3] It was precisely at this stage that his embarrassments commenced. Before the meeting he thought it prudent to request the superintendent of his division to warn the regular police on duty at Holloway Head not to show any sign of recognition.[4] Whether any of them did accidentally betray him is not clear, but a day or two later he was received with cool looks by the Chartists at the Cross Guns, having been suspected of connections with the police.[5] To rid him of his embarrassments, Captain Burgess now proposed to strike him off the regular strength, and to employ him solely on special duties. As there was no financial provision for detectives in Birmingham, the Commissioner had to ask the Home Secretary for an advance from the Secret Service Fund, but Lord Normanby declined to recommend it,[6] and Barnett had to continue as a regular constable. Meanwhile, however, he persisted in his attendance at Chartist meetings, but remained under a cloud of suspicion, more especially as he did not appear to gain his living by labour, yet had not sufficient resources to maintain the appearance of a gentleman of leisure.[7] Verbal messages, sent from the police station to his lodgings, caused him no little inconvenience, and exposed him to his landlady as a policeman. On 2 November 1840 he appealed to Captain Burgess to suspend such messages, as he was cultivating the friendship of Green, one of the most violent physical-force agitators in

[1] Reports of P.C. Barnett dated 29 and 31 July 1840. H.O. 40/56.
[2] *Ibid.*, dated 8 August 1840.   [3] *Ibid.*, dated 10 August 1840.
[4] *Ibid.*, 9 August 1840.   [5] *Ibid.*, 13 August 1840.
[6] Burgess to H.O. dated 13 August 1840 and H.O. minute. H.O. 40/56.
[7] Barnett to Burgess dated 15 and 23 October 1840. H.O. 40/56. Barnett made good use of this in his appeals to the Commissioner for increased payment.

Birmingham, and would need to be especially careful.[1] A few days later Green turned against Barnett, and denounced him as a police agent. His action threatened to produce a further rift in Birmingham Chartism, since Barlow, one of the leaders, took Barnett's part.[2]

But Barnett's most serious embarrassment, arising out of his position as a regular constable, was still to come. Early in December 1840 he was placed on duty in uniform at a Birmingham theatre. He had lost favour with his divisional superintendent, Ryde, who now declined to make any special arrangements in his favour. Barnett escaped from his difficulty by telling the Chartists that he was a private policeman employed by the proprietors of the theatre.[3] Soon afterwards, however, Superintendent Ryde ordered him to go on the beat. Commissioner Burgess countermanded the order through another superintendent, Stephens, but Ryde forced a show-down by suspending Barnett from the force for absence from duty. Barnett resisted, and became involved in an altercation at the police station, after which he appealed to the Commissioner for permission to seek other employment.[4] Nothing further is known of him except that he reported a few more Chartist meetings for Burgess towards the end of the month.[5] In personal character he was never above suspicion,[6] but it is a testimony to the honesty of his reports of Chartist proceedings that he never pretended that a dangerous conspiracy was afoot. The same could not be said of many of the private spies employed by the authorities.

P.C. Barnett's peculiar and embarrassing situation resulted largely from the fact that there was no separate detective establishment in Birmingham.[7] Detective police was in its infancy in

[1] Barnett to Burgess dated 2 November 1840. H.O. 40/56.
[2] Barnett to Burgess dated 12 November 1840. H.O. 40/56.
[3] Barnett to Burgess dated 3, 7, 9 and 14 December 1840. H.O. 40/56.
[4] Barnett to Burgess dated 20 December 1840. H.O. 40/56.
[5] Reports of meetings on 27 and 29 December. H.O. 40/56.
[6] When he joined the Birmingham Police he stated falsely that he was a single man. Barnett to Burgess dated 11 September 1840. H.O. 40/56. His letters and reports demonstrate also a strong desire to obtain money from the Commissioner.
[7] Nevertheless Burgess does appear to have employed one of his inspectors.

the age of the Chartists. The Metropolitan Force had a specialized corps of detectives from 1842 onwards, but the latter consisted of not more than two inspectors and six sergeants,[1] and suffered, for the first quarter of a century of its existence, the disadvantage of being deprived of regular contact with the divisions, in consequence of its being attached exclusively to headquarters;[2] provincial police forces, on the other hand, were well behind the Metropolitan.

Because of the immaturity of the detective force the new police were driven to rely extensively for their knowledge of subterranean activities on information brought in by private spies. Writing of the most typical of the reformed constabularies, the Metropolitan, Mr. Charles Reith asserts that "the Commissioners' growing confidence in themselves and in the success of their principles enabled them to confine their handling of the Chartist menace to methods which were just and unconcealed".[3] Without impugning the justice of the Commissioners' proceedings, however, it may legitimately be doubted, on the basis of evidence to be presented later of the employment by the Metropolitan Police, for purposes of obtaining information, of persons well established in the confidence of the Chartists, whether their methods can fairly be described as unconcealed. Nor is this surprising. Even today, as Sir Basil Thomson, Director of Intelligence at Scotland Yard during the present century, has reminded us, " 'information received', in other words information received from a member of the underworld who has abandoned his criminal career in favour of honest employment, but is still on friendly terms with

Stephens, to collect information from spies and informers about Chartist proceedings in 1839. He was a pioneer detective even if not known as such. See Statement of Expenses incurred by Inspector Stephens, 30 November 1839. H.O. 40/50. Similarly Richard Mayne had been in the habit of employing Inspector Nicholas Pearce and several other officers of the Metropolitan Force regularly on detective duties for about three years before the corps of detectives at Scotland Yard was established. See Belton Cobb, *The First Detectives*, passim.

[1] H.O. to Metropolitan Police Commissioners dated 20 June 1842. H.O. 65/14.

[2] Sir Basil Thomson, *The Story of Scotland Yard*, 163.

[3] Reith, *op. cit.*, 247.

his old associates", is "the starting [point] of all detective work":[1] in an age when the science of detection was largely undeveloped, it tended to constitute the entire process.

The spy, therefore, was still the natural source of secret information, both where professional police forces existed, and where they did not exist. From a perusal of Chartist newspapers, speeches and reminiscences, and of some secondary sources for the period under review, the conclusion might readily be reached that the governments of the day had at their disposal a relentless, unprincipled, highly systematized espionage organization which was responsible not only for unearthing, but also for originating much of the physical-force movement. "I now warn you the Spy System has begun", declaimed Stephens from his Ashton pulpit on 9 December 1838, "Little John recommends it, and Lord John Russell's spy is now in this place."[2] Some time later, commenting in *The Northern Star* on the rôle of spies in the Yorkshire outbreaks of January 1840, Feargus O'Connor called attention to a "complete and systematic plan adopted by the Government to goad the working classes into resistance".[3] The sensational allegations of George Jacob Holyoake led the historian Rosenblatt to assert that "venomous newspaper reports of the Chartist meetings provoked the Government to introduce a wide system of espionage".[4]

There is much to suggest the need for caution in interpreting Chartist reports of espionage. It was natural that the leaders of the movement should seek a scapegoat in the *agent provocateur* for the unsuccessful physical-force adventures which brought so much discredit on the cause. Moreover, Chartism was so riddled with divisions and sects that it was not unknown for the leaders of one faction to attack their opponents by the method of accusing them of being in the pay of the government. Even the venerated

---

[1] Thomson, *op. cit.*, 315.

[2] Deposn. of Robert Ripley enclosed in Clerk of Ashton Magistrates to H.O. dated 24 December 1838. H.O. 40/38.

[3] *The Northern Star*, 21 March 1840, p. 4.

[4] F. F. Rosenblatt, *The Chartist Movement*, Columbia University Studies in History, Economics and Public Law, LXXIII, 161.

Feargus O'Connor was so charged when in March 1840 he advised a conference of delegates at Manchester to think no longer of force.[1] References to secret service in Chartist periodicals and memoirs are also much too vague and general to be accepted without question. Holyoake, having claimed that there were spies in the pay of government in 1839, proceeds to refer to the affair of Cuffay, which in effect occurred nine years later, contenting himself with the comment that it was "about that period". Vaguer still is his reference to the knave who, at some unspecified date, "produced an explosive liquid which he said could be poured into the sewers, and, being ignited, would blow up London from below".[2] The very word "spy" was used so loosely by the Chartists—for a local postmaster reporting on the state of his district,[3] for a constable in plain clothes[4] and even for a magistrate watching an open-air meeting[5]—that their allegations of espionage cannot be taken at their face value.

It is, of course, undeniable that during the Chartist period the authorities charged with the maintenance of the public peace employed spies or private agents to ferret out the secrets of the working-class movements. The view that the age of the spies came to an abrupt conclusion when Peel succeeded Sidmouth at the Home Office in 1821 is clearly a fond delusion without foundation in fact. But it is misleading to speak, without qualification, of government spies as being at work during the period, whilst to postulate a spy system is positively incorrect.

Nothing in the official records gives the slightest confirmation to the contention that the Home Office, Whig or Tory, gave direct employment to spies, as Lord Sidmouth had employed Oliver in the turbulent years of the Regency. On the contrary there is much to suggest that it did not. Whenever Chartism threatened to disturb the public peace, the Home Secretary received numerous applications for employment from individuals

---

[1] Heyrick to H.O. dated 16 March 1840. H.O. 40/55.

[2] G. J. Holyoake, *Sixty Years of an Agitator's Life*, II, 3–4.

[3] Placard dated Fixby Hall 17 January 1838. H.O. 40/40.

[4] Simmons' Report of meeting at Lawrence St. Chapel, Birmingham, on 12 November 1839. H.O. 40/50.

[5] *The Northern Star*, 10 August 1839, p. 3.

O

of doubtful character who claimed to have the means of furnishing information about some diabolical plot which the disaffected were concocting. In January 1839 a man named Towler, claiming to be a delegate from the Old Kent Road Chartists, wrote to Lord John Russell, hinting at a conspiracy of the Cato Street description, which was to come to a head on 4 February, the date of the opening of the Chartist Convention.[1] Similarly, in 1848, a certain 'O. W.', claiming acquaintance with an individual who was engaged in a treasonable plot, offered his services to Sir George Grey as a spy, declaring that in return for the sum of £100 he would mix up with the conspirators and, if they persisted in their deadly purpose, have them arrested at the fitting moment.[2] The records of Scotland Yard show that the Home Office had developed a regular technique of dealing with so many of these offers as it deemed worthy of notice—viz., that of passing them on to the Commissioners of the Metropolitan Police, sometimes with specific instructions to communicate with the parties concerned, sometimes without such directions. The case of William Radley is illustrative of the Home Secretary's refusal to entertain a closer relationship with informers. Radley, who declared himself to be a manufacturing chemist of Cullum Street in the City of London, wrote to the Home Office on 23 June 1848, stating that he had delivered supplies of a very poisonous substance to Birmingham, London and Ipswich, and offering to come up for an interview. According to the accepted practice his offer was passed to the Metropolitan Police, as a result of which Inspector Haynes of the detective branch was sent to seek audience with him. Haynes called seven times at his office without success, but Radley, ignoring these communications, renewed his application direct to the Home Office on 28 July. Sir George Grey remained adamant on the point that the negotiations should be conducted by the police, and in a letter of 2 August Radley scornfully proclaimed his refusal to deal with subordinates.[3] There, we may

---

[1] Towler to Lord John Russell dated 16 January 1839. H.O. 44/52.
[2] Metropolitan Police Records, 'Chartists' Box: Bundle marked 'Special Reports and Documents Relative to Chartist Meetings'.
[3] *Ibid.*: Bundle marked 'Chartist Proceedings, 1848'.

infer, the matter was allowed to rest. The rise of the professional police forces had rendered it no longer so necessary for the Home Secretary to engage his own secret agents.

If the government did not employ spies directly, neither did it intervene to systematize their employment by the local author-ities. The attitudes of the several Home Secretaries whose careers spanned the period towards the question of espionage can only be described as very cautious. In the very month when Rayner Stephens was treating his congregation to a denunciation of Lord John Russell's "spy system", the Whig Home Secretary returned the following answer to the Duke of Newcastle, who, as Lord Lieutenant of Nottinghamshire, sought reimbursement to the magistrates of expenses incurred in employing men to ascertain the extent, progress, and power of arms clubs in the county: "I am glad to find that the magistrates are on the alert. I am aware that they have no funds at their disposal for the purpose of pro-curing information. It is a matter of so much delicacy that I have not thought it right to sanction any outlay of this nature except in some very special case. Perhaps it will be best that the magistrate to whom your Grace refers should write to Mr. Phillipps at the Home Office, when the propriety of the measure can be maturely considered." [1] The Clerk to the Colne magistrates was evidently right when, in a letter of 18 May 1839, he wrote of Lord John Russell's reluctance to resort to espionage.[2]

During the period of office of Lord John's successor, Lord Normanby, the Home Office not only dissuaded the Birmingham Police Commissioner from entering into treaty for information with Fussell, one of the local physical-force leaders, but seized the opportunity to deliver the Commissioner a lecture on the perils of secret service: "With respect to the employment of spies and informers", he wrote, "let me assure you it is the most difficult and dangerous thing to manage, and generally ends in nothing but disappointment. If the fact of your employing a Spy is known to any living being excepting to you and the Spy himself, success

[1] Russell to Duke of Newcastle dated 21 December 1838 (Private). H.O. 41/13.
[2] Bolton to H.O. dated 18 May 1839. H.O. 40/37.

is hopeless."[1] Sir James Graham was almost puritanical in his scruples concerning the employment of secret agents. He lauded himself publicly for having spent only a trifling amount of Secret Service money during three years of office.[2] When, on the morrow of the disturbances of 1842, the news reached him that persons had been employed to attend Chartist meetings for the purpose of procuring information, he called for a more detailed report, and subsequently wrote to John Gregory, the solicitor engaged in the Crown prosecutions: "I am glad to find that no persons were so employed by anyone with whom you had any communication. I would not on any account sanction such a mode of obtaining information. . . ."[3] Twelve months later, experience of the elusive instigators of the Rebecca Riots had caused him to relax his attitude a little, but he was still cautious. Reimbursing Colonel Love's expenditure on espionage he sent the following message to that officer: "Sir James Graham does not wish you to keep any person in your regular employ as an informant, thinking the practice of having informers very hazardous and inconvenient. At the same time he is aware that in some special cases information may be so important and necessary [that] it ought to be procured if possible. In all such cases, considering the situation in which you are placed, he will entirely rely on your discretion; and would not lay any restraint upon you which might thwart your proceedings."[4] That Sir George Grey shared the caution of his predecessors is evident from his treatment of a police report of a Chartist meeting in Holborn on 31 January 1850. He underlined the statement that "a general rush was made to the platform calling for the Spy Clark, one of the Speakers", and wrote by the side of it: 'What does this mean?' Only when the police superintendent explained that the spy in question came from a rival Chartist society did the Home Secretary close the affair with the minute 'satisfactory'.[5]

[1] Draft of H.O. to Burgess dated 21 November 1839 (Confidential). H.O. 40/50.   [2] Hans., 3 Ser., LXXV, 906.
[3] H.O. to Gregory dated 21 November 1842. H.O. 41/17.
[4] H.O. to Love dated 21 November 1843 (Confidential). H.O. 41/18.
[5] Reports of Supt. Pearce of F. Division dated 2 February 1850. H.O. 45/3136.

In short the initiative in the employment of spies came in the main from the localities—from the magistrates and Lords Lieutenant, from military commanders and Chief Constables, and from private individuals who acted as sub-contractors for the authorities.[1] In some cases the Home Secretary agreed to recommend the reimbursement of expenses incurred in such activities from the Secret Service Fund, but this was by no means an unvarying practice. In August 1839 the Huddersfield magistrates found their espionage account disallowed by the Home Office, on the grounds that the sanction of government had not been obtained before the agents were engaged.[2] In February 1842 Sir James Graham bluntly informed Lord Talbot that he could not advise the government to grant indemnity or reimbursement where magistrates employed persons to obtain private information of nightly meetings.[3] Disbursements of Secret Service money by the Home Secretaries of the period were by no means large. Russell spent £1,790 7s. between April 1835 and November 1838.[4] Normanby spent £591 5s. 5d. between September 1839 and August 1841.[5] Graham spent only £232 16s. 3d. during five years of office.[6] These figures appear trivial when viewed against Sidmouth's expenditure of £9,526 0s. 9d. in the period, June 1812 to January 1818.[7] The government's reluctance to foot the spy bills of the local authorities must have limited severely the amount of espionage that could be undertaken, for there was no

---

[1] John Paterson of Bexley drew information about the Chartists in 1848 from a private spy, and passed it on to the Duke of Wellington, Sir George Grey and Sir Richard Mayne. Metropolitan Police Records, 'Chartists' Box: Bundle marked, 'Special Reports and Documents Relative to Chartist Meetings'. Also Mayne to Waddington dated 26 May 1852. H.O. 45/4313.

[2] Laycock to H.O. dated 22 August 1839 and H.O. Minute. H.O. 40/51.

[3] H.O. to Talbot dated 12 February 1842. H.O. 41/16.

[4] Records of the Exchequer and Audit Office: Declared Accounts in Books (A.O.2). Vol. 37, pp. 341-2.

[5] *Ibid.* Vol. 42, pp. 465-6.

[6] Of this, £139 16s. 3d. was expended between September 1841 and February 1844. *Ibid.* Vol. 47, pp. 231-2; and £93 between February 1844 and July 1846. Vol. 53, pp. 383-4.

[7] Records of the Exchequer and Audit Office: Declared Accounts in Rolls (A.O.1). Bundle 2129, Roll 45.

public money available locally which the magistrates could regularly apply to this purpose.[1]

Many such agents were at work during the Chartist period, most of them persons of no great standing, intelligence or moral integrity, men who preferred to live by their wits rather than by honest labour, and who in more tranquil times plied the trade of common informer. They were not usually planted upon the Chartists by the authorities, but tended to ingratiate themselves with the working-class leaders first and then to use their contacts as a bait to induce the authorities to employ them. They also operated for the most part on a purely local basis. The Duke of Portland's informant seems, on his own testimony, to have possessed a roving commission, and to have mixed with the Chartists in places as far apart as Nottinghamshire, Oldham in Lancashire and Bradford in the West Riding,[2] but he was the exception not the rule. A more typical figure was the informer whose purview extended only to the Chartist movement in a single locality.

As 1839 drew to its close, spies in the pay of the authorities were penetrating deeply into the confidence of the Chartists in almost every district where the movement remained alive. Birmingham was a nest of them. W. C. Alston, one of the magistrates, was employing a man named Thomas, alias Wilkins, who claimed to be known to Julian Harney, and was obviously dissatisfied with being the tool of a mere provincial justice, for he showed great keenness to procure an interview at the Home Office.[3] Captain Burgess, the Police Commissioner, paid 21 shillings per week to William Tongue,[4] who attended regularly at the Chartist rooms for two or three months at the end of 1839, went out drilling with parties of Chartists at dead of night,[5]

---

[1] See Russell to Newcastle dated 21 December 1838 (Private), quoted above, p. 201.

[2] Dawson to Portland dated 18 July, 7 August and 3 September 1848. H.O. 45/2410S.

[3] W. C. Alston to H.O. dated 31 August 1839. H.O. 40/50; Burgess to H.O. dated 24 December 1840. H.O. 65/10.

[4] Statement of expenses incurred by Inspector Stephens, 30 November 1839. H.O. 40/50.

[5] 'T' Report, 23 November 1839. H.O. 40/50.

served on Frost's Committee in Birmingham[1] and laid information of a plot to set fire to churches, which, he said, was being considered by a small committee of which he was a member.[2] But a more important person than Tongue, Joseph Fussell, the most prominent of the physical-force leaders of Birmingham, was also compromised by contacts with the authorities. Arrested for sedition in May 1839, he was afterwards mysteriously released,[3] and entered into negotiations first with W. C. Alston[4] and later with Captain Burgess to give information to the authorities. He would have settled with the latter for £2 per week in November,[5] had not Lord Normanby's scruples prevented the conclusion of the deal.[6] Indeed it is not improbable that, as Tongue, the other spy, alleged, he had actually given information to George Redfern, head of the police in Birmingham before Burgess's force was formed.[7]

There were also spies in London as 1839 drew to its close. Towards the end of December Colonel Rowan, Commissioner of the Metropolitan Police, was dealing with a certain W. P. Stuart of Mile End Tollgate, who had previously been employed by the Lord Mayor. Stuart claimed to have been elected secretary to the East London (Chartist) Association and offered to show the books to the police.[8] A little over a fortnight later, on 14 January, Rowan received from a spy whose handwriting strongly resembled that of Stuart, warning of a Chartist outbreak in London that very night. The informant stated that he would be with the disaffected.[9] About that time also Joseph Goulding, a leading figure in London Chartism, passed into the service of the police,[10] who, by virtue of their channels of secret information, were able

---

[1] Wilson's Report, 9 December 1839. H.O. 40/50.
[2] Tongue's Report, 8 November 1839. H.O. 40/50.
[3] Gill and Briggs, *History of Birmingham*, I, 246.
[4] W. C. Alston to H.O. dated 31 August 1839. H.O. 40/50.
[5] Burgess to H.O. dated 20 November 1839, Private. H.O. 40/50.
[6] See above, p. 201.
[7] Burgess to H.O. dated 11 January 1840. H.O. 40/56.
[8] Rowan to H.O. dated 24 December 1839 and enclosures. H.O. 61/24.
[9] Report to Colonel Rowan dated 14 January 1840. H.O. 61/25.
[10] Reith, *British Police and the Democratic Ideal*, 240 et seq.

to pounce on a meeting of armed Chartists in the Trades Hall, Bethnal Green, on 16 January.

The West Riding too had its complement of spies. In Sheffield, during the week before the rising of 12 January 1840, the magistrates had notice of impending disturbance from a private source; Lord Howard was forewarned by a Chartist from Rotherham.[1] The abortive insurrection at Bradford on 27 January was betrayed to the authorities by James Harrison, who had been active as a spy for at least six weeks prior to the event.[2] He was employed by Brigg, the Head Constable,[3] who spent £45 7s. 6d. in obtaining information.[4] Meanwhile, at Huddersfield, the magistrates formed a committee for employing two persons to report on whether the Chartists held secret meetings, and administered secret oaths or discussed treasonable projects at them.[5] Similar reports of espionage came from Leicestershire,[6] Manchester[7] and Todmorden[8] at the end of 1839 and the beginning of 1840.

Informers in the pay of the authorities followed the turnout mobs on their tours of ejection in August 1842,[9] and sounded the depths of the Rebecca-ite conspiracy in 1843.[10] In 1848 Chartism was again the recipient of the attention of secret agents. The Metropolitan Police drew the information which led to an extensive round-up of London physical-force extremists on 16 August mainly from Thomas Powell and George Davis, who were themselves deeply implicated in the proceedings. Powell had been masquerading as a Chartist, under the assumed name of Johnson,

[1] Parker to H.O. dated 15 January 1840. H.O. 40/57.

[2] See deposition by him enclosed in Paley, Thompson and Hird to H.O. dated 17 December 1839. H.O. 40/51.

[3] *The Manchester Guardian*, 25 March 1840, p. 2.

[4] Clerk of Bradford Magistrates to H.O. dated 7 February 1840. H.O. 40/57.

[5] Battye, Brook and Walker to H.O. dated 22 January 1840. H.O. 40/57.

[6] Mowbray to H.O. dated 28 November 1839 and enclosed deposition. H.O. 40/44; Heyrick to H.O. dated 3 February 1840. H.O. 40/57.

[7] Shaw to H.O. dated 18 December 1839, Private and Confidential. H.O. 40/43.

[8] Shaw to H.O. dated 3 January 1840, Private. H.O. 40/54.

[9] Charles Smith, *Stockport in the Age of Reform* (1822–70), (unpublished) 309.

[10] By November 1843 Colonel Love, the military commander in South Wales, had spent above £30 in procuring secret information. Love to H.O. dated 18 November 1843. H.O. 45/453.

since shortly after 10 April, and for most of that time he had been in communication with the Commissioners of the Police who had paid him £1 per week. Little by little he had wormed his way into the confidence of the London Chartists, being elected first to the council of management of his district association (Cripplegate), then as a delegate from Cripplegate to a co-ordinating committee for the metropolis formed about 20 July, and finally to a smaller ulterior committee charged, as he alleged, with planning an insurrection.[1]

Davis was a second-hand book and furniture dealer from Greenwich.[2] He was a member of the Wat Tyler brigade of Chartists at Greenwich and attended meetings of a central co-ordinating committee of London Chartism.[3] For at least two months prior to the arrests of 16 August, Davis reported regularly to Inspector Mark of R Division, who took down written statements of his information.[4] He did not receive a regular wage, but was paid £150 in compensation for the loss of his business, as he was compelled, as soon as it was known that he had been a spy, to flee from Greenwich to the security of Southampton.[5] The Metropolitan Police were also getting information from at least two other Chartists, Charles Tilden[6] and a class leader from Lambeth, Charles Baldwinson,[7] when they struck on 16 August to forestall the armed outbreak which they had been warned to expect.

Meanwhile from the provinces came a similar tale of intrigue, deception and betrayal. At Bradford the two Flynns, father and son, were at the disposal of the authorities as spies. The elder Flynn

[1] See his examination at the trial of Dowling. *The Manchester Guardian*, 27 September 1848, p. 6; also H.O. to Commissioners of Metropolitan Police dated 27 November 1848. H.O. 65/16.

[2] *The Northern Star*, 7 October 1848, p. 8.

[3] *Ibid.*, 30 September 1848, p. 7.

[4] In the Home Office Papers there is a memorandum of a conversation between Davis and Inspector Mark dated June 1848. H.O. 45/2410/2. Davis, himself, asserted at the trial of Cuffay that he attended Chartist meetings down to 16 August, and "reported within two hours all that had occurred at each meeting to the inspector of police". *The Northern Star*, 30 September 1848, p. 7.

[5] Davis to H.O. dated 27 October 1849. H.O. 40/59.

[6] Metropolitan Police Records: 'Chartists' Box: 'Confidential Information Relative to Chartist Proceedings.'

[7] *The Northern Star*, 30 September 1848, p. 7.

gave information from time to time to the superintendent of the local police division.[1] Michael Flynn, one of the two, became a secretary of the Chartist Executive Council in Bradford; in August 1848 he disclosed to W. B. Ferrand, an active magistrate of the West Riding, particulars of a Chartist conspiracy to murder unpopular personages and to destroy property.[2]

The policy of drawing upon the services of private spies was attended by two very serious dangers. The first of these was that the informant, desirous of perpetuating the conditions of alarm which made his employment appear indispensable, would submit to his employers groundless or exaggerated reports of subversive activity. Less than twelve months after the abortive Newport Rising of 1839 the county of Monmouthshire was put into a state of alarm by reports circulated by George Frowen, a secret agent employed by Capel Hanbury Leigh, the Lord Lieutenant, to the effect that combustibles were being imported into the area for the purpose of destroying gentlemen's houses.[3] So great a credence did his information receive, from those who had the ear of government, that it was decided in October 1840 to reinforce the garrison at Pontypool, where the Lord Lieutenant's residence was situated, even though this could not be done without placing the troops in billets. The military commander remonstrated.[4] A man of more than usual sagacity, he deduced from the lack of corroboration of the current alarming rumours that there was probably no truth in them. "It is strange", he wrote to Lord Fitzroy Somerset, "how all the reports one hears, when investigated, are so invariably brought home to the same one or two individuals, and a consideration of this one circumstance has induced me to suspect that there is not so much cause for alarm as they would lead us to believe."[5] His suspicions were not unfounded. Frowen informed the magistrates of the borough of

[1] Wickham and Clayton to H.O. dated 19 June 1848. H.O. 45/2410AC.
[2] W. B. Ferrand to H.O. dated 16 August 1848. H.O. 45/2410AC.
[3] Hawkins to H.O. dated 24 October 1840, and enclosed deposition by Frowen. H.O. 40/55.
[4] Brown to Fitzroy Somerset dated 14 October 1840. H.O. 50/16.
[5] Brown to Fitzroy Somerset dated 29 September 1840. H.O. 50/16.

Newport that the combustibles had been brought by sea from Bristol to Cardiff, where they were deposited at the Five Bells Inn, and later removed to the Coach and Horses, Blackwood, to be called for by the consignees. On 21 October 1840 the Mayor of Newport, his suspicions aroused, carried out a thorough search of the Coach and Horses, finding nothing. The landlords of the Coach and Horses and the Five Bells vigorously denied that any packages had been deposited with them.[1] Frowen now endeavoured to retrieve the situation by claiming that the combustibles had reached the house of one, Alexander, in Newport. Before verifying this statement the Newport magistrates took the precaution of swearing Frowen to it, and when a further search had proved its utter falsity, they committed him to Monmouth Gaol to stand trial for perjury.[2] "Since this gentleman has been shut up", wrote the military commander, "we have no more alarming tales, and I trust that the Lord Lieutenant sleeps all the more soundly." [3]

The second danger arising out of the employment of secret agents was that the spies might become the instigators of violence and rebellion. There was a twofold logic which turned the spy into an *agent provocateur*. In the first place he had to gain the confidence of those whose designs it was his duty to betray, and could best do this by pretending an unrivalled zeal for the cause. When he became suspected, as often he did, he proclaimed in even louder tones his enthusiasm for violent courses, hoping thereby to throw dust in the eyes of his victims. Secondly the fomentation of plots, where none would otherwise have existed, was obviously good business for the spy, for it kept the authorities in a state of anxiety and willingness to spend money on secret service. It is not difficult to discover examples of provocation by the agents of the authorities during the Chartist period. Tongue, the Birmingham informer, took the chair at a Chartist meeting,[4]

[1] Hawkins to H.O. dated 24 October 1840 and enclosed depositions. H.O. 40/55.
[2] Mayor of Newport to H.O. dated 9 November 1840 and enclosed depositions. H.O. 40/55.
[3] Brown to Fitzroy Somerset dated 8 November 1840. H.O. 40/55.
[4] Burgess to H.O. date 30 October 1839. H.O. 65/10.

and, on one occasion, aired the view that the Birmingham Chartists were a set of cowards for allowing Frost to be transported.[1] Goulding, whose activities assisted the government in procuring the conviction of the London Chartists arrested at an armed meeting in the Trades Hall, Bethnal Green, on 16 January 1840, had urged persons to attend that meeting armed,[2] and had read the Queen's speech aloud to the gathering, to an accompaniment of derisive cheers and groans,[3] notwithstanding the fact that several days earlier he had put himself at the disposal of the Home Secretary as a spy.[4] Harrison, the Bradford spy of 1839–40,[5] and Michael Flynn who operated in the same district in 1848[6] both occupied positions of importance and trust in the movements which they betrayed. The turnout mob which visited the mills at Hyde on 14 August 1848 was actually headed by a spy—Daniel Lee, the cotton spinner, who had been in the habit of giving information to Brown, the constable.[7]

But the most flagrant example of provocation was to be found in the activities of Thomas Powell, the spy in the employment of the Metropolitan Police in 1848. Placed in the witness-box to testify against his fellow conspirators, and subjected to a stringent cross-examination, Powell confessed to innumerable villainies. He had drawn up a plan for the assassination of the police. He had made caltrops to cripple the horses of the cavalry.[8] He had induced men to fire houses and other premises.[9] He would not swear that he did not talk about "milk and water moral force——".[10] He

[1] Tongue's Report dated 17 March 1840. H.O. 40/56.

[2] *The Northern Star*, 7 March 1840, p. 8.

[3] *Times* report quoted in *The Northern Star*, 25 January 1840, p. 2.

[4] Goulding to H.O. (undated) quoted in Reith, *op. cit.*, 242.

[5] In the rising of 26 January 1840 he was entrusted with the task of summoning the delegates from the outlying districts, a task which he failed to carry out. *The Manchester Guardian*, 25 March 1840, p. 2.

[6] See above, pp. 207–8.

[7] *The Manchester Guardian*, 9 December 1848, p. 10: "They ordered me to go in the front", Lee explained somewhat unconvincingly afterwards. Deposition dated 25 August 1848. H.O. 48/40. It is possible, however, that he was pushed into the front because his motives were suspected.

[8] *The Northern Star*, 30 September 1848, p. 7.

[9] *Ibid.*, p. 5.

[10] *Ibid.*, p. 7.

had cast bullets for Gurney, one of the prisoners.[1] "I entered the Association", he admitted, "for the purpose of getting information and communicating it to the Police Commissioners. I encouraged and stimulated these men in order to inform against them." [2] A correspondent of the Duke of Wellington and the Metropolitan Police Commissioners, obviously well affected to the government, and having his own means of watching working-class political activity in the capital, wrote on 19 August 1848, before the full extent of Powell's iniquities had been disclosed in a court of law: "The witness, T. Powell, I fear, will do the Government no credit whatever. This is the same man to whom I alluded in a communication I made to the Duke of Wellington some time ago, as the person who had a large quantity of spike heads made of cork and lead at the bottom, to be thrown in the way of the cavalry horses. He also boasted that he had a large quantity of muskets and cutlasses which he offered for sale, and all this was before he became a member of the Chartists. He was one of the leaders on 29 May." [3] Only slightly less culpable was the other main government witness, George Davis, described by a witness for the defence, as "the great Chartist leader at Greenwich". He had sold guns to the Chartists, made use of a good deal of violent language against the Queen and the police, and encouraged attendance at meetings of the Chartist Club at Greenwich.[4] "I may have asked as many as 150 to come",[5] he admitted under examination.

These facts make it abundantly clear that the agents of the authorities shared responsibility for the illegal activities in which the Chartist movement became involved, but the precise extent of their contribution to physical-force Chartism is much more difficult to assess. The view taken here is that that contribution was not of tremendous magnitude, that it was certainly far less than Feargus O'Connor and other apologists of the movement

[1] *The Manchester Guardian*, 27 September 1848, p. 6.
[2] *The Northern Star*, 26 August 1848, p. 8.
[3] Metropolitan Police Records, 'Chartists' Box: Bundle marked 'Metropolitan Police—Confidential Information'.
[4] *The Times*, 30 September 1848, p. 7.
[5] *The Northern Star*, 7 October 1848, p. 8.

urged, for reasons which are not difficult to understand. None of the first-rank Chartist leaders falls under suspicion of being in the pay of the authorities, with the possible exception of Harney, and the evidence against him is circumstantial and, in the light of his rôle in the history of the movement, unconvincing. It is true that Alston, a Birmingham magistrate, wrote in 1839 that he had sent his spy to London "at the desire of Julian Harney", but since he added that he had had no personal communication with Harney, the remark proves nothing.[1] This, we may perhaps presume, is the incriminating letter in the Home Office Papers alluded to by Mark Hovell.[2]

From the responsibility for so much of physical-force Chartism as resulted from the deliberations and impassioned utterances of the major leaders of the movement, spies and informers may reasonably be acquitted. But much of the initiative in the outbreaks of the period, particularly those which were planned and premeditated, came not from the great public figures of Chartism, but from men of a less distinguished breed. The possibility remains open, therefore, that the agents of the authorities, moving in this latter circle, generated most of the violence which they subsequently disclosed to their employers. A closer examination of the evidence, however, makes this conclusion suspect. Gammage, the Chartist historian, thought the Newport Rising of 1839 to be partly the work of *agents provocateurs*, citing in support of this view that 25 out of 37 witnesses at the trial of Frost gave what was commonly termed Queen's Evidence.[3] Against this it must be remembered, however, that many of these accomplices had been taken up by the mob, and forced against their will to accompany the rioters, whilst others were undoubted Chartists, who had clutched at this opportunity of saving their skins after the failure of the Rising. It has been contended further, in favour of attributing the authorship of the Newport affair to *agents provocateurs*, that "a man with a glazed hat" and a deserter from the

---

[1] Alston to H.O. dated 31 August 1839. H.O. 40/50.

[2] *Op. cit.*, p. 178, n. 1. See also A. Schoyen, *The Chartist Challenge: A Portrait of George Julian Harney*, pp. 87–8.

[3] Gammage, *op. cit.*, 166.

army spurred on the mob to attack Newport, but it is by no means certain that these parties had real existence,[1] and, even if they did exist, supposition alone would place them in government employment.

O'Connor, writing in *The Northern Star* on the 'Government Spy System', presented the case that the risings at Sheffield and Bradford in January 1840 were largely fomented by the authorities through their agents:

> Rayner, the Superintendent of Police at Sheffield [he wrote] was forced to admit upon his cross-examination that for nine days previous to the outbreak at Sheffield he had seen, and been in the habit of conversing with, a Frenchman of the name of Hartley, or some such name; while every article of combustible preparation found at poor Holberry's house, and upon which alone he was convicted, was of French manufacture; and without any previous information against Holberry, save what must have been gathered from the Frenchman, he went to the poor fellow's house, and "He who hides can find".[2]

Had O'Connor's readers turned on to the columns of the *Star* in which the evidence given at Holberry's[3] trial was reported, they would have found difficulty in reconciling it with his commentary. Rayner was explicit in denying that he had ever spoken to Hartley,[4] whose name in any case hardly suggests French origin. Nor does it appear that, in searching Holberry's house, the police went straight to the garret where the bulk of the arms were hid, but rather that they first explored Holberry's bedroom, finding nothing, and, as they were leaving, spotted the staircase leading up to the garret.[5] O'Connor's allegation with respect to the Bradford Rising, that the spy Harrison led Brook the Chartist up to the forces of the authorities[6] sounds more credible, though Harrison denied it, but the general trend of the latter's evidence, as far as it is capable of credence, tends to support the view that

[1] D. Williams, *John Frost*, 214 and 222.

[2] *The Northern Star*, 21 March 1840, p. 4.

[3] Holberry was the Chartist leader referred to in the introductory chapter, in whose house a collection of hand grenades and fireballs was found by the Sheffield police. See above, p. 23.

[4] *The Northern Star*, 21 March 1840, p. 6.   [5] *Ibid.*

[6] *The Northern Star*, 21 March 1840, p. 4.

by his failure to distribute messages to the delegates of the out-lying districts, the task committed to him by the Chartists, who trusted him, Harrison damped down the insurrection, and thus diverged from the rôle of *agent provocateur*.[1]

Though spies were deeply implicated in the revolutionary movements in Lancashire and London frustrated by the author-ities in August 1848, their rôle must not be exaggerated. *The Northern Star* was not warranted in asserting, with reference to the events in the metropolis, that Powell, the government witness, "was the fomenter of the whole conspiracy".[2] My reasons for dismissing this allegation are as follows. In the first place develop-ments in London were only part of a wider conspiracy which extended to the north of England, and had Manchester as its focus.[3] If Powell is to be regarded as the *fons et origo* of the entire plot, then it must be shown that he originated the movement in the north. The *Star* endeavoured to prove just that by publishing an undated letter written by Powell to Feargus O'Connor, explaining that he, Powell, had sent missionaries to bring out the Chartists of the north, and summoning O'Connor to attend a meeting of delegates in London.[4] The fact that this letter was signed Thomas Powell, when Powell was moving in Chartist circles under the name of Johnson, leads one to suspect that it was a fabrication. It is also difficult to believe that Powell could have been fool enough to write so incriminating a letter, or that, if he had written it, the Chartist defence would not have produced it in court at the trial of Cuffay. Secondly, such evidence as we possess, derived it is true from tainted sources, but partially con-firmed by its dependence upon the testimony of more than one witness,[5] gives grounds for believing that Powell was not actually

---

[1] *The Manchester Guardian*, 25 March 1840, p. 2; F. Peel, *The Risings of the Luddites, Chartists and Plug Drawers*, 324 et seq.

[2] *The Northern Star*, 26 August 1848, p. 4.   [3] See above, pp. 24–6.

[4] *The Northern Star*, 26 August 1848, p. 4.

[5] See Powell's own evidence at the trial of Ritchie, Able, Gurney, etc. (*The Manchester Guardian*, 27 September 1848, p. 6) and at the examination of prisoners at Bow St. (*The Northern Star*, 26 August 1848, p. 8). This is cor-roborated by the evidence of Davis (*The Northern Star*, 30 September 1848, p. 7). Davis gave evidence after Powell and would, therefore, be aware of what Powell had said, but since his reports to Inspector Mark of the Metropolitan

a member of the highest executive committee of the London physical-force Chartists at the time when the police arrested the leaders. Powell and Davis, the two approvers who gave evidence at the Chartist trials at the Old Bailey in September 1848, both testified to the existence not only of a sort of metropolitan central committee consisting of delegates from the several localities of the metropolis, but also of a smaller ulterior committee of four or five members, which laid plans for a rising. Powell claimed to be a member of the former, but both Powell and Davis were certain that he was not a member of the ulterior committee when the London plot matured, and that he did not withdraw with that committee from the larger meeting at the Lord Denman, Suffolk St., Blackfriars Rd., on 15 August, to take counsel with Lacey, newly returned from Manchester, and to make the final plans for an outbreak on the following day. According to his own evidence he had been a member for a few days early in August, but had been ejected along with three others for not producing plans of insurrection. The wretched informer was by no means guiltless of leading others into lawlessness, but his contribution to whatever was afoot in London on 16 August 1848 was a purely secondary one. In inducing others to undertake the task of firing houses and other premises he merely carried out the instructions issued to all delegates by Mullins, a surgeon and member of the small ulterior committee, who distinguished himself by a forthright and uncompromising advocacy of physical force.

The spies of the Chartist movement were active, therefore, in encouraging disorder, but they were not on the whole the prime movers; and from this it follows that, in the absence of modern methods of detecting crime and conspiracy, the employment of such agents was justified. Moreover, in places where a professional police system had come into existence, spies were treated with a healthy suspicion by their employers. The Birmingham

Police prior to the arrest of the Chartist leaders, were produced in court, he can hardly have departed seriously from the contents of them. Superintendent Mallalieu's police reports of 14 and 15 August 1848 confirm in the main the testimony of Davis and Powell, one of whom was probably the source of the information contained in them. H.O. 45/2410(2).

P

Police Commissioner engaged additional informers to watch the behaviour of the spy Tongue, and to test the accuracy of his informations.[1] The Metropolitan Police conducted detailed enquiries into the circumstances and characters of persons offering to give information about the Chartists in the London area. The records of the Metropolitan Police Office and the Home Office for the years 1839 and 1848 contain abundant details of such investigations, the majority of which terminated in a decision to reject the offer of information, on the grounds that the individual offering it was merely trying to get money out of the government, and had nothing useful or reliable to communicate.[2] When, at the end of January 1849, Julian Harney forwarded to the Home Office a letter which he had just received, suggesting methods of preparing weapons for offensive warfare against the government, and insinuated that it might have come from a spy in the service of the authorities, Commissioner Mayne went to the trouble of comparing the handwriting with that of the numerous correspondents who had written to the police in the previous year, offering to disclose information of seditious conspiracies.[3]

In Sir Charles Shaw's Manchester police force the attempt was made, on at least one occasion, to replace the services of the spy by a more direct method of observation which eliminated the dangers of distortion and provocation. In December 1839, when Chartists all over England were meeting behind closed doors to devise some means of rescuing the unfortunate Frost from his doom, Shaw prevailed upon the landlady of the premises used by the Manchester Chartists as a committee room to allow him to place himself and his officers in concealed positions within the building, from which they might observe without being observed. Since the Chartist committee was in arrears of rent to the extent

[1] Burgess to H.O. dated 31 October 1839. Also reports of Thomas Simmonds, 2–4 November 1839. H.O. 40/50.

[2] Metropolitan Police Records, 'Chartists' Box: Bundles marked 'Chartist Proceedings, 1848', and 'Special Reports and Documents'. See also H.O. 44/52 and 61/25.

[3] Metropolitan Police Records, 'Chartists' Box: 'Special Reports and Documents'.

of £15, the landlady was not unwilling to comply, and the police obtained a vantage point which afforded them a complete insight into Chartist proceedings.[1] The point is often made that modern methods of crime detection differ from those of the Bow Street Runners as "diligent observation" differs from "familiar association". In taking this step Sir Charles Shaw's force had advanced from the latter method to the former.

Akin to the employment of spies was the practice of procuring information from accomplices about offences already committed, by offering a reward coupled with the promise of a pardon to the informer for his share in the offence. Once arrests of Chartist leaders had been effected, it was not usually too difficult to prevail on one or two of the prisoners to tender Queen's Evidence—i.e. to testify against their fellows, on condition of the abandonment of the prosecution against themselves, and also, perhaps, of a promise of free transport overseas, away from the vengeance which awaited them at the hands of their neighbours.[2] There were times, however, during the Chartist period, when, owing to threats and intimidation, it was well-nigh impossible to procure such evidence as would justify either arrest or prosecution. In these circumstances, it was customary for the local authorities to make a public offer of a small reward for information of this character, and for the Home Secretary to supplement it with an additional sum from the Secret Service funds, and with the promise of a free pardon to informers who happened to be implicated in the criminal proceedings. Normally the offer related to a specific offence which had already been committed, and could not, therefore, tend to the concoction of crime, but it is possible that the knowledge that such offers were habitually made may have encouraged unscrupulous men to get up

[1] Shaw to H.O. dated 18 December 1839 (Private and Confidential). H.O. 40/43.

[2] The Crown witnesses against the Chartists arrested for the disturbances at Ashton-under-Lyne in August 1848 were assisted by the Colonial Land and Emigration Commissioners acting on the recommendation of the Ashton magistrates, to emigrate to New South Wales. Correspondence enclosed in Elliott to Waddington dated 27 May 1850. H.O. 45/3136.

conspiracies, or at least to fan them, for the sake of the reward. It is undeniable that several of the Crown witnesses in Chartist trials had themselves occupied positions of trust and authority in the movement.[1] When, in times of emergency, the government resorted to proclamations of a general character offering rewards and pardons for information concerning any offence of a particular kind which might occur,[2] the risk of provocation was enhanced. Moreover, the persons who could be prevailed upon to betray their fellows were sometimes of such a character that their evidence was worthless in a court of law. James Abraham Ball, an accomplice, produced as a witness against the Manchester Chartists and Confederates at the Liverpool Assizes in 1848, so perjured himself that he was hissed by the persons present, and finally ordered out of court by the judge.[3] To make the offer of a reward conditional upon the conviction of an offender, as was often the practice during this period, was to encourage approvers to falsify their evidence in order to ensure a verdict of guilty.

One further means of obtaining information resting at the disposal of the authorities remains to be noted—viz., the opening of letters at the Post Office. Notwithstanding the Englishman's proud boast that his correspondence is inviolable, English law recognizes the right of the Secretary of State to issue his warrant to the Postmaster-General calling upon him to open the letters of suspected persons, and send them for inspection. The practice of intercepting correspondence (which was based on prerogative) dates from the Tudor period, and was recognized by the Post

---

[1] Thompson, the witness against the Sheffield Chartists in 1840, was a class leader. *The Manchester Guardian*, 18 January 1840, p. 3; Lattimore, who appeared against the Ashton rioters in December 1848, had been a sergeant in the National Guard in command of one of the prisoners. *The Manchester Guardian*, 20 December 1848, p. 7.

[2] Such a proclamation was issued during the Plug-Plot disturbances. P. W. Slosson, *The Decline of the Chartist Movement* (Columbia University Studies in History, Economics and Public Law, Vol. LXXIII). During the Rebecca Riots £50 and a pardon was offered "for the conviction of every person concerned in pulling down a tollgate or destroying a toll house". H.O. to Walsh dated 7 October 1843. H.O. 41/18.

[3] *The Manchester Guardian*, 20 December 1848, p. 7.

Office Acts of 1710 and 1837 as being vested in the Secretary of State.[1]

Eighteenth-century warrants had been vague and indefinite in character. Large numbers of persons were included in a single warrant, and during the '45 Rebellion the Duke of Newcastle went so far as to order the detention of all letters "suspected to contain matters of a dangerous tendency". After the close of the Napoleonic War the warrants continued to be issued, but became more definite in their specification. Names were cited in each case, and even minute differences of name or address were considered sufficient to justify separate mention or the issue of a separate warrant. The number of persons mentioned in one warrant did not now generally exceed six, and a check was imposed on the use of warrants after 1806, by the introduction of the practice of entering them in a book accessible to the Under-Secretaries of State and the Chief Clerk of the Domestic Department.[2]

Warrants fell into two main categories—criminal warrants designed to facilitate the exposure of crime, and security warrants issued for the purpose of disclosing proceedings dangerous to the State, or deeply involving British interests overseas. The former were issued by the Secretary of State at the request of magistrates and solicitors in charge of prosecutions, but the initiative as to the latter rested with the Home Secretary. Criminal warrants were entered in the ordinary Public Office Book kept by the Home Office,[3] whilst security warrants were recorded in a special Private and Secret Entry Book.[4]

Warrants of the second type increased significantly in number and importance during the first half of the nineteenth century, reflecting the heightened tempo of political activity. Whereas in the period 1712–98 warrants issued in connection with cases of treason and sedition constituted only 5 per cent of the whole (i.e.

[1] For a study of how this kind of secret service was organized in the eighteenth and early nineteenth centuries, see K. Ellis, *The Post Office in the Eighteenth Century*, especially Chapter VI and Appendix IV.

[2] The foregoing information concerning the early exercise of the prerogative of opening letters is derived from the *Report of the Secret Committee of the House of Commons on the Post Office*, 1844 (582) XIV.   [3] H.O. 34.   [4] H.O. 79.

5 out of 101), the percentage rose to 20 (77 out of 372) for the years 1799–1844.[1] A detailed examination of the later period reveals a fluctuation of the number of warrants in sympathy with the political movements of the time, peaks being attained in 1812, 1817, 1831, 1839 and 1842, all years of intense social disturbance.[2] The first warrant issued against the Chartists appeared on 8 February 1839, four days after the commencement of the Convention in London, and ordered the opening of the correspondence of four delegates to that body. It was worded as follows: "My Lord—I am to desire, and do hereby authorize your Lordship to detain, open and send for my inspection all letters received at the General Post Office addressed to Dr. Wade, Pembroke Terrace, Pimlico—Richardson, Arundel Coffee House, S. Clements churchyard and Strand—Vincent, 5 Greenland Grove, Cromer St.—Hartwell, 5 Commercial Rd., Lambeth—and for so doing this shall be your sufficient warrant—I am sir, J. Russell (H.S.)—Secret."[3]

Soon the intercepted letters of these parties began to find their way to the office of the Secretary of State for Home Affairs.[4] If they were expected to disclose evidence of a top-secret seditious conspiracy, they must have proved disappointing, for they contained little of importance concerning the Chartist movement that could not equally well have been derived from other sources. The warrant authorizing the detention of these letters was held in force for more than five months,[5] notwithstanding the fact that Dr. Wade, one of the parties named in it, had by that time withdrawn from the Chartist Convention in dissent from the violent measures which were in contemplation. Meanwhile, in May 1839, the scope of the letter scrutiny had been extended to include the correspondence of Henry Hetherington[6] and Feargus O'Connor.[7]

---

[1] *Secret Committee on Post Office*, Rept., pp. 10–11.
[2] See Appendix II to this volume.
[3] Warrant dated 8 February 1839. H.O. 79/4.
[4] H.O. 40/53 contains copies of letters intercepted.
[5] The order freeing this correspondence from inspection was issued on 13 July 1839. H.O. 79/4.
[6] Warrant dated 9 May 1839. H.O. 79/4.
[7] Warrant dated 23 May 1839. H.O. 79/4.

Early in August, when a general strike in favour of the Charter was apprehended, the letters of Lowery, Fletcher, Carpenter and O'Brien were placed under surveillance.[1] These men belonged to a committee of seven meeting in London, to which the Convention, before dispersing, had delegated its responsibilities in respect of the strike.[2] On 5 August a warrant was issued against the correspondence of John Frost,[3] and in late December, when rumours were rife of secret plotting to secure Frost's release, and when the conduct of the Chartist agitation had largely passed into new hands, the scrutiny was put into operation against Harney, Cardo, Peddie, Hansom, Dr. John Taylor and a Carlisle news-agent named Arthur, with whom Taylor was staying.[4]

During the Plug-Plot disturbances and afterwards the letters of a large number of individuals scattered throughout the country, but mainly in the provincial towns of the north, were regularly opened and read for nearly two months.[5] The addressees were mostly Chartists, e.g. O'Connor, MacDouall and Cleave, but the correspondence of middle-class radicals was by no means inviolate. The warrant against Richard Cobden dated 19 August 1842 reflected the Conservative government's suspicions as to the complicity of the Anti-Corn Law League in the upheaval. This method of obtaining information was also used during the Rebecca Riots when the letters of Hugh Williams, the radical solicitor of Carmarthen, who was suspected of actually being Rebecca, were subjected to inspection.[6]

Of course, the system was not maintained without difficulty. When too many warrants were allowed to accumulate, the Post Office was apt to complain. "We shall be very much obliged", wrote Colonel Maberley, the Secretary to the Post Office in November 1839, "if you can relieve us from any of the secret orders now in force. We have no less than ten now in operation, which greatly embarrass the general business for the search must be made, although no letters are found to be sent to you, every

---

[1] Warrant dated 3 August 1839. H.O. 79/4. [2] West, *op. cit.*, 139.
[3] Warrant dated 5 August 1839. H.O. 79/4.
[4] Warrant dated 21 December 1839. H.O. 79/4. [5] H.O. 79/4.
[6] Warrant dated 6 October 1843. H.O. 79/4.

day."[1] More acute were the problems arising out of the need to allay suspicion. Numerous subterfuges were adopted to avoid detection. According to an allegation made in Parliament pains were taken to ensure that the cut across the seal of the letter was "so delicate that it almost required a magnifying glass to follow its trace", and a double stamp was frequently applied to render illegible the postmark of the hour when the letter reached the G.P.O.[2]

The greatest danger of exposure arose, however, from the delay in forwarding interrupted letters. "If you do not wish what you are doing to be known", Maberley warned the Under-Secretary at the Home Office in February 1839, "I think it right to tell you you run a great risk, as in both the instances the original communications must be detained a day."[3] It was only natural that the suspicions of Hetherington should be aroused, when, as in the summer of 1839, the retardation of his correspondence by the Post Office was such that the customers of his newspaper business began to complain of delay in attention to their orders.[4]

The perils of delay were multiplied, when the addressee of the intercepted correspondence resided in the provinces, and the decision to open the letters of John Frost of Newport in August 1839 raised this problem in an acute form. To require the Newport postmaster to stop all letters addressed to Frost and send them back to London for inspection by the Home Secretary would be to court a delay which, if incurred in several consecutive cases, could only result in disclosure. The alternative, of allowing the postmaster at Newport to open the letters, make transcripts for the Home Secretary's use, and forward the originals to their destination was scouted by the General Post Office,[5] probably on grounds of security. It was, therefore, decided to intercept and copy Frost's letters at the G.P.O., London,[6] but this expedient

---

[1] Maberley to H.O. dated 20 November 1839. H.O. 33/4.
[2] Hans., 3 Ser., LXXV, 1267.
[3] Maberley to H.O. dated 15 February 1839. H.O. 40/53.
[4] Maberley to H.O. dated 12 July 1839 (Secret). H.O. 33/4.
[5] Phillipps to Maberley dated 5 August 1839 (Secret). H.O. 79/4.
[6] Phillipps to Maberley dated 8 August 1839 (Confidential). H.O. 79/4.

must also have been attended by considerable delay, since the
sorting of mails destined for distant places in the provinces was
not normally undertaken until the bags had left London.[1] Two
years later, during the Plug-Plot disturbances, the postal authorities preferred to despatch three confidential clerks to the provinces
to copy the letters of the parties under observation at the local
post offices, and to send the originals direct to their addressees.[2]
Where a letter had been so retarded as to arouse strong suspicions,
both Home Secretary and Postmaster-General were prepared to
contemplate drastic steps. In April 1839 the latter returned to the
Under-Secretary at the Home Office a letter written by Lord
Stanhope to R. J. Richardson, the Chartist delegate, refusing to
present a petition in favour of the restoration of Frost to the
magistracy. "I return you the letter", he added, "as we think
suppression on the whole the most advisable. Detention would
give rise to suspicion as it would be the second letter put out of
course within a few days, and we can easily get over any further
enquiry."[3] Before the end of the year the Home Office tendered
similar advice. "I return to you the letter addressed to Dr. Taylor
at Mr. T. Arthur's, Newsagent, Carlisle", wrote Phillipps to the
Postmaster-General on 27 December 1839. "Lord Normanby
thinks it had better not be forwarded unless you can suggest any
course, either as a 'Missent' letter or any device, by which the
delay in its reaching Dr. Taylor's hands can be accounted for."[4]
The following day Lord Normanby gave directions for stopping
only such of Taylor's letters as bore the London postmark.[5]

Despite the elaborate precautions taken to maintain secrecy the
practice of opening letters was not unknown to the public, and its
efficiency was thereby diminished. A little more than a fortnight
after the issue of the warrant against R. J. Richardson, Wade,
Vincent and Hartwell, the first-named of these parties told the
Chartist Convention that his letters had been "most unaccountably detained, in most cases opened, and in some cases suppressed

[1] Howard Robinson, *The British Post Office: A History*, 332.
[2] *Secret Committee on the Post Office*, Rept., p. 13.
[3] Draft of Lichfield to Maule dated 7 April 1839. H.O. 40/53.
[4] Phillipps to Maberley dated 27 December 1839 (Secret). H.O. 79/4.
[5] Phillipps to Maberley dated 28 December 1839 (Secret). H.O. 79/4.

altogether". A number of other delegates having made similar complaints, a committee of the Convention consisting of Dr. Taylor, Bailie Craig and one other was appointed to enquire into the matter and report.[1] Readers of Thomas Cooper's autobiography will also recall that Cooper despatched his letters from the Potteries to Leicester in August 1842 by a private messenger, because he feared to send them through the post.[2]

These were mere glimmers of suspicion. In June 1844, however, the searchlight of public opinion was focused upon this method of obtaining information. By a peculiar stroke of fortune, the exposure arose, not from the widespread use of the Home Secretary's warrant as an instrument of the preservation of internal order, but from its employment in the interests of British diplomacy. On representations from abroad that Mazzini, the Italian exile in England, was conspiring to excite insurrection in Italy, Lord Aberdeen, the British Foreign Secretary, had requested his colleague at the Home Office, Sir James Graham, to order the opening of Mazzini's letters. This having been effected, Duncombe, the ultra-radical member for Finsbury, presented a petition to Parliament, on behalf of Mazzini and three others, protesting against interference with their correspondence. What followed—Sir James Graham's disdainful refusal to give information to the House of Commons, the storm of public indignation within and without the doors of Parliament, the appointment of secret committees of both Houses to investigate the use of the Home Secretary's powers—has been adequately related elsewhere.[3] Despite the bitter criticisms directed against it, the law authorizing the Home Secretary to order the interception of letters remained unchanged, and it is impossible to say with any certainty how far the practice was affected by the crisis of 1844–5. The entering of warrants in the Private and Secret Entry Book kept by the Home Office ceased abruptly after the month of June 1844, but this does not prove that political warrants were no longer issued. It may well be that the Home Secretary merely decided to make no further entries in a book which might be

---

[1] *The Northern Star*, 2 March 1839, p. 5.   [2] Cooper, *op. cit.*, p. 193.
[3] Robinson, *op. cit.*, Chap. XXIV.

scrutinized by a future parliamentary committee. It was stated
in the report of the Secret Committee of the House of Commons
in 1844 that from 1822 onwards the original warrants were
preserved at the Post Office.[1] If, therefore, these could be located,
some light might well be thrown on the issue of political warrants
after 1844, but the writer has been unable to trace any nineteenth-
century warrants for the opening of letters at the G.P.O.,
London.[2] Rowland Hill, Secretary of the Post Office 1854–64,
declared that during his time warrants were issued only in a very
few instances "relating, so far as I can recollect, exclusively to
burglars, and others of that stamp",[3] but allegations were made in
the less tranquil years of the later nineteenth century that letters
were being opened once again in cases of a political character.[4]

It must, therefore, be concluded that, in their handling of the
problem of disorder during the period under review, the authorities continued to have recourse to the devices of secrecy and concealment. There was no clear break with the oft-decried methods
associated with the names of Sidmouth and Castlereagh. The
growth of the new police forces did not indeed produce a repudia-
tion of spies and informers, for these were employed as much by
the officers of the Metropolitan Force as by the magistrates of the
still inadequately policed rural districts. But if the spy was not
ejected from his employment he was now at least suspected by the
more enlightened of those who engaged his services, and the
establishment of professional police forces supplied the means of
subjecting him to a more systematic vigilance and control.

[1] Rept., p. 9.
[2] For assistance in this investigation I am indebted to Mr. G. W. P. Devenport of the G.P.O. Record Room.
[3] Robinson, op. cit., 351.
[4] The use of warrants was questioned in 1881 when Irish matters were at
tension. Ibid., 352.

CHAPTER VII

CONCLUSION: THE MACHINERY IN MOTION

BROADLY speaking we may distinguish in the several major disturbances[1] of the period under review a common cyclical pattern, at every stage of which we may see the interaction of the disorders and the governmental machinery which confronted them.

The initial phase was one in which the contest was waged by the local magistrates of town and county with those resources which rested locally at their disposal—the constables of the parishes, the police of the boroughs, the rural police forces (where such existed), the special constables whom the magistrates were able to recruit from among the local tradesmen and Chelsea out-pensioners, the regular military force already stationed within the disturbed district and the county Yeomanry corps. The Home Office, under Whig and Tory governments alike, at first held aloof, tendering advice when consulted and sometimes sending down to the scene of disorder a few Metropolitan Policemen, who would assist rather than supersede local endeavour by organizing the special constables sworn in by the magistrates into an efficient force, but declining to take the initiative in directing operations or materially to augment the resources of the local authorities.

This local machinery on which so much depended proved quite unequal to the task. The magistrates were at first notoriously supine. In the early spring of 1839 the Whig Home Secretary and his associates depicted them to Napier as "a poor set on whom no reliance can be placed".[2] Rather than make full use of their own resources they preferred to clamour helplessly to the government for military assistance or new repressive legislation. Some of this

---

[1] The term 'disturbances' is here used to signify not individual riots but the prolonged periods of disorder distinguished in Chapter I. See above, pp. 8-9.
[2] Napier, op. cit., II, 6.

226

inertia occasionally sprang from disaffection such as was felt against the New Poor Law by the Tory gentry of the West Riding and against Sir Robert Peel's Conservative administration by millowning magistrates in Lancashire in August 1842. Some was due to a rather optimistic outlook on the subject of disturbances common in radical town councils whose members had been accustomed in the early stages of the Chartist movement to a considerable measure of co-operation with the Chartists. Principally, however, it was a consequence of fear—of want of confidence in the resources locally available to maintain the peace.

This apprehension did not lack justification. In fact the most serious charge that can be sustained against the authorities of borough and county alike is their failure to establish adequate professional police forces before the outbreaks occurred, although they had been given the requisite legal powers by the Municipal Corporations Act of 1835 and the Rural Police Acts of 1839-40. Once the disturbances had broken out there was little that the magistrates could have done to produce immediate useful effect. Except in one or two of the largest towns, the permanent civil force was inadequate both in quality and size, and there were not enough troops regularly stationed in the large manufacturing area of Lancashire and Yorkshire to supply the means of dealing with any large-scale outbreak. Denied the security of military protection and on some occasions, like the magistrates, actuated by sympathy with the mob, the local inhabitants refused all co-operation with the authorities. It was thus a feature of this early phase in the disturbances that special constables could only with difficulty be enrolled and that every conceivable obstacle was presented to the prosecution of offenders. In the absence of means of protecting witnesses the task of collecting evidence was an unenviable one, and jurymen, exposed to all manner of intimidation, showed a marked unwillingness to convict. In brief the government looked to the local authorities; the local authorities looked to the government; with the result that no effective resistance was offered to the disorders.

During the Chartist disturbances of 1838-9 this early phase lasted until the end of April 1839. The corresponding period of the Plug-Plot extended for about a week after the outbreak of rioting in Lancashire on 8 August 1842, and the Rebecca Riots in Wales passed through a similar phase prior to the middle of June 1843.

The weaknesses in the machinery of public order permitted the disturbances to gain a foothold. Thus, for example, during the so-called Plug-Plot Riots vast mobs were allowed to gather and to transmit the turnout from town to town and from district to district with very little attempt to check their progress. In those cases where the authorities took it upon themselves to interfere, the paucity of the force employed was such as to encourage the rioters to resist fiercely, and bitter clashes ensued, frequently accompanied by loss of life. Within a week of the beginning of the outbreak in Lancashire the mob found itself for a while virtually in command of large towns like Stockport and Bolton, and that violence and destruction of property did not take place on a large scale was solely due to the restraint of the working men. The situation was such as might readily have been harnessed to revolutionary purposes by leaders of zeal and determination. In fact a local postmaster, writing to the G.P.O. from Accrington in Lancashire at the height of the disturbances, affirmed in terror: "It is more like a Revolution than anything else in this neighbourhood, and we fear that plunder and mischief is not at an end".[1]

It must be remembered, however, that the danger was very largely due to the fact that ministers were consciously and deliberately refusing to put forth their whole strength against the disturbances until the local machinery had been fully tested and a positive necessity had arisen. Eventually the point was reached when assistance from the central government could no longer be withheld. Then a new phase opened in the cycle of disorder— a phase in which, under the stimulus imparted by the government, the entire machinery acquired a new momentum. The action taken by the Home Office assumed a variety of forms. Royal Proclamations were issued declaring the law in respect of particular offences as a warning to the disaffected and calling upon magistrates in the Queen's name to do their duty. Circular letters

[1] Hutchinson to Maberley dated 17 August 1842. H.O. 45/249.

were despatched to Lords Lieutenant and to the magistrates in their several petty sessions and borough benches, tendering advice on how to act in particular circumstances. Once the decision had been taken large military reinforcements were poured into the manufacturing districts of the North with all speed from Ireland, or by rail from the garrisons of the south of England. Rewards to informers were offered at the government's expense. Arms were supplied to special constables and persons wishing to form voluntary defence associations. Shorthand writers were sent down to the provinces to report seditious speeches, and the investigation of offences against the public peace was taken out of the hands of the magistrates and committed to agents of the central government, such as the Treasury Solicitor and the Chief Magistrate of Bow Street.

The intervention of the Home Office certainly reduced the strength of the insurrectionary movement. All else apart it had a strong moral effect which was quickly perceptible. One has only to read through the files of *The Northern Star* newspaper for May 1839 to appreciate the extent to which the need for caution was imposed upon the Chartists by the Royal Proclamation issued early in that month, and the military movements then set on foot. On 9 May Bronterre O'Brien moved an Address in the Convention urging the Chartist followers not to parade arms at public meetings and attributing the practice of illegal drilling, which had been specifically denounced by the Proclamation, to the machinations of spies. This was reported in the issue of the *Star* for 18 May, together with an article warning the people against carrying arms at the proposed Whitsuntide demonstrations. Similarly the Proclamation which was issued at the height of the Plug-Plot disturbances offering a general reward to all informers, and the strong military reinforcements sent by rail to Manchester and other parts of the disturbed districts, had a profoundly depressing effect on the spirits of the Chartists not only in Manchester, but in towns as far distant as Oldham and Stockport.[1]

Moreover the situation was affected by the greater vigour with

[1] See reports in *The Times* and in H.O. 45/249 and 249C.

which the magistrates began to perform their duties and the propertied inhabitants to enrol themselves on the side of order, when prodded by the government and assured of proper support. During the summer of 1839 the magistrates acted against the Chartists with greater energy than had been demonstrated earlier in the year, before the Whig government's intervention in May. Much of their activity was misplaced—directed towards the breaking up of meetings which, as Napier saw, would have been better left alone—but of its reality and of the depressing effect it had upon the Chartist fortunes there can be little doubt. In very much the same way the supineness of the magistrates of Lancashire in the first week of the Plug-Plot disturbances gave place, after the Proclamation and the sending of troops, to vigorous measures. The borough authorities of Bolton, Wigan and Preston took steps to repel the turnout mobs at the entrance to their towns, and little by little order was restored to the great towns of Lancashire and the West Riding.

During this second phase of the cycle, however, the restoration of order was only partial, and the extent to which it was achieved varied with the character and circumstances of the disorders. In the late summer of 1839 and the early summer of 1848 Chartism was driven underground. When their meetings were interfered with by the authorities the Chartists simply ceased to hold them openly, and met in classes and committees behind closed doors. Soon after the government had shown its hand the semi-Chartist strike movement of August 1842 shed many of its most dangerous features, including its political character, but continued as a strike for higher wages. Violence still occurred in the form of attacks on factories and mines which dared to resume work, but it was pushed out from the towns into the remote country districts where the mob could effect sharp hit-and-run raids on isolated factories, and disappear long before the soldiers arrived on the scene.[1] It was possible to keep the disturbances going in this form for many weeks after order had been restored to the towns, because the military commanders firmly refused to allow their

---

[1] Winder to H.O. dated 17 August 1842. H.O. 45/249. See also report of meeting of Staffordshire magistrates. *The Times*, 7 September 1842, p. 6.

troops to be divided into small parties for guarding individual workplaces, and there was insufficient civil force to do this duty. The despatch of troops into Wales in June 1843 had little effect upon the Rebecca Riots, as they were almost entirely conducted in the countryside, and the terrain offered every advantage to the insurgent peasantry and every obstacle to the forces of order. A decisive check was indeed administered to the more overt disorders which had been developing in the preceding weeks, and had been most strikingly illustrated in the Carmarthen workhouse riot; but attacks on isolated toll-gates and lonely farm-houses continued unabated throughout the summer.[1]

In general, disorder narrowed down during this phase into a form which was capable of being sustained against heavy official opposition. More emphasis than previously was now laid upon eluding and harassing the forces of the Crown rather than upon resisting them. The inability of the troops to act in dispersion, the shortage of magistrates in many districts, and the continued refusal of many of them even to lead the troops which were sent to their assistance were all exploited by the rioters. Fundamentally, however, the situation was far less dangerous than in the period before the government intervened, for the towns at least had been restored to order and a sufficiently large military force was available at the main centres to counter any major outbreak.

The third and last phase of the cycle began when the authorities tackled the disorder in its new form. If the danger was from secret meetings the magistrates and chief constables penetrated the inner conclaves with their spies and plain-clothes officers. To cope with the problem of the hit-and-run raid, they either resorted to a system of civilian horse patrols, as in Cheshire and Staffordshire in 1842, or set up numerous small posts manned by police and military and distributed throughout the disturbed countryside, as in Wales in October 1843.[2] Though much of this endeavour, notably the horse patrols, arose from the self-help of the propertied inhabitants of the county, belatedly organized and directed by the magistrates in general sessions, further assistance

[1] See H.O. 45/453 and 454.
[2] Rice Trevor to H.O. dated 18 October 1843. H.O. 45/454 ii.

Q

from the central government was frequently called for at this final stage. Re-imbursement was sometimes granted to the local authorities for the money which they had expended in obtaining information, and in Wales in 1843 the Home Office was obliged to send down persons to assist the magistrates to organize resistance to the Rebeccaites.

By these means the disturbances were gradually brought to a close. The lengthy cycle through which they had run reflected badly upon the efficiency of the machinery of public order. It pointed the need for the establishment of a force which, while preserving the freedom of legitimate political action, would arrest disorder before it obtained a foothold. That such a force should already have been operating efficiently in the capital, the centre of government, was obviously a tremendous stabilizing factor in English society. No longer was Parliament liable to hold its deliberations, as at the time of the Gordon Riots of 1780, under threat of violence from a mob which held the metropolis in fee, burning, looting, destroying without let or hindrance. In France's capital in the year of revolutions, the insurrectionists of June were allowed to work uninterrupted at the establishment of barricades, as the military commander, Cavaignac, was unwilling to divide his troops to deal with the numerous parties of barricade builders. It can scarcely be doubted that, if a London mob had manifested a disposition to erect barricades, its efforts would have been speedily arrested by a force which believed prevention to be better than cure.

But police reform had scarcely outgrown the experimental stage. The task of applying it in a uniform fashion to the counties and boroughs of England was a long way from having been accomplished. The orderliness of the British people, which has since become proverbial, was foreshadowed in the better-policed areas during the Chartist period. It was not yet fully attained.

BIBLIOGRAPHICAL NOTE

ORIGINAL SOURCE MATERIAL

Manuscript Sources

The principal manuscript source for the history of the machinery of public order is undoubtedly the Home Office Papers in the Public Record Office, and in particular the books of out-letters relating to disturbances classified as H.O. 41, and the bundles of in-letters dealing with the same subject in H.O. 40. It should be noted, however, that owing to some administrative change most of the in-letters relating to disturbances after the year 1840 were transferred to H.O. 45, Registered Papers, Old Series, where they are arranged in bundles according to counties, with separate bundles for correspondence with the military commanders. The same mode of arrangement is followed in H.O. 40 for in-letters prior to 1840.

These sections include most of the correspondence with Lords Lieutenant, magistrates and military commanders, transacted during outbreaks of disorder and having direct reference to them. There are, however, many other sections of the Home Office Papers which throw light on the nature and operation of the machinery of public order. H.O. 52, Counties Correspondence, gives valuable insight into the condition of the magisterial bench, and together with H.O. 48 and 49, Law Officers' Reports and Correspondence, supplies useful information about the prosecution of Chartist leaders. H.O. 50/16, Military Correspondence, 1838-9, contains a number of letters from the Commander-in-Chief and the Military Secretary, many of which bear on the subject of internal disturbances. H.O. 51, Yeomanry Correspondence, Appointments, etc., is also useful.

A good deal of information about the working of the new police forces may be gleaned from the correspondence contained in H.O. 61, Metropolitan Police Correspondence—In-letters, and from H.O. 65, Police Entry Books relating to the Metropolitan Police, the Birmingham Police and the Rural Police. H.O. 45/724 relates to the establishment of a detective branch of the Metropolitan Police Force.

H.O. 79, Entry Books, Private and Secret, is mainly concerned with warrants for opening the letters of suspected persons at the Post Office. H.O. 64, Rewards, Pardons and Secret Service, despite its exciting title, contains little more than some correspondence about the offer of

233

rewards and pardons as a means of eliciting information in cases of incendiary fires.

The War Office Papers, which are also in the Public Record Office, contain an interesting bundle of memoranda drawn up by the Duke of Wellington with reference to the precautions adopted in London prior to the Chartist demonstrations of 10 April and 12 June 1848.

The records of the Metropolitan Police, preserved at Scotland Yard, include Entry Books of Police Orders and a box of papers marked 'Chartists', which contains bundles of police reports on the Birmingham Riots of 1839 and Chartist disturbances in London in 1848, and on persons offering to give information to the government relative to Chartist proceedings.

Departmental records such as the above suffer to some extent from their formality, and when the student wishes to penetrate below the surface of a decision taken by one of the departments of government or by the Cabinet he is frequently compelled to resort to the private correspondence of ministers of state and other influential persons. The Russell Papers at the Public Record Office (P.R.O. 30/22) contain occasional references to disturbances in 1838–9 and again in 1848, but on the whole they are disappointing. The letters of Lord Melbourne in the Panshanger Papers (now at Windsor Castle) are slightly more fruitful. Volume No. 15, Correspondence of Melbourne and Lord John Russell, is the most rewarding part of the collection.

The Peel Papers in the British Museum (especially Additional Manuscripts 40,447, 40,448 and 40,459) and the Graham Papers at Netherby (microfilm copy in the Cambridge University Library) deal much more fully with the subject of disturbances. Sir James Graham seems to have reserved for his private files some of the most vital correspondence relating to the suppression of the riots of August 1842. Most of these letters do not appear in either of the two works of C. S. Parker—*The Life and Letters of Sir James Graham, 1792–1861* (London, 1907) and *Sir Robert Peel from his Private Papers* (London, 1891–9).

The papers of Sir George Grey relating to his Home Secretaryship have been destroyed by fire, but much useful information may be culled from a *Memoir of Sir George Grey, Bart., G.C.B.* by Mandell Creighton (privately printed, Newcastle upon Tyne, 1884).

Some references to disorder which do not appear in the published *Letters of Queen Victoria, 1837–1861*, ed. Benson and Esher (London, 1908), may be found in the Correspondence of Queen Victoria in the Royal Archives, Windsor Castle. There is a file (C 56) exclusively devoted to 'Chartists and Working Classes, 1848'.

Printed Sources

Printed material includes a limited number of parliamentary papers chiefly relating to police, reference to which has been made in the footnotes of the present work. Newspapers are valuable for the details of disturbances and reports of the evidence tendered at Chartist trials, and also for the light which they throw on movements of public opinion, which are often of vital importance in that they affect the behaviour of the machinery of public order. To obtain a fair and balanced picture I have consulted newspapers representing divers political outlooks, notably *The Times, The Manchester Guardian, The Manchester Times, The Bolton Free Press, The North Cheshire Reformer, The Stockport Advertiser* and *The Northern Star*. The *Place Collection of Newspaper Cuttings* at the British Museum has also been used.

Newspaper reports of Chartist trials may be supplemented by full accounts of some of the leading prosecutions of the period in *State Trials, 1839–1843* (London, 1888–98).

Hansard's *Parliamentary Debates* (Second and Third Series) are useful for the treatment accorded in Parliament to disturbances.

The following memoirs and other contemporary or near-contemporary writings of a literary character add to our knowledge of disorder, its social background and the measures taken to combat it.—A. Alison, *Some Account of My Life and Writings* (Edinburgh, 1883); W. Cooke-Taylor, *Notes of a Tour in the Manufacturing Districts of Lancashire, 1842* (London, 1842); W. Cooke-Taylor and Charles Mackay, *The Life and Times of Sir Robert Peel* (London, to 1851); T. Cooper, *The Life of, Written by Himself* (London, 1872); Lord Ellesmere, *Personal Reminiscences of the Duke of Wellington* (London, 1904); R. G. Gammage, *A History of the Chartist Movement* (London, 1894); C. C. F. Greville, *A Journal of the Reign of Queen Victoria from 1837 to 1852* (London, 1885); G. J. Holyoake, *Sixty Years of an Agitator's Life* (London, 1893); Charles Kingsley, *His Letters and Memories of His Life* (London, 1877); Lord Malmesbury, *Memoirs of an Ex-Minister* (London, 1884); W. Napier, *The Life and Opinions of General Sir Charles James Napier, G.C.B.* (London, 1857); A. Prentice, *A History of the Anti-Corn Law League* (London, 1853); Earl Russell, *Recollections and Suggestions, 1813–73* (London, 1875); A. Somerville, *The Autobiography of a Working Man* (London, 1848); W. M. Torrens, *Memoirs of the Rt. Hon. William, Second Viscount Melbourne* (London, 1878); Absalom Watkin, *Extracts from his Journal, 1814–56* (London, 1920); E. W. Watkin, *Alderman Cobden of Manchester* (London, 1891).

SECONDARY WORKS

(1) *Social, Economic and Political Background of the Disturbances:* The best general history of the Chartist Movement is still Mark Hovell, *The Chartist Movement* (Manchester, 1918); but this work now requires

to be supplemented by information contained in more up-to-date books, such as S. Maccoby, *English Radicalism, 1832–52* (London, 1935); G. D. H. Cole, *Chartist Portraits* (London, 1941); L. C. Wright, *Scottish Chartism* (Edinburgh, 1953); J. Saville, *Ernest Jones* (London, 1952); A. R. Schoyen, *The Chartist Challenge: A Portrait of George Julian Harney* (London, 1958); and David Williams, *John Frost: A Study in Chartism* (Cardiff, 1939). Cecil Driver, *Tory Radical* (New York, 1946) and S. E. Finer, *The Life and Times of Sir Edwin Chadwick* London, 1952), are useful for the study of the New Poor Law and the movement of resistance to it. The Rebecca Riots have been fully dealt with by David Williams, *The Rebecca Riots: A Study in Agrarian Discontent* (Cardiff, 1955).

The following throw light on the economic fluctuations which played so important a part in generating disorder—A. D. Gayer, W. W. Rostow and A. J. Schwartz, *The Growth and Fluctuation of the British Economy, 1790–1850* (Oxford, 1953); R. C. O. Matthews, *A Study in Trade-Cycle History* (Cambridge, 1954).

(2) *The Central Government and the Home Office:* E. Troup, *The Home Office* (Old Whitehall Series, London, 1925) contains some useful information applicable to this period, Howard Robinson, *The British Post Office: A History* (Princeton, 1948) deals with the opening of letters at the Post Office and the Mazzini case. K. Ellis, *The Post Office in the Eighteenth Century* (London, 1958) throws important new light on the history of this practice. The following biographies also bear on the response of government to disturbances—Spencer Walpole, *The Life of Lord John Russell* (London, 1889); A. W. Tilby, *Lord John Russell* (London, 1930); Lord David Cecil, *Lord M. or the Later Life of Lord Melbourne* (London, 1954); A. B. Erickson, *The Public Career of Sir James Graham* (Oxford, 1952).

(3) *Local Government:* Though focused on the period prior to the passing of the Municipal Corporations Act, S. and B. Webb, *English Local Government from the Revolution to the Municipal Corporations Act*, is a mine of useful information. The relevant volumes are I—*The Parish and the County* (London, 1906); II and III—*The Manor and the Borough* (London, 1908); IV—*Statutory Authorities* (London, 1922). J. Redlich and F. W. Hirst, *Local Government in England* (London, 1903), H. J. Laski, W. I. Jennings and W. A. Robson, *A Century of Municipal Progress* (London, 1935) and W. E. Tate, *The Parish Chest* (Cambridge, 1946) should also be consulted. Much valuable material about the local machinery of public order is also to be found in studies of individual towns such as—A. Redford and I. S. Russell, *History of Local Government in Manchester* (London, 1939–40); Conrad Gill and

Asa Briggs, *History of Birmingham* (Oxford, 1952); A. T. Patterson, *Radical Leicester* (Leicester, 1954); W. H. Chaloner, *The Social and Economic Development of Crewe* (Manchester, 1950); B. D. White, *A History of the Corporation of Liverpool* (Liverpool, 1952); C. Welch, *A Modern History of the City of London* (London, 1896).

(4) *Police:* Numerous books on police history have appeared in recent years. Charles Reith has published—*The Police Idea, Its History and Evolution in England* (London, 1938); *Police Principles and the Problem of War* (London, 1940); *A Short History of the British Police* (London, 1948); *The Blind Eye of History* (London, 1952); *A New Study of Police History* (Edinburgh, 1956); but the most useful of his books for the light it throws on the period which is being studied is *British Police and the Democratic Ideal* (London, 1943). J. M. Hart, *The British Police* (London, 1951) has a brief but valuable historical intro-duction. Other recent contributions to police history bearing upon the subject of this book are D. G. Browne, *The Rise of Scotland Yard* (London, 1956); R. L. Gribble, *Triumphs of Scotland Yard: A Century of Detection* (London, 1955); J. M. Hart, 'The Reform of the Borough Police, 1835–1856' (*English Historical Review*, LXX, 1955); Belton Cobb, *The First Detectives* (London, 1957). Older police histories which are still of value are W. L. M. Lee, *A History of Police in England* (London, 1901); E. H. Glover, *The English Police, its Origin and Development* (London, 1934).

(5) *The Military:* The history of the British Army in the years of peace which followed the battle of Waterloo is not very well covered in secondary works. Sir John Fortescue, *A History of the British Army* (London, 1899–1930) treats the subject very sketchily. E. Halévy, *A History of the English People, Vol. I—England in 1815* (London, 1949) gives a vivid description of the condition of the Army in 1815, and much of what he says is applicable throughout the first half of the nine-teenth century. Cecil Woodham-Smith, *The Reason Why* (London, 1953) presents a very readable word-picture of the military situation in the quarter-century before the outbreak of the Crimean War in the form of biographical studies of the officers chiefly implicated in the charge at Balaclava. Other useful information about the Army and its rôle in maintaining public order may be gleaned from published lives of military leaders, e.g. G. Lathom Browne, *Wellington* (London, 1888), and Rosamond, Lady Lawrence, *Charles Napier* (London, 1952). The part played by the Yeomanry is indicated by O. Teichman, 'The Yeomanry as an Aid to Civil Power, 1795–1867' (*Journal of the Society of Army Historical Research*, XIX, 1940); the rôle of the pensioners in F. C. Mather, 'Army Pensioners and the Maintenance of Civil Order in Early-Nineteenth-Century England' (*Ibid.*, XXXVI, 1958).

APPENDIX I

Table Showing the Strength of the Borough Police in the Three Main Years of Chartist Unrest

The following table is based mainly upon a parliamentary return drawn up in 1854.[1] It includes only those police forces which were set up in accordance with the Municipal Corporations Act of 1835. Hence no entry is made for boroughs which are known to have amalgamated their forces with those of the neighbouring county, or for Manchester, Bolton and Birmingham at the time of the disturbances of 1842, when the policing of those three towns was being carried out by special statutory forces.

The table contains particulars of $56\frac{1}{2}$ per cent of the English and Welsh boroughs in 1839, $62\frac{3}{4}$ per cent in 1842 and $69\frac{1}{2}$ per cent in 1848. As to the remaining towns the 1854 return is silent. It may be assumed that in the earlier years the majority of these would have no police force, but it also seems likely that by 1848 a substantial part of the residue would consist of boroughs which had merged their police into the county force.

I have corrected the return in cases where I have positive information that it is wrong. Manchester had a force of 343 men under the Corporation in 1839,[2] whereas the return gave no figure for that year. Bolton had 10 borough policemen,[3] but these were not mentioned. On the other hand the return gave figures for Andover and Stafford in 1848, when these towns were served by county constables.[4] That such changes should be necessary does not create confidence in the remaining data, but as it is impossible to obtain figures for this period which are 100 per cent reliable, I have decided to reproduce these, thinking that statistics which may possibly embody defects are better than no statistics at all.

The police/population ratios are calculated by dividing the population by the number of constables. Population figures for 1839, 1842 and 1848 have been obtained by distributing the increase in the population evenly over the intercensal years.

[1] *Return of the Several Cities and Boroughs of Great Britain, their Populations Respectively, the Number of Police and the Cost of Same in Each Year from their Establishment*; 1854 (345) LIII.

[2] A. Redford and I. S. Russell, *The History of Local Government in Manchester*, II, 42.

[3] Darbishire to H.O. dated 19 May 1839. H.O. 40/37.

[4] *S.C. on Police*: First Report, Mins. of Evidence, pp. 434–5; 1852–3 (603) XXXVI. Second Report, Mins. of Evidence, p. 6; 1852–3 (715) XXXVI.

Name of Borough	1839		1842		1848	
	No. of Police	Ratio	No. of Police	Ratio	No. of Police	Ratio
Abingdon	7	1 : 789	6	1 : 937	5	1 : 1169
Arundel	3	1 : 887	3	1 : 879	3	1 : 904
Ashton-under-Lyne	—	—	—	—	17	1 : 1660
Banbury	9	1 : 428	11	1 : 354	11	1 : 362
Barnstaple	5	1 : 1538	5	1 : 1650	5	1 : 2066
Basingstoke	3	1 : 1323	3	1 : 1362	3	1 : 1401
Bath	122	1 : 432	99	1 : 538	98	1 : 550
Beccles	2	1 : 2020	2	1 : 2058	2	1 : 2151
Bedford	12	1 : 728	12	1 : 786	12	1 : 911
Berwick upon Tweed	2	1 : 6895	3	1 : 4705	4	1 : 3692
Beverley	9	1 : 955	9	1 : 966	9	1 : 982
Bideford	—	—	1	1 : 5267	1	1 : 5606
Birmingham	—	—	—	—	314	1 : 694
Bolton	10	1 : 4837	—	—	24	1 : 2411
Boston	10	1 : 1260	10	1 : 1312	10	1 : 1420
Bradford	—	—	—	—	69	1 : 1343
Bridgnorth	2	1 : 3009	2	1 : 3097	2	1 : 3090
Bridgwater	11	1 : 902	7	1 : 1491	7	1 : 1480
Bridport	5	1 : 1419	4	1 : 1803	3	1 : 2483
Bristol	228	1 : 521	228	1 : 543	248	1 : 536
Buckingham	3	1 : 1322	4	1 : 1013	4	1 : 1007
Bury St. Edmunds	11	1 : 1120	10	1 : 1267	13	1 : 1038
Calne	2	1 : 1257	2	1 : 1244	2	1 : 1263
Cambridge	28	1 : 848	28	1 : 885	23	1 : 1165
Canterbury	18	1 : 838	18	1 : 874	14	1 : 1251
Carlisle	—	—	18	1 : 1240	25	1 : 999
Chester	29	1 : 785	19	1 : 1241	22	1 : 1199
Chesterfield	16	1 : 383	16	1 : 394	22	1 : 311
Chichester	9	1 : 940	9	1 : 947	8	1 : 1077
Chippenham	—	—	4	1 : 417	4	1 : 423
Chipping Norton	1	1 : 2530	1	1 : 2630	1	1 : 2831
Colchester	10	1 : 1746	11	1 : 1632	11	1 : 1722
Congleton	—	—	1	1 : 9994	3	1 : 3448
Coventry	17	1 : 1765	17	1 : 1841	17	1 : 2033
Deal	9	1 : 756	7	1 : 961	8	1 : 869
Derby	17	1 : 1819	16	1 : 2095	32	1 : 1195
Devizes	—	—	—	—	4	1 : 1494

Name of Borough	1839		1842		1848	
	No. of Police	Ratio	No. of Police	Ratio	No. of Police	Ratio
Devonport	21	1 : 1621	15	1 : 2284	23	1 : 1603
Doncaster	6	1 : 1754	9	1 : 1179	9	1 : 1286
Dorchester	6	1 : 920	6	1 : 957	6	1 : 1029
Dover	19	1 : 951	15	1 : 1275	15	1 : 1413
Droitwich	2	1 : 1381	2	1 : 1430	2	1 : 1518
Durham	5	1 : 2415	7	1 : 1803	7	1 : 1857
Exeter	—	—	—	—	24	1 : 1349
Eye	6	1 : 409	6	1 : 417	6	1 : 426
Faversham	4	1 : 1007	4	1 : 1024	4	1 : 1107
Gateshead	8	1 : 2392	13	1 : 1590	16	1 : 1496
Gloucester	18	1 : 762	18	1 : 805	18	1 : 919
Godmanchester	2	1 : 1075	2	1 : 1085	2	1 : 1140
Grantham	2	1 : 2452	2	1 : 2511	2	1 : 2628
Gravesend	9	1 : 1603	15	1 : 1051	15	1 : 1090
Grimsby	—	—	—	—	7	1 : 1045
Harwich	—	—	—	—	4	1 : 1025
Hastings	11	1 : 1028	11	1 : 1105	9	1 : 1707
Helston	1	1 : 3318	1	1 : 3327	1	1 : 3346
Hereford	15	1 : 764	15	1 : 786	15	1 : 800
Hertford	5	1 : 1082	5	1 : 1113	5	1 : 1252
Honiton	—	—	—	—	2	1 : 1783
Huntingdon	3	1 : 1153	3	1 : 1181	3	1 : 1256
Ipswich	19	1 : 1281	17	1 : 1537	16	1 : 1916
St. Ives	—	—	1	1 : 5752	1	1 : 6267
Kendal	5	1 : 2037	5	1 : 2077	5	1 : 2269
King's Lynn	16	1 : 969	16	1 : 1023	16	1 : 1147
Kingston upon Hull	94	1 : 682	104	1 : 662	121	1 : 656
Lancaster	8	1 : 1650	9	1 : 1497	10	1 : 1423
Launceston	1	1 : 2414	1	1 : 2554	1	1 : 3116
Leeds	112	1 : 1306	133	1 : 1158	137	1 : 1213
Leicester	50	1 : 970	54	1 : 961	54	1 : 1069
Leominster	5	1 : 795	5	1 : 805	5	1 : 963
Lincoln	23	1 : 665	23	1 : 704	25	1 : 685
Liverpool	590	1 : 458	622	1 : 475	822	1 : 425
Louth	8	1 : 979	8	1 : 1136	8	1 : 1251
Lyme Regis	5	1 : 546	4	1 : 687	4	1 : 672
Maidstone	16	1 : 1096	10	1 : 1835	14	1 : 1424
Manchester	343	1 : 655	—	—	447	1 : 633
Monmouth	2	1 : 2670	2	1 : 2736	2	1 : 2815
Newark	8	1 : 1261	9	1 : 1148	9	1 : 1222

Name of Borough	1839		1842		1848	
	No. of Police	Ratio	No. of Police	Ratio	No. of Police	Ratio
Newcastle upon Tyne	85	1 : 788	105	1 : 686	115	1 : 718
Newport, I.W.	6	1 : 1198	5	1 : 1481	5	1 : 1567
New Sarum	—	—	10	1 : 1024	12	1 : 942
New Windsor	11	1 : 695	11	1 : 724	11	1 : 820
Norwich	66	1 : 940	78	1 : 806	78	1 : 852
Nottingham	—	—	56	1 : 956	56	1 : 1002
Oswestry	—	—	—	—	4	1 : 1191
Oxford	11	1 : 1990	11	1 : 2064	12	1 : 2141
Penzance	11	1 : 743	12	1 : 720	13	1 : 694
Plymouth	31	1 : 1143	31	1 : 1229	44	1 : 1080
Pontefract	—	—	—	—	4	1 : 1244
Poole	13	1 : 583	9	1 : 889	9	1 : 982
Portsmouth	30	1 : 1750	30	1 : 1831	30	1 : 2213
Preston	—	—	—	—	26	1 : 2451
Reading	22	1 : 852	18	1 : 1100	25	1 : 855
E. Retford	—	—	2	1 : 1353	2	1 : 1432
Richmond	3	1 : 1300	4	1 : 1001	3	1 : 1357
Ripon	2	1 : 2909	2	1 : 3005	2	1 : 3028
Rochester	25	1 : 544	22	1 : 645	15	1 : 1023
Rye	2	1 : 1984	2	1 : 2017	2	1 : 2029
Salford	—	—	—	—	43	1 : 1411
Scarborough	—	—	2	1 : 5172	2	1 : 6029
Sheffield	—	—	—	—	122	1 : 1050
Shrewsbury	—	—	—	—	17	1 : 1133
South Molton	—	—	2	1 : 1842	2	1 : 2108
Southwold	2	1 : 1039	2	1 : 1076	1	1 : 2288
Stamford	10	1 : 743	10	1 : 792	9	1 : 941
Stockport	13	1 : 3806	12	1 : 4281	12	1 : 4418
Stratford on Avon	5	1 : 671	5	1 : 665	5	1 : 671
Sunderland	38	1 : 1337	46	1 : 1190	43	1 : 1469
Tamworth	—	—	2	1 : 1907	2	1 : 1985
Tenterden	3	1 : 1177	3	1 : 1216	3	1 : 1272
Tewkesbury	5	1 : 1169	5	1 : 1173	5	1 : 1175
Thetford	21	1 : 183	21	1 : 188	21	1 : 192
Tiverton	—	—	—	—	4	1 : 2703
Truro	6	1 : 681	6	1 : 797	6	1 : 1458
Wallingford	3	1 : 912	3	1 : 928	3	1 : 936
Walsall	3	1 : 6299	8	1 : 2555	10	1 : 2393
Warrington	—	—	—	—	6	1 : 3620

Name of Borough	1839		1842		1848	
	No. of Police	Ratio	No. of Police	Ratio	No. of Police	Ratio
Wells	4	1 : 1742	4	1 : 1705	4	1 : 1357
Weymouth and Melcombe Regis	—	—	—	—	10	1 : 893
Wigan	6	1 : 4097	6	1 : 4362	10	1 : 3002
Winchester	8	1 : 1292	8	1 : 1379	10	1 : 1281
Wisbech	8	1 : 1034	8	1 : 1092	8	1 : 1247
Worcester	20	1 : 1202	20	1 : 1281	21	1 : 1280
Gt. Yarmouth	—	—	37	1 : 761	37	1 : 810
York	13	1 : 2179	14	1 : 2113	19	1 : 1793
Aberystwyth	3	1 : 1586	3	1 : 1649	2	1 : 2568
Beaumaris	1	1 : 2660	1	1 : 2691	1	1 : 2630
Brecon	—	—	4	1 : 1424	4	1 : 1420
Cardiff	6	1 : 1550	8	1 : 1363	13	1 : 1221
Carmarthen	7	1 : 1373	7	1 : 1375	8	1 : 1278
Carnarvon	2	1 : 3953	2	1 : 4021	2	1 : 4231
Swansea	7	1 : 3416	7	1 : 3686	14	1 : 2112
Tenby	1	1 : 2755	1	1 : 2919	2	1 : 1480
Welshpool	3	1 : 2000	3	1 : 2074	9	1 : 717

APPENDIX II

Return of the Number of Home Office Warrants for the Opening of Letters in the Years 1799–1844[1]

Year	Number of Warrants	Year	Number of Warrants	Year	Number of Warrants
1799	9	1815	2	1831	[17]
1800	11	1816	0	1832	5
1801	7	1817	[11]	1833	4
1802	6	1818	9	1834	6
1803	7	1819	[6]	1835	7
1804	2	1820	6	1836	7
1805	7	1821	1	1837	4
1806	9	1822	12	1838	8
1807	13	1823	7	1839	[16]
1808	2	1824	2	1840	7
1809	11	1825	6	1841	18
1810	6	1826	[8]	1842	[20]
1811	8	1827	8	1843	8
1812	[28]	1828	4	1844	7
1813	8	1829	5	Total	372
1814	3	1830	14		

[1] Quoted from *Report of the Secret Committee of the House of Commons on the Post Office, 1844,* p. 11; 1844 (582) XIV. The square brackets, which are my own, indicate years of maximum unrest.

INDEX

R